An Introduction to Design and Culture

An Introduction to Design and Culture provides students with an comprehensive guide to the changing relationship between design and culture from 1900 to the present day, with an emphasis on five main themes:

- design and consumption;
- design and technology;
- the design profession;
- design theory; and
- design and identities.

Design is defined broadly to cover product and furniture design, interior design, fashion design and graphic design. The new edition is international in scope and emphasises the increasingly global role played by design as it gets nearer to the present day.

Taking a broadly chronological approach, Professor Sparke employs historical methods to show how these themes were all implicated by design's progress through the twentieth century and into the twenty-first century. Illustrations throughout the text demonstrate the breadth of design and its multiple contexts, and design examples – such as those of the Sony Walkman, contemporary design in China and James Dyson – are used to elaborate key ideas.

Penny Sparke is Professor of Design History and Pro Vice-Chancellor (Research), Director, Modern Interior Research Centre, Kingston University. Her research interests include modern design and the modern interior with special interest in role of gender. She is currently researching the meaning of plants and flowers in the modern interior.

An Introduction to Design and Culture

1900 to the Present

Third edition

Penny Sparke

Routledge
Taylor & Francis Group

LONDON AND NEW YORK

First published 2013
by Routledge
2 Park Square, Milton Park, Abingdon, Oxon OX14 4RN

Simultaneously published in the USA and Canada
by Routledge
711 Third Avenue, New York, NY 10017

Routledge is an imprint of the Taylor & Francis Group, an informa business

British Library Cataloguing in Publication Data
A catalogue record for this book is available from the British Library

Library of Congress Cataloging in Publication Data
A catalog record for this book has been requested

ISBN: 978-0-415-68618-1 (hbk)
ISBN: 978-0-415-68619-8 (pbk)
ISBN: 978-0-203-12999-9 (ebk)

Typeset in Sabon
by FiSH Books Ltd, Enfield

MIX
Paper from
responsible sources
FSC® C004839

Printed and bound in Great Britain by the MPG Books Group

Contents

Illustrations

Acknowledgements

This book could not have been written without all the support and stimulation I received over eighteen years spent teaching on the joint Royal College of Art/Victoria and Albert Museum History of Design Programme. My thanks go to all the staff I worked with there, among them Dr Gillian Naylor, Professor Jeremy Aynsley, Professor Christopher Breward, John Styles, Marta Ajmar and Helen Clifford. Special thanks go to the many visiting scholars – too numerous to list here – who presented seminars over the years and opened my eyes to new ideas emanating from a number of disciplines hitherto unfamiliar to me and which changed the way I thought about design. Above all it is to the students – at both MA and PhD levels (especially, in the latter category, Quintin Colville, Trevor Keeble, Susie McKellar, Nik Maffei and Viviana Narotzky) – that I owe the greatest thanks, as it is they who pushed the boundaries forward through their research, continually challenging my assumptions. I continue to be challenged by the PhD students I have supervised – among them Emma Ferry, Fiona Fisher and Patricia Lara-Betancourt – and I am supervising at Kingston University, as well as by the staff who teach Design History there. My contact with design tutors and students across a range of disciplines, both at the Royal College of Art and at Kingston University, has also ensured that I understand not only where design is coming from but also, I hope, where it is going.

At Routledge I would like to thank Rebecca Barden, Julene Knox (for energetic picture research) and Helen Faulkner. Above all I must thank John, Molly, Nancy and Celia for putting up with my spending too many holidays and weekends working on my laptop.

Introduction
Twentieth-century design and culture revisited

Perhaps we should speak of a 'political economy of design'.[1]

This third edition of this book is a revised and updated version of the 2004 edition, itself an almost completely rewritten version of the original text I wrote back in the early 1980s, entitled *An Introduction to Design and Culture in the Twentieth Century*. Sitting down to rewrite the second edition, I had initially set out with the idea that I would simply add some new sections to accommodate the events of the intervening years. Very swiftly, however, I had realized that that was not going to be possible. Not only had many more things happened in the world of design since the 1980s, my perspective on the subject had also been utterly transformed by the vast amount of theoretical literature that had emerged since then. While the broad themes which directed the earlier text remained valid, something very substantial had happened in the intervening years, which meant that, if the new text was going to constitute a valid contribution from the perspective of the early twenty-first century, a much more radical overhaul was going to be needed.

Eight years later, yet more significant changes have occurred and the definition that design still had in 2004 is no longer valid. Thirteen years into the twenty-first century, such is the impact of the massive global economic, technological, social and cultural shifts that have occurred that design, and designers, can no longer see themselves as continuing either to be rooted in nineteenth-century industrialization or in twentieth-century cultural modernism and mass consumption. Instead, design is currently looking for a role to play in a world in which debt is more of a reality than wealth, in which environmental disasters are part of daily life and advanced technologies have transformed social relations beyond recognition. That realignment is still taking place and, to date, it is difficult to know how it will pan out. It is the aim of this third edition of *An Introduction to Design and Culture* to try to capture where design has been, where it is now and to speculate on where it might be going.

Where the 2004 text was concerned, the essential story of design's passage through the twentieth century had, of course, not changed substantially from the original account. However, the vast amount of new primary research and intellectual debate that had emerged between the mid-1980s and the early twenty-first century under the umbrella heading of postmodernism, relating, in particular, to the general area of the culture of consumption, required the concept of design to be approached quite differently. Back in 1986, I had written that, 'Within the framework of industrial capitalism, which created it and continues to dominate it in contemporary society, design is characterized by a dual alliance with both mass production and mass consumption and these two phenomena have determined nearly all its manifestations. *Like Janus, design looks in two directions at the same time: as a silent quality of all mass-produced goods it plays a generally unacknowledged but vital role in all our lives. As a named concept within the mass media it is, however, much more visible and generally recognized.*' That same statement still held true for the 2004 study. The difference, however, was that, while the 1986 text acknowledged design's important role within consumption, it paid little more than lip-service to the ways in which designed artefacts and images negotiated the arenas of the social and the cultural through the mediation of consumption. This was not because it didn't deem it important but rather because, at that time, there was little research available with which to demonstrate the depth of that relationship, the extent to which, that is, the modern concept of design was born of market demand and facilitated by mass manufacturing industry, designers and their institutional support structure in the public and private sectors. Material relating to these last three areas filled the majority of the pages of the 1986 book but little detail was presented with which to illuminate the first. As the 2004 book demonstrated in some detail, however, design's relationship with production and the world of professional practice could not, as it is in so many studies emanating from the field of 'cultural studies', be ignored. Without it, none of the complex contradictions, that are the very stuff of design, can be adequately engaged with.

Having said that, if the rapidly changing society that characterized the era of modernity had not required a visual and material means of expressing its aspirations and its identities, design and, by implication, designers, would not have played such a prominent role in modern life. Design and designers are, and have been for many years, a sine qua non of the modern commercial system, ensuring, through the activities of production and consumption, that people's needs and desires (whether consciously acknowledged or not) are met by the visual and material images and artefacts that enter the marketplace and the spaces we inhabit help us define who we are.

This simple idea provided the starting point for the 2004 introductory study of the relationship between design and culture since 1900. The structure of the book, which has remained in place in this 2013 edition, divides the twentieth and early twenty-first centuries into two main periods: 1900–1939 and 1940 to the present. They correspond, in broad terms, to the historical periods of 'modernity' and 'postmodernity' (even though there is not a sudden transition from one to other but, rather, a considerable overlap). Each of the ten chapters is divided into two sections to allow a broad chronology to guide the narrative. The first sections in the first five chapters of the book cover the years 1900–1914, while their second sections deal with the period 1915–1939. In the second part of the book, the first sections of the next five chapters cover the period 1940–1969, while the second sections of those chapters provide an account of design's trajectory over the period 1970 to the present day. Because design's role in the marketplace is deemed to be so fundamental to its cultural one, the first chapters of each of the two main parts of the book focus on the broad context of the 'culture of consumption'. Much writing related to this subject emerged in the 1980s and '90s and focused on themes as diverse as department stores, shopping, the city, spectacle, gender, ethnicity, class, taste and the influence of the mass media, not to mention the vast amount of theoretical work emanating from such diverse disciplines as history, social history, cultural history, art history, decorative arts history, architectural history, design history, visual culture, material culture, American studies, Italian studies, gender studies, cultural studies, media studies, sociology, anthropology, social psychology and cultural geography. This broad-based body of literature has positioned design, whether overtly or by implication, as a cultural phenomenon. At the same time, design's inherent multidisciplinarity is such that it has also been continuously dependent for its changing self-definition over the period in question, on its close links with the worlds of economics, technology, art and politics. However, by the end of the twentieth century, it had become clear that design's main imperative was to create and reflect meaning in the context of everyday life. Back in the early 1980s that had not been quite so evident. In the first decade of the twenty-first century, that primary role has been usurped by the multiple crises that have occurred and design has significantly reoriented itself to become a facilitator for innovation, creativity and change across a range of contexts – commercial, social and cultural. As a tool for development – a role it has had for some time – it has now been adopted by those countries that are entering the global marketplace for the first time: China, Taiwan, Singapore, India and Brazil among them.

In my 1986 book, I failed to provide any useful working definitions or defining frameworks for the two main concepts – design and culture – that I was at pains to document. This is still a daunting task, as they are both difficult, complex concepts which have transformed themselves significantly over time and which have been defined by different people at different times in different ways. However, there are some useful defining characteristics that are worth mentioning, if only tentatively. In linguistic terms, for example, the word 'design', with its obvious (although misleading) roots in the Italian *disegno* and French *dessin*, can be used both verbally – 'to design' and substantively – 'design', the latter deriving as a direct result of the former. This allows one the freedom to treat it ambiguously both as a process and as the result of that process. From the perspective of this study, therefore, it was deemed important to discuss both 'designing' and 'design' – and their interface with culture. This double level of meaning imbues the concept with a particular richness. The word 'culture' is even harder to define, denoting, as it can, so many different things, from its normative meaning, when it is used to describe highly-valued, highly aestheticized activities – such as opera, poetry, theatre, and fine art, which are believed, by many people, to represent mankind's greatest achievements – to its anthropological sense in which it refers, more simply, to 'a way of life'. Interestingly, like 'design', the word 'culture' also has a verbal derivation, linked to the idea of 'growing' or 'nurturing'. In recent times, the word has been transformed into a noun denoting the result of the above activity. Putting the two words, design and culture, together immediately compounds their complexities and they impact upon each other in interesting ways. Design's relationship with culture, is, for example, significant at both of the latter's levels, whether 'high' or 'popular'. Indeed, this dualism constitutes an important leitmotif in this text. The tension between the high-minded idealism underpinning modernist design ideas and the value-free approach of the postmodernists, who embraced the importance of cultural 'difference', can be seen as one of the dominant themes of the period and the one which stimulated the strongest design debates. In its visual, material and spatial incarnations, design embodied and continues to embody that tension.

The structure of this book reflects the multiple contexts of design as it evolved through the twentieth century and into the twenty-first century and the text emphasizes the ways in which it has been both an agent and a mirror of change. While many other accounts of design and material culture see them performing a primarily 'illustrative' role, this study credits design with having a formative function within society and culture, believing, through its visual and material language, and the ideological values and messages it embodies and carries within it, that it can communicate complex messages. In turn these can be negotiated and transformed but they are difficult to ignore. In this sense, design is seen here as being part of the dynamic process through which culture is actually constructed, not merely reflected.

If the culture of consumption makes design necessary, technological progress makes it possible. Engendered, as a process, by the division of labour which played a part in the development of industrial production, design carries technology's messages with it into the sociocultural context. It both mediates the philosophical underpinnings of industrial production – its essential rationality for example – and the cultural messages of the materials of manufacture, transferring them into the arena of consumption. The second chapters in the two main parts of this book address design's relationship with the culture of technology. In determining production technologies and specifying materials, the designer plays a key part within the production process of goods and images. In essence, design acts as a bridge between the worlds of production and consumption as the process of 'designing' is transformed into the sociocultural concept, 'design'. Materials are of special significance in this context. Until they have been 'designed' and have become material 'somethings' they have minimal cultural content. The designer holds enormous power in this respect and can manipulate materials to create multiple meaning, in spite of the fact that they will, inevitably, be transformed, subsequently, within the contexts of consumption and use.

The third chapters in each section of the book turn from the worlds of consumption and production to that of the designer whose primary function is to act a bridge between the two distinct spheres. It is not the intention here to suggest that he/she (mostly he) is a monolithic, heroic figure but rather to demonstrate the fact that design is a practice as well as an abstract concept and that the cultural context of that practice is part of the bigger picture. Design practice has always been fragmented and diverse with enormous chasms separating its specialist fields – the fashion designer and the car designer, for example, have always inhabited different universes. Today, however, those boundaries are being eroded and multidisciplinarity is widely discussed. It is also a moving target, constantly transforming itself to suit the economic, technological, political and cultural climate within which it functions at any one time. Owing to the fact that twentieth century professional design practice emanated from two main roots, there have, however, always been areas of commonality across some specialized design fields. While one face of modern design originated within a commercial tradition, manifesting itself either in two-dimensional graphic advertising or in various kinds of display or spectacle which overtly set out to promote consumption in various ways, its other important face emerged as an extension of the work of architects who believed they could control the whole visual, material and spatial environment and make the world a better place to live in. These chapters document the evolving, complex and overlapping routes taken by these two traditions and the design practices they engendered. They also track the emergence and development of designer culture, one of design's most potent contributions to twentieth-century life, which is predicated on the need, at one level of the market, for design to maintain a link with fine art in order the ensure it a high level of cultural significance and to distinguish certain products from other, more mundane, goods in the marketplace. Most significantly, perhaps, this strategic cultural referencing also enabled goods with an overt 'design' context, frequently made manifest by a marketing or a branding link with a designer's name, to command higher prices than 'anonymous' products. While today this still has some relevance for developing countries, it is less visible in countries with vulnerable economies. In that context, design has largely reverted to its earlier modernist function as an aid to problem solving.

The fourth chapters in each section of the text focus on the ideas and discourses which have underpinned design practice since 1900. As a set of ideas that emerged in the years between 1900 and 1939 as an ideological base-line for design practice, and as a aesthetic ideal which influenced a new generation of designers, as well as numerous nations which sought to distinguish themselves as modern after the Second World War, modernism dominates the picture, even though the period of its demise, which began in the 1960s, has been almost as long as the one in which it was hegemonic. In the final analysis, modernism's impact was felt most acutely by those cultural institutions – museums and educational establishments among them – which embraced its ideology most fully. However, the concept of modernity, or rather of multiple modernities, experienced by the mass of consumers, had an enormous effect on everyday life as it was lived by vast numbers of people through the twentieth century. Designed goods and images played a key role in providing them with access to it.

The last chapters in both sections of the book take as their subject the ways in which, once its key contexts and discourses had been established, design has been used by powerful political and economic groupings, nations and corporations in particular, both to define and express their identities and to empower themselves. In this context, design's ability to embody and express the idea of international modernity was especially meaningful, although local inflections were inevitably developed to reflect the special features of the nations and corporations which used design as an intrinsic feature of their modernizing strategies. These chapters demonstrate the power of design both to form and to express identities, whether for personal, political or commercial ends. They also touch on its capacity to construct and represent the stereotypical characteristics of a range of culturally-defined categories, such as class, gender and ethnicity, offered up for negotiation by individuals in the marketplace.

These ten chapters offer a picture of design as it relates to culture from a number of key perspectives and describe different facets of that complex relationship. As we have seen 'design' and 'culture' are both complex phenomena. If there is one concept that lies at the heart of their relationship in the twentieth century, however, and which holds this study together, however, it is that of 'identity' or 'identities'. The way in which individuals and groups depend upon the mass media as a means of defining themselves is a key characteristic of modern life. Increasingly, through the twentieth century, values were communicated to people less and less through interaction with their local communities and more and more through the mass media. Through its inherent relationship with industrial production, a key agent of mass mediation and its presence in the mass-disseminated goods, images, spaces and services that resulted from that process, design became a key component of all the messages that were communicated. To extend Marshall McLuhan's analysis of the mass media, not only is the 'medium' the 'message', it is the design of the medium which is crucial in this context, as it determines the way in which the message is read and negotiated.

Arguably, by the late twentieth century, design had become more significant than the medium itself, as it played an increasingly ubiquitous role in influencing the ways in which individuals and groups defined themselves. In other words the lifestyle implications of the media became the most significant part of their messages. Design expresses itself visually, materially, spatially and virtually, primarily (although not exclusively) in the context of consumption and, in that context, it is frequently negotiated through the agency of taste which underpins consumer choice. It is a complex language, however, which can operate, simultaneously, as representation and as material actuality.

This way of thinking about design prioritizes its role within identity formation. In the words of the cultural critic, Grant McCracken, 'without consumer goods, certain acts of self-definition and collective definition in this culture would be impossible'.[2] These definitions are, inevitably, as numerous as the individuals and the groups that relate to them. At the same time, however, a number of key overarching identities emerged in the twentieth century, notable among them one we call 'modern'. The visual style developed by the modernists – simple, undecorated, etc. – was one way of recognizing the modern but the definition of modernity went beyond that to include the experience of engaging in a lifestyle which embraced all that modern life had to offer, from technologically sophisticated goods to access, for women, to the public sphere. Inevitably, that experience varied according the situations of individuals or groups which were dependent upon the vagaries of class, gender, race, etc. Design became everyone's bridge to their own brand of modernity.

In the first half of the twentieth century, the term 'design' can be understood as being synonymous with modern design, although its characteristics varied according to whose modernity was in question and, in certain instances, modern could even be expressed by the adoption of an historical style. The latter half of the century presents a more complex picture, one which, in this book, is characterized by the umbrella term 'postmodernism', used as a catch-all to describe the pluralistic cultures that emerged in those years. Within postmodernity, arguably, design had an even more integrated role, its very existence being one of the prerequisites of the 'condition'. However, even within postmodernity, the concepts of 'design' and 'modernity' continued to be linked and it remained very hard to disengage them from each other.

This text is dependent upon a number of theoretical texts and situates itself within the body of literature relating to the culture of consumption which emerged in the 1980s and 1990s. Feminist ideas developed in the same decade have also been a strong influence. It is especially indebted to two texts published in 1986: Andreas Huyssen's *After the Great Divide: Modernism, Mass Culture and Postmodernism* and Pierre Bourdieu's *Distinction: A Social Critique of the Judgement of Taste*. The ideas articulated in the first book can be seen to relate directly to design, even though

Huyssen stopped short of pushing very hard in that direction himself, as it was not the focus of his study. Bourdieu's book, written first in the 1970s, but translated into English in the mid-1980s, also provided an important framework for this study of design and culture.[3] It positioned design within a sociocultural framework which made sense of it and which took Thorstein Veblen's innovative ideas of the late nineteenth century forward several stages. Although much of the material in Bourdieu's book is dated now, and the case studies were very specifically French, his proposition that the exercising of taste underpins both the shape and the dynamic of modern society and culture is one which has still not been fully acknowledged, so preoccupied, until recently, have historians and theorists been with post-Marxist ideas and with prioritizing production over consumption. Bourdieu's ideas help challenge the modernist framework which has tended to dominate most accounts of design to date.

In trying to encompass a wider spectrum of design activities and objects, the 2004 text was more ambitious than its 1986 predecessor. The primary focus on product design remained but more effort was made to include fashion, graphic, interior, environmental and, in this 2013 edition, environmental, interaction, social, inclusive and virtual design, where appropriate. This was not simply for inclusiveness for its own sake but rather because the author has come to understand that modes of professional practice and ideas flowed from one area to another through the twentieth and early twenty-first centuries and that consumers and users do not compartmentalize designed goods and images in the same way as the manufacturing industry. Ideas generated within specialized design fields went on to influence others over a period of time. The role played by identity within fashion design, for example, permeated the world of interior decoration in the early century and subsequently went on to play a role within car design. Similarly, the emphasis on spectacle, visible in the early twentieth century shop-window display, moved into objects themselves through the agency of industrial designers. Also, the aesthetic relationship that consumers have long had with decorative art objects – ceramics, glass and textiles among them – has finally been transferred to computer-generated images. These are just some of the insights that it has been possible to gain by considering design across a range of media and within a historical context.

Most importantly, however, this text sets out to avoid the historicizing tendencies of the 1986 edition. In spite of efforts to withstand their often strident claims, the dominance of modernist texts in the early 1980s was such that the 1986 study was inevitably influenced by them and unwittingly reproduced their rhetoric and their tendency to reductivism to some extent. All that has changed since the disciplines of cultural and media studies have matured and the impact of postmodern ideas in the broadest sense has become greater. It is now much easier to understand that design had, and continues to have, no fixed definition or meanings nor one ideal path to follow. Rather, it is a constantly transforming concept, reflected in a set of practices and influenced by a broad context of changing ideologies and discourses that have affected its shifting parameters. If a discourse of design can be developed it must be one which recognizes the high level of relativism, pragmatism and contextualization that has determined the concept's past and which will, undoubtedly, continue to affect its future. Design will continue to be influenced by consumption, the fashion system, identities of all kinds, production, whether industrial or craft-based, as well as by broader ideologies and discourses and economic, environmental and social conditions and crises outside its control. It is a constantly moving target, although its future is, like everything else, significantly influenced by its past. In short, the picture of design and designers is constantly being repainted. This book can only, therefore, present a sketch of it, as the colours will constantly change.

Part 1

Design and modernity, 1900–1939

1   Consuming modernity

Conspicuous consumption and the expansion of taste

> The department stores had fostered an extravagant taste not only for clothes but also for 'things one might do without'.[1]

Although the term 'design' did not have any common currency until the middle years of the twentieth century, the idea of imbuing goods and images with aesthetic and functional characteristics that attracted consumers and met the needs of users has a long history. That history was closely linked to the development of modern society and culture.

As a modern concept, design developed as a direct result of the expansion of the market for consumer goods and the democratization of taste. For centuries, hand-made furnishings, ceramics, glass, metalwork, dress, printed artefacts and carriages had impacted on the lives of members of the upper classes, acting as providers of comfort, as markers of propriety, as the glue of social, family and gender relations and as visible signs of fashionableness, taste and social status. As modernity influenced the lives of ever larger numbers of people, however, design – the visual and conceptual component of the mass-produced goods and images that facilitated mass production, made goods attractive to a mass market and helped to give meaning to people's everyday lives – took on the role that, for the social élite, had been performed up until that point by the decorative arts. In both Europe and the USA, industrialization began to create new levels of social mobility and the increased access to goods began to blur traditional class distinctions. Indeed, as increasing numbers of consumers embraced new goods, new classes emerged. Within that context, the link between design and taste was reinforced. Gradually, as industrially produced goods became more accessible, designed goods and images took over from the decorative arts the task of demarcating social difference and becoming the key messengers of fashionableness and modernity.

There has been much debate about the moment at which the process of modernization first came to be formed by and expressed through material culture. Some studies have documented conspicuous consumption as a sixteenth-century phenomenon, while others have located it in the eighteenth century.[2] The historian, Lorna Weatherill, for example, has demonstrated the way in which, in the latter century, the levels of the ownership of new goods in Britain varied considerably in urban and rural areas. 'Saucepans', she explained, 'associated with cookery on enclosed stoves, were four times as common in London and in other towns as they were in the countryside, where about only one in twenty households used them. Earthenware, although used in farming as well as in households, was more common in London than in provincial towns'.[3] Weatherill's groundbreaking study claimed that mass demand preceded and, indeed, helped to bring about the changes in manufacturing techniques associated with the industrial revolution. She provided data relating to both aristocratic and demotic consumption and to the ways in which certain goods – textiles, ceramics and metal goods in particular – played key social and cultural roles for new consumers.

In the nineteenth century, the middle classes expanded in number and their capacity to consume continued to grow. Studies of the patterns of their consumption in Britain are few and far between, however, and the picture that is presented by those historians who have addressed that question has tended to focus on goods destined for the domestic arena.[4] Work has been undertaken, for example, on the customers of high-end manufacturers, such as the furniture maker and interior decorating firm, Holland and Sons, but there is still much more to be done on the consumption patterns of people inhabiting the other end of the social spectrum.[5] W. Hamish Fraser has provided an overview of the way in which the expansion of the nineteenth-century British market for manufactured goods was a direct result of the growth in the population, an increase in spending power and of shifts in taste that encouraged people to transfer their spending from one set of goods to another. In the 1860s, he explained, more gas cookers became available as a result of a fall in the price of gas; by 1914, new household objects, such as the US Bissell carpet sweeper, came on to the British market; following its success in the US marketplace, the domestic vacuum cleaner made its appearance in Britain at the turn of the century and, by the first decade of the new century, the bicycle and the automobile had become common appendages of the urban scene. The strategies involved in catering for, sustaining and expanding the new mass market subsumed the question of design through its links with advertising, marketing and retailing.[6]

While visual elaboration enhanced the appeal of the new goods, technological novelty played a key role in most consumer choices at that time. Given that many consumers saw it as a threat, however, visual strategies were sometimes employed to conceal that novelty. That was especially the case in some of the new domestic electrical products to which surface pattern was often added to enhance familiarity and relieve anxiety (see Figure 2.3).

While Britain was the first country to witness the advent of mass consumption, it also emerged in the USA and in a number of European countries. Although it took longer than in Britain to bring about an expansion of production figures, when it finally did so in the USA a much more dramatic and rapid growth of consumer activity and a more forward-looking approach towards the development of new, technological products destined for both the public and the private spheres could be observed. In his study of the changing nature of the American middle classes, the historian, Richard L. Bushman, has shown how, as a direct result of material and environmental developments, they had achieved refinement by the mid-nineteenth century. Gentility, he argued, went hand in hand with the emergence of a sophisticated model of domesticity, the growth of cities and the acquisition of taste.[7]

Focusing more specifically upon changing consumption patterns and their relationship with material culture, the essays in S. J. Bronner's collection, *Consuming Visions: Accumulation and Display of Goods in America 1880–1920*, have documented the impact of modernity on American society as expressed through consumers' choices of their material environments.[8] The growth of consumption was understood as a key feature of the emerging modern world. Karen Hultenen's essay has described the subtle transformation of the parlour into the living room and the modernizing effect of the female inhabitant's enhanced association with that newly defined space.[9]

Consumption had a material face that was visible in both the public and private spheres. Although historians have tended to move away from the idea that those spheres were entirely separate – men inhabiting the latter, that is, and women being confined to the former – the changing material culture of the two different spheres was largely specific to each in the years leading up to 1914.[10] Cultural historians have discussed the public sphere at length, in particular the expansion of city culture in the late nineteenth and early twentieth century, focusing on the impact of modernity on people's changing experience of everyday life. They have said less about the concept of design, however, in spite of the fact that the visual, material and spatial environment undoubtedly played a key role within those transformations. The extensive work on the concept of the *flaneur* – the poet, Charles Baudelaire's, term for the male city wanderer – and Walter Benjamin's writings about the commercial face of the city, has explored the new experience of the city and equated it with modernity.[11] Elizabeth Wilson has concentrated on women's experience of the city in that period, seeing it as an escape from domesticity.[12] While the modern urban experience has been described in terms of the high level of spectacle visible to city dwellers, most accounts have privileged its reception rather than its production or its designed components.

Although the idea of modernity existed before architects and designers had created a visual, material and spatial representation of it, the first signs of a man-made shift in the look of the city itself – whether London, Paris, Vienna or New York – emerged at the end of the nineteenth century. The impact of, first, gas and subsequently of electric lighting transformed the city into a dramatically new kind of night-time environment, while the advent of new retailing outlets, department stores in particular, transformed the act of shopping and, perhaps more significantly, that of window shopping. New objects of transportation, trains and cars among them, also contributed to the new experience of everyday urban life.

The American cultural historian, William Leach, has written at length about the way in which the new plate-glass store windows created a level of spectacle for the city dweller or visitor.[13] Seen from the street, the illuminated contents of those public theatres offered a new and dramatic form of popular entertainment that was created by a new visualizer, the show-window display artist. His task was to create a dramatic visual focus for the *flaneurs*, whose growing presence transformed the streets of the city. The overtly commercial role of window displays offered a foretaste of what later came to be called design for industry and the nineteenth-century store display artists were the forerunners of the inter-war creative artists, known as industrial designers, who went on to transform the appearance of goods themselves rather than merely that of the frame that surrounded them.

Literary historians, social and economic historians and architectural historians have provided numerous accounts of the birth of the department store (Figure 1.1).[14] The contemporary fascination with that subject on the part of historians emanated from a desire to capture the experience of

Figure 1.1 Dickens and Jones department store in early twentieth-century London (courtesy of London Metropolitan Archives)

modernity and to uncover the roots of contemporary consumer and commodity culture. Feminist historians have been particularly active in the field, seeing the department store as middle-class women's first encounter with the public sphere and commercial culture. The department stores established in the second half of the nineteenth century consolidated the modern emphasis on the experience of seeing and, as a consequence, the marginalization of the other senses. In sharp contrast to the act of buying goods from a market stall, which had involved touch and smell as much as sight, the dominance of the eye characterized the modern way of shopping and of interacting with the modern world.[15] That shift marked a moment when the material culture of modernity took on an extra level of potency and became a key characteristic of the modern world.

Within the public sphere, numerous visual, material and environmental markers of modernity – from the new objects of public and private transport, to dress, to posters to spaces within public buildings – were in evidence on the late nineteenth century.[16] So novel were the engineered forms of many of the new objects of transportation – bicycles, railway trains, transatlantic liners and early aeroplanes among them – that they took on an iconic significance. Indeed, so powerful was their visual and symbolic impact that, a little later, modernist architects and designers were to take their aesthetic lead from them. The rational kitchen of the 1920s, for example, took its inspiration from Pullman trains, where space was at a premium.[17] In the years leading up to 1914, designers began to borrow from one new form to create another. The smooth, aerodynamic forms of early automobiles, for example, were inspired by the bulbous shape of the prows of boats and the fuselages of aeroplanes.[18] The new aesthetic that was thus created owed its existence to engineers but, re-interpreted by designers, it was transformed into a visual marker of modernity.

While the material culture of the public sphere openly embraced modernity, the private sphere was slower to respond. Nowhere was that more apparent than in the domestic interior, especially in those areas of the home where everyday life and its accompanying rituals were enacted (Figure 1.2). In turn-of-the-century USA, for example, following the advice of Edith Wharton and Ogden Codman that was articulated in their book on the subject, the interior fashion of the day favoured the French eighteenth-century style, understood by a newly rich sector of society as the perfect messenger of good taste.[19] Even in that most conservative of contexts, however, modernization was present in the form of new technologies, such as gas and electric lighting and heating.[20] While not every aspect of material culture moved equally quickly towards modernity, there was a strong sense, at the turn of the century, that important transformations were taking place that were changing the experience of everyday life for increasing numbers of people.

Dress, or fashion as it had become for the majority of people by that time, played a role in both the private and the public spheres. Several studies

Figure 1.2 Late nineteenth-century middle-class American parlour
(courtesy of the Society for the Preservation of New England Antiquities)

have looked in detail at the relationship of men and women's clothing with modernity. Elizabeth Wilson, for example, has shown how fashion and modernity developed hand in hand with each other in the urban context, especially in the formation of identities, while Christopher Breward's account of male clothing in the period has explained that men were not, as has frequently been claimed, operating outside the fashion cycle or the world of consumption.[21] The widespread idea that men's dress was standardized at that time was, in fact, formed later, influenced by the modernist belief that men were governed by rationality rather than desire and that they resisted the urge to join the fashion cycle. As the French cultural critic, Roland Barthes, has explained, the language of material culture in the context of consumption operates simultaneously on two levels and is dependent upon an important contradiction. To follow the logic of the capitalist economy, he has claimed, it has to evoke desire while also aligning itself to the rationality of the production system.[22] From the outset, design was characterized by that dual alliance, its main *raison d'être* being its role within industrial production but its primary function being to stimulate desire in the marketplace. It was the task of the designer to reconcile those conflicting requirements.

In 1899, the social scientist, Thorstein Veblen, published his seminal text,

Theory of the Leisure Class, an early attempt to analyze the system underpinning conspicuous consumption.[23] Later, Georg Simmel also set out to unravel the same conundrum.[24] Veblen focused his study on the way in which society was driven by conspicuous leisure. In the consumption of women's fashionable dress, he recognized the existence of a social process that applied to that of other goods as well, although with less intensity. The situation, he observed, was characterized by fashionably dressed women acting as markers of their husband's social position and continually seeking new, ever more fashionable clothes in emulation of their immediate social superiors (Figure 1.3). He isolated the concept of upward emulation: the phenomenon, that is, which, according to Veblen, drove the continual process of conspicuous consumption and fashion change. Although he did not focus his attention on design, on the process that made fashionable dress attractive to consumers in the first place, it was a necessary (albeit unacknowledged) component, nonetheless, of the social process he had described.

Figure 1.3 Late nineteenth-century women's dress from *Myra's Journal of Dress and Fashion*, 1 September 1885, published by Weldon, London
(courtesy the V&A images at the Victoria and Albert Museum, London)

Veblen was more interested in the sociocultural function of dress than in its inherent characteristics. For the designers who created fashion items, however – among them the French couturiers, Charles Frederick Worth, Jacques Doucet and Jeanne Paquin – detail was everything. Their task was to continually refine the language of dress through the application of new colours, decorative details, shapes and levels of elaboration, such that they were continually desirable. Although in outlining his theory of upward emulation Veblen referred to dress, it was equally relevant to a range of other visual and material artefacts, among them interiors, furnishings, toasters, knives and forks and eventually automobiles. So fundamental was the role of design in maintaining social stability and cohesion in the context of continuous change that the existence of visually skilled individuals who could conceptualize and continually renew the visual appearance of consumer goods was paramount.

The goods in question continued to include the traditional decorative arts, which incorporated the safety of familiarity and were therefore risk-free for those consumers who were insecure about their taste. As the idea of fashion and modernity began to affect the lives of increasing numbers of people, however, the two-dimensional world of commercial promotions that embraced advertisements, magazines and the packages created for branded goods, began to reflect that fact, making consumers aware of what was available to them and communicating to them ideals to which they could aspire. The growth of modern advertising and of modern mass-media magazines, aimed in the first instance at women, served to create new levels of desire and to accelerate the growth of modern consumer culture.

Women's magazines, especially those focusing on fashion and the elabo-ration of the home, played a crucial role in the expanding consumer culture of the second half of the nineteenth century. Margaret Beetham has provided an account of the expansion of those magazines in Britain in the years in question, while Jennifer Scanlon has documented the development of the American woman's magazine, *The Ladies' Home Journal*.[25] Both studies have emphasized the ways in which those publications served to position women at the heart of modern consumer culture. As well as acting as consumer guides, however, they also contained advertisements for the countless consumer goods on offer in the marketplace. In tandem with the growth of magazines, the numbers of household advice books also swelled in at that time on both sides of the Atlantic, offering yet another source of information for housewives keen to perform their tasks properly, as well as a wide range of idealized images of domesticity to inspire them.

One of the subtlest ways in which advertising and marketing penetrated the consciousness of consumers was through the use of brands. Changes in retailing systems from market stalls to fixed shops and urban department stores put a greater emphasis on the roles of packaging and branding (Figure 1.4). Rather than buying loose foodstuffs, shoppers increasingly bought pre-packed goods that had been prepared in factories and

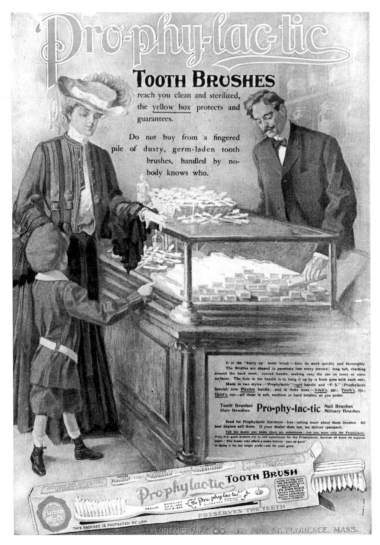

Figure 1.4 Late nineteenth-century packaging in the USA
(courtesy of the Archives Center, National Museum of American History,
Smithsonian Institution)

distributed in bulk to retail outlets.[26] Susan Strasser has described the
changes that took place in retailing in those years and the accompanying
rise of branding as a means of identifying goods.[27] It was the era in which
the names of companies, used as brands – Kellogg's and Hoover among
them – came to replace those of the commodities themselves in the minds of
consumers. Packaging and branding necessitated the emergence of yet

another group of visualizers, whose role was to create attractive, memorable images that helped promote the brand over the product. Although brand names were often visible on packets, they were essentially immaterial concepts that sold products through their appeal to a desirable lifestyle.

The rise of branded goods in the USA represented a major shift in the way in which goods were bought and sold and created a new link between design and marketing that was to become increasingly complex over the next century. Companies found names for their products that evoked particular lifestyles. The Pittsburgh Reduction Company, for example, a manufacturer of aluminium kitchenware items, coined the name *Wearever* for its range of products, building on the assumption that their potential consumers were rational beings who wanted value for money. It employed artists to develop a range of magazine advertisements to promote the *Wearever* range and shops were encouraged to place banners in their shop windows with the name emblazoned on it. A sophisticated visual promotional framework was thus developed around the campaign to sell aluminium pots and pans. Importantly, it required the input of visually skilled specialists in the areas of graphics, packaging and show-window display. In the years before 1914, however, few attempts were made to make goods themselves – aluminium saucepans, for example – look attractive. Rather, they retained a utilitarian appearance and their desirability was communicated through the visual information that accompanied them. That early means of conveying the added value of mass-produced items represented a first stage in a process that eventually led to the emergence, in the inter-war years, of industrial design. By that time, manufacturers had realized that the visual impact of goods themselves gave them a competitive edge that advertisements, packaging and shop-window displays could not achieve on their own.

By the early years of the twentieth century, in its attempt to stimulate and satisfy consumer desire, the commercial world had developed a set of sophisticated marketing strategies that involved a wide range of visualizing and conceptualizing practices. The expanded market, the phenomenon of new consumers using visual, material and spatial culture as a means of defining and communicating their identities and social aspirations and the availability of more and more goods, images and services in the marketplace, combined to create the necessary backcloth for the emergence of a concept of modern design that began to merge those strands. Most significantly, design, as it came to be called, was characterized by its unique position at the interface between consumption and production and by its ability to relate both to the irrational behaviour of consumers and the increasingly rational process of mass manufacturing. Above all, its ability to represent modernity made it one of the key social and cultural forces of the early twentieth century. By 1914, the framework was in place for a new, modern visual, material and spatial culture that was defined by its role within conspicuous consumption and the requirements of the marketplace.

Consumer culture and modernity

> Consumer culture is in important respects the culture of the modern west.[28]

In the years between the two world wars, more and more inhabitants of the western industrialized world began to engage with modernity in a multitude of ways. Sometimes, as the social historian, Sally Alexander, has so evocatively shown, it was expressed by gestures as simple as a touch of lipstick or the puff of a cigarette.[29] At other moments it was represented by the wholesale reshaping of the visual, material and spatial environment, as demonstrated, for example, by New York's 1939 World's Fair.[30] Modernity existed to the extent to which people could imagine the future and bring that vision to bear on the present. It was frequently experienced as an idealized concept, something that promised to add value to people's lives and that went beyond need into the world of desire. Presented to them through the mediation of mass manufactured goods, magazines, films and advertisements, it had something of the unattainable about it while being, at the same time, attainable. Luxurious, it was also democratic. Modernity's key characteristic, therefore, as it was presented to the inhabitants of the industrialized world, was its inbuilt ambivalence. Designers, paid to be imaginative and visually innovative, played a key part envisioning modernity, in ensuring that it remained just out of reach and in appearing to resolve its inherent contradictions, if only temporarily.

The outward signs of modernity continued to be most obviously visible in the public arena. Europe and the USA witnessed the arrival of urbanization and increasing levels of wealth in those years. As a result, consumption grew dramatically, with far-reaching effects on the mass environment. Car ownership grew, for example, creating in its wake a roadside material culture of motels, drive-in cinemas and petrol stations (Figure 1.5). Also in the public arena the consumption of goods for personal embellishment – from frocks to make-up – and the enhanced visibility of women meant that city life was visually transformed. The ever increasing impact of graphic advertising and commercial display added to that effect, providing a mass environment that, in urban and suburban centres, was visually transformed.

Those changes were driven by the commercial machine that underpinned the expansion of consumer culture. It was especially successful in the USA, where the art of marketing was at its most sophisticated. Much has been written about its development. Susan Strasser and R. S. Tedlow, for example, have documented the rise of mass marketing in the USA.[31] Case studies have demonstrated how marketing ensured that mass-produced goods reached a large audience of consumers. In her essay, *The Marketing of Cutex in America, 1916–1935*, for example, Kate Forde has shown how the J. Walter Thompson Advertising Company set about selling nail varnish to a female mass market.[32] The Cutex brand was heavily advertised through

Figure 1.5 Texaco gas station designed by Teague Associates, USA, 1930s
(© Walter Dorwin Teague Associates)

women's magazines, the readership of which was expanding exponentially.[33] Forde has explained that JWT's strategy was to sell the name of Cutex, in line with a range of other modern hygiene products, among them Borax, Kleenex, Lux and Pyrex, as if it were a kind of deity.[34] The use of strikingly modernist packaging was also an important selling point. Kathy Peiss's essay, *Hope in a Jar: The Making of America's Beauty Culture*, has also explained that consumer fantasies were created, controlled and fulfilled by the commercial system, which embraced design.[35]

The financial hardships of the 1930s did not dampen people's desire to consume a particular range of goods – cars, refrigerators and other domestic appliances among them. The new products of the technological industries came with a vision of modernity built into them. Cars, for example, were manufactured by new production techniques and, from the late 1920s, styled to appeal to a spectrum of consumers. General Motors' (GM) range included its up-market Cadillac and its down-market Buick at that time.[36] The market segmentation of goods not only reflected consumer difference but it also played a key role in creating it. The result was the emergence of a subtle consumer–design relationship that increasingly applied right across the social spectrum. While it was not possible for GM to predict consumer tastes, as Sally Clarke has explained, its venture into industrial design constituted a business risk that it was, nevertheless, willing to take.[37]

The democratization of taste and luxury brought about by design's alliance with mass production industry was intensified through the inter-war years across the industrialized world, bringing with it a new mass sensitivity to stylistic change. The fashion cycle, described by Thorstein Veblen some decades earlier, became a widespread reality, particularly in those areas of material culture – fashionable dress and motor-cars in particular – that were most susceptible to it. Along the way, a gendering of material culture was established whereby women used their dress, their beauty products and their interiors to express their fashion awareness, and thence their social standing (Figure 1.6), whereas men began to invest their status and identities in the new consumer machines.

Much was written about the female consumer of the inter-war years. Within the period, it was widely acknowledged that women were the key consumers. In *Selling Mrs. Consumer* of 1929, the household management expert turned consumer advisor, Christine Frederick, described what she believed to be the characteristics of 'feminine consumption'.[38] In a section entitled 'Guessing at Mrs. Consumer's Character' she explained that, 'Mrs. Consumer habitually proceeds more along the lines of instinct than upon theory or reason and accommodates herself more readily to practical realities. Man is more thoroughly theoretical'.[39] In his article, 'Consuming

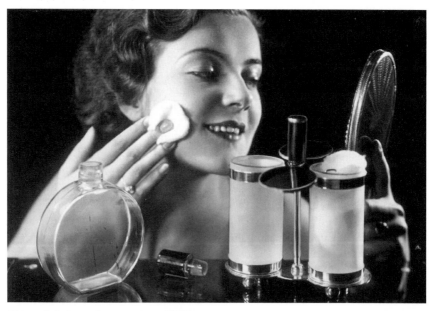

Figure 1.6 A modern woman, 1930s
(courtesy of the author)

Brotherhood: Men's Culture, Style and Recreation as Consumer Culture, 1880–1930', Mark A. Swiencicki has claimed, however, that, 'men were a very large and important consuming constituency'.[40] His evidence indicates that men were indeed significant consumers in the period, with their range of possible consumables including ready-to-wear clothing, sports equipment and recreational activities. Unlike women, Swiencicki has argued, men did not acquire their goods from shops and department stores but rather from a range of nonretail outlets, such as saloons, lodges, clubs, barbershops and dime theatres.[41] Designed goods, images and services clearly played an important role in both motivating sales and meeting the needs and desires of both men and women, albeit in different ways.

In his book, *Auto Opium*, the sociologist David Gartman has argued that the growing emphasis upon colour and appearance in consumer decision making was a result of the fact that women were increasingly involved in purchasing decisions. Although, he has suggested, men were also involved, they did not admit that they were equally interested in the visual aspects of everyday life. He has also explained that, with the advent of mass manufacturing, inasmuch as the assemblers of mass-produced cars also became their consumers, the worlds of production and consumption became increasingly intertwined. A form of compensation for the loss incurred by their labour being sold to the capitalist system was thus provided.[42]

Automobile graphic advertising appealed to a world on wheels and was designed accordingly. The design historian, David Jeremiah, has researched the expansion of petrol stations in Britain in the period, showing how they, 'irreversibly changed the shape of the rural and urban landscape'.[43] That change did not come about without resistance, however, as many people saw it as a regrettable influence from America that was ruining the environment.

From the outset, consumer culture had its aggressive opponents who did not want the natural landscape polluted by unnatural constructions and garish graphics. Early twentieth-century aluminium cooking pots, for example, were believed to spread disease and the new chemical substances contained in nail polish, such as the nitrocellulose, were also thought to be dangerous. Whether in the form of graphic advertisements, packaging or as a component of goods themselves, design played an important role in offsetting such anxieties and appeasing consumers through the evocation of a pleasant, beautiful world in which progress was always depicted as benevolent.

Arguably, the advent of the motor-car was the most radical modernizing material cultural force of the interwar years, most dramatically in the USA but also significantly in Europe. In their preface to *The Automobile and American Culture*, the editors, David L. Lewis and Laurence Goldstein, have discussed society's ambivalent relationship with the automobile. 'We still complain' they wrote, 'that vehicles disturb tranquillity, pollute the environment, kill us off in large numbers, and strain our pocketbooks. But only a handful of us have traded motor vehicles for mopeds, much less bicycles'.[44] In his study of the influence of the motor-car on British society in the period in question, Sean O'Connell has emphasized the inherent masculinity of that new form of transportation which, he has argued, 'has ultimately prevented millions of women from taking to the driving seat'.[45]

Designed public environments, especially those linked to work, shared leisure and shopping, also played a key role within the formation of urban modernity. In all the modern metropolises of the western industrialized world, shops and the experience of shopping were important agents of modernization for large sections of society. Building on pre-1914 innovations when the means of selling to a mass market were first put in place, shops presented themselves as overtly modern. The effect was a circular one, in that the new environments simultaneously reflected and created a modern consumer culture. Indeed, shops were among the first buildings the interior spaces of which were influenced by the modern styles of the day, from the austere form of high modernism in the most up-market stores (London's Simpsons of Piccadilly, for example) to the more decorative, American-influenced curved forms of streamlining, sometimes referred to as 'modernistic' and the French-influenced '*moderne*' style.

French designers played a special role in the modernization of the shopping environment. In that country, manufacturing was dominated by the luxury trades – those of haute couture, perfume, interior decoration and craft-made furniture among them. Shopping was geared, therefore, to the socially and financially privileged, who purchased their goods from élite outlets, while it also offered aspiring consumers access to a luxurious lifestyle. The latter's first experience of modernity was often in a department store or a boutique. In her study of 1920s Paris, Tag Gronberg has explained that the '*devanture de boutique*' (shop front) was 'frequently cited as the most appropriate means of modernizing Paris'.[46] The model of modernity she presented was strongly bound up with the concepts of fashion and luxury.

Modernity was especially evident in post-war dress. After the First World War, a revolution in women's dress and general profile meant that the soft flowing forms of the early century were replaced by a more linear, angular silhouette. The idealized female body was dramatically transformed as fashionable women aspired to a look that owed much the modernist 'machine aesthetic'. Men's idealized bodies also changed to reflect a new image of modernity. Transformations in hairstyling were particularly apparent. New technology allowed women to curl their new short hair and present it in the fashionable styles of the day. Innovative hairdressers, such as Antoine of Paris, turned hairdressing into an art form that was emulated in urban centres across the globe. The spaces in which such activities took place combined the advances made possible by technology in the public sphere and the traditionally private and intimate activity of having one's hair dressed at home, resulting in a new democratized fusion of luxury and modernity.[47]

Even within the tradition-oriented arena of the home, modernity was also making its mark. It was especially noticeable in kitchens and bathrooms where there was little resistance to the improvements that the new technologies could make. The kitchen was affected by advances in organization, inspired by the scientific management advice provided by Christine Frederick in the early century. Continuous work surfaces were installed by those householders who could afford them and the new labour-saving appliances – as much status objects as time-savers – were consumed in large numbers by the '30s. The refrigerator, in particular, took on an iconic significance at that time, representing as it did the arrival of technological modernity in kitchens across the globe.

The entry of modernity into the domestic arena went hand in hand with the housewife's changing role and status. From a rational scientist, in charge of her laboratory, she was transformed into a caring wife, mother and consumer. By the 1930s, however, she had turned into a charming hostess, inviting visitors into her home and showing them her impressive modern goods.[48] A seductive idealized image was created by manufacturers and their advertisers to convince women that they should see themselves as consumers first and foremost and that they could construct their identities and the social status of their families through consumption (Figure 1.7).

Figure 1.7 Xanti Schawinsky, Olivetti poster, 1935
(courtesy of the Associazione Archivio Storico Olivetti, Ivrea, Italy)

In spite of the successful efforts made by manufacturing industry to intro-
duce modern styles into the domestic arena, the home also retained its
traditional face. That was especially apparent in the living room, the site of
family values which depended on memory for their continuity. It frequently
featured a wide range of material references to the past and inherited
objects also had an important role to fulfil. Nonetheless, several signs of an
encroaching modernity were also in evidence. The claustrophobic Victorian
parlour was gradually being replaced by lighter, brighter living rooms
containing fewer pieces of furniture and less clutter. That cautious, evolutionary approach to an acceptance of a transformed environment has been
described by the literary historian, Alison Light, as being characteristic of a
preference for a 'conservative modernity'.[49] A number of historians have
demonstrated that the path to modernity was not the same for everyone and
that factors such as gender, class, age and ethnicity affected the ways in
which it was negotiated.[50] Most women engaged with some level of modernity in the inter-war years, however. In all but the most affluent of homes,
interior decoration was undertaken by housewives themselves, facilitated by
consumption and tradesmen. Examples of modern interior schemes were
available to them in magazines, shop windows and films – Hollywood films
played a key role influencing both interior décor and dress – providing
important sources of inspiration.[51]

Nowhere was the adoption of modern styles disseminated through the
mass media more apparent than in the new suburban residential areas that
were developed around the key cities in the USA and Europe. Inhabited for
the most part by the new upper working class and middle class, those areas
developed an alternative to sophisticated metropolitan taste. The social and
cultural geography that separated the city from the suburb was recogniza-
ble across the industrialized world, albeit with inevitable local variations.
The suburbs engaged with what the cities had consumed some time earlier
and had subsequently rejected as being unfashionable. In addition, the
suburb and the city supported completely different systems of production
and consumption that remained separated from each other. It became
apparent that it was possible for distinctive taste cultures – all of them
modern according to their own definition of the term – to coexist in close
proximity to each other. Ben Fine and Ellen Leopold's theory of 'systems of
provision' was developed to explain that phenomenon. They have maintained that people's tastes are formed in the economic context of the
particular system of provision available to them.[52] However, they ignored
the role played by the globally disseminated media, to which most people
had access in the inter-war years and which were as effective as agents of
taste formation as what was available in the local shops.

By the late 1930s, a concept of modernity had penetrated the lives of
many people living in the western industrialized world. The effects of
marketing, advertising and branding were widespread and there was a high
level of awareness about the stylistic languages of mass-produced goods,

images and spaces. Self and group identities were increasingly being negotiated through consumption and it had become clear that, while meanings were injected into images and objects at the moment of their production, they were supplemented and transformed as they entered into everyday life. In turn, new desires were stimulated that required the creation of new goods and images to satisfy them. Thus was the fashion cycle fuelled. Consuming modern visual, material and spatial culture, and thereby embracing modernity, had, by the inter-war years, become one of the primary means through which the majority of the inhabitants of the industrialized world acquired their identities and positioned themselves in society. Such was the intensification and expansion of that process that designers found themselves at the very epicentre of modern consumer culture.

2 The impact of technology

New production methods, new materials

> Mass production is the focussing upon a manufacturing project of the
> principles of power, accuracy, economy, system, continuity, and speed.[1]

In the first four decades of the twentieth century, one face of modern design
was defined by its sociocultural role within the expanding picture of
consumption and the newly defined marketplace – an area of modern life
that could not be easily rationalized and systematized. Its other important
defining context was the more rationally based world of mass manufacturing and technological innovation. In that context, large numbers of
standardized goods were produced to meet expanding demand but, because
of the high investment costs required, they had to be aggressively sold.
Design crossed the technology/culture divide. A process that was intrinsic to
mass manufacturing, the results of which communicated sociocultural
values, it was embedded equally firmly within the worlds of consumption
and production. Arguably, it was one of the few phenomena that linked
those two worlds together.[2]

Technological innovation made possible the manufacture of vast numbers
of newly conceived products that entered the marketplace from the late nineteenth century onwards. As well as constituting a whole new area of visual
and material culture, complementing the more traditional decorative arts,
the new goods also challenged and excited designers' imaginations. The
wide availability of such novel objects as vacuum cleaners, electrical appliances and new modes of transportation, as well as the new forms of
advertising and retail display developed to promote their sales in those years,
provided a primary means through which consumers could create new identities for themselves and negotiate their entry into modern life.

The modern concept of design, which moved beyond the traditional
decorative arts and the craft process that had generated them, was a direct
consequence of a defining feature of industrial manufacturing – the division
of labour. The new means of producing goods caused the work of the traditional craftsmen to become fragmented into a number of new, differentiated

tasks, one of which – the initial conceptualization of the product – required the development of a new process. From the outset, designers had a two-fold responsibility. As well as conceiving new products and planning their manufacture, they also had to work in the context of consumption to ensure that their products contained appropriate sociocultural meanings. Designers were uniquely placed, therefore, to express modernity in the contexts of both production and consumption.

Industrialization was one of the key defining phenomena of the modern world. In Britain, the discovery of steam power inspired the invention of numerous new machine tools and production techniques.[3] In turn, those new tools facilitated the manufacture of new consumer machines. New materials, cast iron among them, were responsible for dramatic changes in the design of products and the environment, making possible new forms of decoration. Those discoveries transformed the production of the traditional decorative arts. In textile production, for example, the Spinning Jenny and the Jacquard loom revolutionized the ways in which textiles were both conceived and made, requiring designers to make decisions in advance of manufacture, unlike craft workers, who had been able to make aesthetic and material choices as they went along. That seemingly simple modification represented an important shift from the working process of the craftsman, who depended upon tacit skills, to that of the designer, who needed to engage in rational planning. It brought with it radical changes in many manufacturing sectors, among them fabric printing ceramics production.[4]

While Britain witnessed transformations in the manufacturing of the traditional decorative art industries, textiles, ceramics, glass and furniture among them, the USA made huge advances in the efficient organization of labour and production in the new, technologically oriented industries, in the development of highly specialized machine tools and in the manufacture of new goods with a technological bias. Much has been written about what was dubbed, 'the American System of Manufacture'. H. J. Habakkuk, for example, has described the developments in both Britain and the USA, explaining that mechanization was much more advanced in the latter country because, given the greater availability of farming land, manual labour was in short supply.[5] Siegfried Giedion's seminal text, *Mechanisation Takes Command* of 1948, focused on the importance of the machine to American culture and to that country's pre-eminence in modern, functional design.[6] Indeed, modernism – the dominant design movement of the mid twentieth-century – considered the machine, with its links function and rationality, as the key metaphor and the source of aesthetic inspiration for modern designers.

David A. Hounshell's book, *From the American System to Mass Production 1800–1932: The Development of Manufacturing Technology in the US*, has focused on the fundamental continuities within the story of American manufacturing in this period.[7] He has outlined a story that began with the changes that took place in American arms production in the nineteenth century and moved through to automobile manufacturing in the

1920s. His narrative has taken in clocks, sewing machines, bicycles, agricultural machinery and automobiles along the way and he has maintained that each industry learnt from the one before it, and that continuity was provided through the use of steel as a basic material, the development of standardized components and the use of specialist machine tools. Hounshell has argued that the production of Henry Ford's 'Model T' automobile represented a model of pure mass production (Figure 2.1). It was, in his view, only to last twelve years, however, as Alfred. P. Sloan at General Motors brought in flexible mass production, which superseded Ford's ideal of completely standardized manufacture. Sloan's flexible model, Hounshell has argued, was a response to the demands of the market, which required product differentiation. Hounshell's text concludes just at the point when the industrial designer – better known as a stylist at that time – in the form of Harley Earl at General Motors, was catapulted into the automotive industry to create a level of differentiation for GM's automobiles. By the 1920s, according to Hounshell, the emergence of a second-hand car market, the urbanization of the mass of the American population and the importance of buying a second car that was not black and which was more impressive than one's neighbour's model, meant that pure standardization

Figure 2.1 Henry Ford's 'Model T' production line at the Highland Park factory, 1913
(from the collections of Henry Ford Museum and Greenfield Village)

could no longer be a commercial reality. Hounshell's study has emphasized an important moment in the story of modern design, one in which technology and culture came into direct conflict with each other. In the event, culture won the day and design provided the means by which the two forces could achieve a workable compromise. From that point onwards, the products of the new mass production industries became as sensitive to the vagaries of the fashion system as the decorative arts had long been. In addition, the role of the 'visualizer' (or designer) became highly valued by those industries that understood that they had to accommodate an element of art within their otherwise highly efficient, rational operations.

The arrival of new materials helped to transform the appearance of the modern environment and provided new challenges for the designer. The impact of plate glass windows on the cityscape, for example, was dramatic, as we have seen, while the forms made possible by cast and wrought iron and concrete came to represent a language of modernity for the inhabitants of the modern world. To create visual, material and spatial symbols of modernity, architects and designers were keen to exploit both the physical and the symbolic potential of new materials. In Vienna, for example, the architect, Otto Wagner, embraced the properties of aluminium in the interior of his Post Office Savings Bank building.[8]

The architects and designers associated with the Art Nouveau movement, who sought to create a new style that had no historical baggage attached to it and which replaced nineteenth-century historicism, looked to new materials to achieve that ambition. As Helen Clifford and Eric Turner have explained, 'Metal architecture stood for modernism. Cast iron was employed by Art Nouveau designers and architects for its practical qualities and aesthetic possibilities...cast iron...was particularly suitable for the expression of the suppleness and tensile strength of the Art Nouveau "whiplash curve".'[9] Blending together the achievements of the engineers with a new language of modern decoration, the Art Nouveau designers created a new aesthetic language of modernity.

Technology could make new products and materials available but it could not ensure their acceptance in the marketplace. It was left to designers to play a role in gauging popular taste and aspirations and in transforming new materials into desirable goods. That was sometimes a relatively easy task and sometimes not. The semi-synthetic material, Celluloid, for example, could easily be used as a substitute for more expensive, highly desirable materials such as jet, ebony, coral, amber and ivory and it was quickly accepted as such. Aluminium proved much more challenging to designers. Indeed, it was not until the turn of the century that that new metal could be produced cheaply and began to replace enamel and brass as materials for cooking pots. Even then, it was regarded with some suspicion because of its proximity to food. Only in the inter-war years of the twentieth century were designers able to visualize aluminium products as modern objects in their own right.

The sense of a new material modernity was most visible in the public sphere. The traditional context of domesticity witnessed a growing acceptance of them. The gradual absorption of new materials into the home began with the acceptance, in the early century, of items made of pressed glass, a replacement for more expensive cut crystal, and others made of the new plastic, Bakelite, used for electrical accessories such as plugs and switches.[10] A number of other materials that had traditionally been used within the domestic sphere also found themselves used in new ways to create a sense of modernity. In the USA, for example, the use of chintz in interior furnishings came back into fashion, replacing the earlier heavy velvets and brocades and ushering in a new feeling of lightness.[11]

Although the home was slower than the public arena to rise to the challenge of new materials and technologies, gas and electricity transformed both the public and the domestic spheres. A search for rationalism and for increased efficiency underpinned factory practice in the last years of the nineteenth and the early years of the twentieth century. In both the factory and the office, this was achieved through the application of Taylorism and by the increasing modifications made to the 'American system of manufacture'. In the factory, the creation of standardized, interchangeable parts was combined with the moving assembly line.[12] That new system was demonstrated in its most refined form at Henry Ford's Highland Park Factory, where the 'Model T' automobile was first manufactured in 1913. The moving assembly line and the use of standardized parts were reflected in the appearance of the automobile, which was characterized by the complexity of its component elements. In spite of its overtly engineered aesthetic, because it was marketed at first-time buyers whose needs were reflected in low price and reliability, the 'Model T' had a strong consumer appeal. Ownership was, in itself, a mark of social distinction for the members of the rural population at whom the car was targeted and who, up until that time, had had to make do with horses. As Hounshell has shown us, however, it was a marketing strategy that had a limited life as, once it was no longer a question of first time ownership and competition existed in the marketplace, the outmoded 'Model T' was unable to continue to stimulate that same level of consumer desire.

Taylorism, the scientific measuring system that was used to analyze the ways in which tasks were carried out and which led to the proposal of more efficient, time-saving alternatives, entered the office and the factory in the early years of the twentieth century, bringing with it a strong ethos of rationalism. A few years later, that desire for rationality was transferred from the factory and office into the domestic arena. The desire to rationalize housework also owed its existence to the tradition of household advice that had been initiated by the writings of Catherine Beecher and her sister Harriet Beecher Stowe (Figure 2.2).[13] To demonstrate that a history of woman's labour in the home needed to be written to complement existing accounts of male labour in the public workplace, Ruth Schwartz Cowan

Figure 2.2 Household management, early twentieth-century USA
(courtesy of the Wisconsin Historical Society)

and Susan Strasser, among others, have charted the development of women's advice literature.[14] They have both emphasized the importance of labour-saving principles to the late nineteenth- and early twentieth-century homes but have questioned whether, given that it was not clear what the home was meant to produce, the concept of efficient production was relevant to the domestic context. With much productive work – preserving fruit, sewing clothes, etc. – having been transferred to the factory, they have both explained, housework was dedicated to nurturing and consuming rather than to producing. In that new context, the introduction of efficiency into the household was a more complex proposition with a less obvious purpose.

As it had in the factory, reorganization preceded mechanization in the implementation of efficient practice in the home. Christine Frederick's 1913 book, which had been serialized a little earlier in the pages of the *Ladies' Home Journal*, outlined the ways in which tasks could be simplified by a reorganization of the kitchen that reduced the number of steps needed to prepare a meal and clear up after it. She also proposed that housewives should be made to look like professionals by donning white gowns, in emulation of laboratory technicians, and that food preparation tools should be positioned in close proximity to the housewife, in emulation of an artisan's workbench.[15] In the years before the First World War, the attempt to bring rationality into the feminine sphere, hitherto perceived as an arena dominated by emotional values and consumer desire, was brought about by a transformation of existing elements rather than by the introduction of new, technologically innovative, domestic tools. Through the absorption of her ideas into 1920s modernist kitchen planning and design in Europe, the impact of Frederick's work was felt later in the inter-war years.

Although Frederick's proposals had only envisaged a reorganization of simple, traditional tools, they nonetheless encouraged manufacturers to approach housewives as rational beings for the first time and stimulated consumers to think in terms of rational consumption. They also put housewives in the right frame of mind to accept the new domestic tools – electrically powered ones in particular – when they eventually became available. The newly formed electrical companies – General Electric and Westinghouse in particular – and the smaller domestic appliance manufacturers – Hoover and Sunbeam among them – were quick to develop marketing strategies that stressed the role played by the new appliances both in professionalizing the housewife's role and in making her life easier. Producers of aluminium pans, for example, set up experimental kitchens in department stores where home economics experts demonstrated the benefits of using the new products.[16] Although the emphasis was upon their role as servant replacements, one historian has suggested that they were also purchased by women who had been lucky enough to retain their servants as a means of encouraging them to stay.[17] Although they represented an engagement with modernity, when they first appeared, the new household tools – toasters, electric frying pans, electric chafing dishes and food heaters among them – had crude, engineered forms. Like the 'Model T', they sold on the basis of their use value and their technical novelty was enough to provide their owners with an enhanced social status.

The distinction between invention and design was very clear in the years leading up to 1914. While the inventor's role was to create new applications for available technologies, the designer acted as the key interface between those applications, manufacturing industries and consumers. In the late nineteenth and early twentieth centuries, new concept followed new concept, such that the consumer machines with which we are all now familiar – the sewing machine, the telephone, the refrigerator, the bicycle and the automobile – all saw the light of day. Most of those new products emerged first in the USA. Given the abundance of manual labour, the push to create new domestic machines was inevitably less energetic in Europe.[18]

Once invented, the new goods had to be manufactured and sold in the open market place. It was the designer's task to ensure, firstly, that they could be made at an affordable price but, perhaps more importantly, to render them both meaningful and desirable. Gradually, the new products began to be visually and symbolically aligned with the environments for which they were destined. Kitchen-based items, often restricted to use by the servant or housewife, for example, usually retained a crude, mechanical appearance, whereas others, such as Hoover's 'Model O' electric suction sweeper, which boasted an Art Nouveau pattern on its metal housing (Figures 2.3 and 2.4), destined, as they were, to be seen throughout the house, were given a more sophisticated appearance. Toasters intended for the breakfast table frequently had decoration applied to their surfaces. Thus were technological inventions transformed into meaningful objects of desire, their technical and utilitarian features having been joined by others that stressed their role as aesthetic and symbolic artefacts with powerful sociocultural functions.[19]

Figure 2.3 Hoover 'Model O' suction sweeper, 1908
(© The Hoover Company, North Canton, Ohio)

Figure 2.4 Hoover advertisement, USA, 1920s
(© The Hoover Company, North Canton, Ohio)

By the First World War, the objects, images and spaces in both the public and the private spheres of the industrialized world had been transformed by the presence of a wide range of new goods that were the results of the technological inventiveness and manufacturing capabilities of the era. Their emergence engendered a strong belief in the power of science and reason to transform the world for the better. That belief existed alongside the importance of the irrationality of conspicuous consumption upon which the capitalist economy was so dependent. Increasingly, however, advertisers and marketing men began to engage with rational arguments to sell many of their goods – especially those destined for use by the housewife herself in the kitchen – but the appeal of accessible luxuries continued to play a strong role within the psychology of consumption. Defined as a process within manufacturing, marketing and advertising, design continued to flourish in and act as a key messenger of the modern world.

The materials of modernity

> Base metals were transformed into marvels of Beauty, expressive of our own age.[20]

Through the twentieth century and beyond, the discovery of new materials and innovations in production technologies have constantly challenged designers to find new forms and meanings for the objects and images that flowed from them. Ever keen to augment their profits, manufacturers sought inexpensive ways of creating their goods and, wherever possible, substituted the traditional materials of craft manufacture with new, cheaper, ones suitable for mass production. Because the technological and economic momentum needed to be complemented by consumer acceptance, aggressive sales techniques were developed to stimulate desire and enhance the modern appeal of the new materials. Design acted as an important bridge between technology and culture, anticipating consumer demand and making new technologies and materials both available and desirable.

The nineteenth and early twentieth centuries had seen iron and steel transform the environment, while plate glass had brought an unprecedented level of spectacle into the urban streets. In the hands of the lady interior decorators, as we have seen, chintz had moved from the country to become a *sine qua non* of the stylish urban interior. Abstract forms, developed by fine artists in response to the new environment, had inspired change and the democratization of modernity had encouraged a new aesthetic for everyday life. Indeed, it could be argued that new materials made everything feel and look different and were seen, therefore, as being highly appropriate to an era that celebrated modernity.[21]

At no time had the urge to create new substances been stronger than in the nineteenth century. The materials of mid twentieth-century modernity owed their existence to a number of key individuals who had been active in those years, as well as to a considerable amount of capital investment. Two key materials of inter-war modernity – plastics and aluminium – had been discovered in the middle of the nineteenth century. Plastics were developed as substitutes for more expensive substances that were in short supply but aluminium did not have an application at the time of its invention. While the developments of the two materials had several characteristics in common, they also diverged significantly. By the 1930s, however, they had both come to be perceived, by designers and consumers alike, as modern materials par excellence. The French cultural critic, Roland Barthes, came nearest to explaining why plastics had such a charismatic presence for consumers of modern material culture when he wrote, some years later, that 'plastic . . . is the stuff of alchemy'.[22]

Plastics and aluminium have both been considered by historians as important agents of cultural change. In his book, *Pioneer Plastic: The*

Making and Selling of Celluloid, Robert Friedel has explained that the semi-synthetic material succeeded in establishing itself through its links with the early film industry, as well as through its application to products, such as billiard balls, and its ability to make novelty goods – hatpins and letter openers among them – available to a wide audience.[23] Plastics have received more attention than aluminium, partly because of their countless applications and partly because they are easily recognized by the public. Throughout their history, plastics have been linked with specific products: Celluloid, for example, the first plastic, is known as the material of billiard balls and cinematic film, while Bakelite is the material of electrical fittings and 1930s radio cabinets (Figure 2.5).

Figure 2.5 Fada baby radio, USA, 1934
  (courtesy of the author)

The most far-reaching account of plastics' history and their links with modernity has been provided by Jeffrey Meikle in his book, *American Plastic: A Cultural History*, which has focused on the meanings of plastics to what the author has described as 'a civilization that seemed to be abandoning its ideals in pursuit of material goods'.[24] The acceptance of plastics, for Meikle, mirrored the growing materialism of modern society. They became both a metaphor for it and a material manifestation of it. Bakelite, Meikle suggested, became synonymous with the modern streamlined style as the products with which it became linked – radios for the most part – themselves became icons of modernity. Modern technology was made into a consumable form in the capable hands of far-sighted designers such as Peter Muller-Munk and Paul T. Frankl. Muller-Munk is quoted as saying that 'plastics became almost the hallmark of "modern design" . . . the mysterious and attractive solution for almost any application requiring "eye appeal",,' thereby anticipating Barthes' observations by some years.[25] Designers, Meikle has suggested, were responsible for imbuing plastics with an identity. Referring to the aesthetic ideas of Walter Benjamin, he has claimed that, 'If there was in truth no uniform "bakelite style" the stuff certainly projected a distinctive aura'.[26]

Plastics were the ideal materials for mass production and their progress through the twentieth century was intrinsically linked to the idea of the democratized product. In the inter-war years, as the material which housed radios, television sets and domestic appliances, plastics were not competing with more traditional materials and did not, therefore, constitute a threat to consumers. Even plastic jewellery found a place alongside more precious objects and mundane household artefacts, such as hairbrushes, powder containers and ashtrays, acquired a level of acceptance through their symbolic links with modernity. Such objects served to reinforce middle-class women's new found freedom in being able to indulgence in the luxury of self-beautification in the comfort of their own homes (see Figure 1.6).

After 1945, plastics lost their aura for a time, however, and became associated with the cheap objects fabricated in places such as Hong Kong that had very little social kudos attached to them. The materials were quickly rescued, however, and returned by Italy's leading designers of the 1950s and 1960s to the safe arena of high culture. In their decorative applications, plastic objects frequently emulated the forms of existing items, although the bright colours that could be achieved meant that they inevitably brought their own appearance with them to those cheap artefacts. Where new products, such as radios, were concerned, however, there was plenty of room for innovation. A number of designers rose to the challenge, creating many exciting new forms that quickly became icons of modernity and which have now become classic objects of modern design.[27] The aesthetically innovative plastic radio cabinets designed by Serge Chermayeff and Wells Coates in Britain in the 1930s, for example, have become collectible items. Their striking body shells performed a dual function, both concealing the complex workings of the machines they covered and, simultaneously, providing a powerful new image redolent of modernity. Given the strong cultural significance of the radio as part of the expanding interest in mass communications and its dramatic impact on the lives of modern citizens in the '30s, the symbolism of plastics was far-reaching and ensured them a high level of popular acceptance.

The example of the radio demonstrates the way in which – with the exception of precious materials, such as gold, which have an intrinsic monetary value attached to them, and others, such as worn stone, which carry memories within them – materials are impotent to convey meanings without the helping hand of the designer. Other classic designs of the inter-war years included Raymond Loewy's famous 1934 reworking of the Gestetner duplicating machine, the scale of which, given the technical limitations of casting plastic objects in moulds at that time, was exceptional. Inevitably, production technologies limited what designers could do. Although casting, machining, laminating and rolling were all processes that could be applied to plastics, moulding was by far the most frequently used. In the 1930s, the curves associated with the popular design style known as 'streamlining' became widespread, partly as a result of the fact that, in the manufacture of plastic products, sharp corners were hard to extract from moulds. In addition, crowned surfaces were used to compensate for the fact that the surfaces of plastic products often appear to be sinking inwards. The designer's role was to provide an appropriate look for artefacts made from those materials based on their knowledge of their physical properties. Countless new objects emerged from the factories of plastics manufacturers in the USA and Europe in those years – from sewing machines, to items of office equipment, to vacuum cleaners – all of them owing their modern identities to the designers who worked on them.

In spite of the efforts made by many manufacturers to persuade consumers that it had the potential to be one, aluminium was much less obviously accepted as a modern material for the public in its early applications. By the end of the 1930s, however, through its use in aeroplane bodies, airships, tableware items, car bodies and avant-garde furniture, it had acquired a modern image.[28] Unlike plastics, however, even with the assistance of marketing and design, the new metal had to work hard to acquire an aura of modernity, owing to the fact that aluminium saucepans stained in use and were thought to engender illness. In an effort to refute the belief that it was a malevolent material, a number of manufacturers, including the Aluminum Reduction Company of Pittsburgh, invested large sums of money in promoting the material to housewives. In an effort to sell their products, they organized department store demonstrations and advised on shop window displays.[29]

The most effective use of aluminium was in early transportation objects, especially aircraft, where its light weight was a huge advantage. Through its use in such objects, the material gradually began to acquire a contemporary aura. In the inter-war years, designers, such as Marcel Breuer and later the Dutchman Gerrit Rietveld, experimented with it in their furniture designs, often using it to replace steel, which was significantly heavier. Through its adoption by the American designer, Russel Wright, it also entered the domestic sphere. Aimed at the housewife, with her newly acquired identity as a hostess, Wright's stylish spun aluminium tableware was welcomed into the home and on to the dining-table (Figure 2.6). Following Wright's lead and with the assistance of the designer, Lurelle Guild, the American company, Alcoa, also moved into the production of household products and small decorative items made of aluminium.

Ultimately, however, it was as a material for the new objects of transportation that aluminium gained its most potent modern identity. It appeared as the shiny fuselages of aircraft, for example, which could defy gravity. In turn, airplanes became sources of inspiration for numerous other

Figure 2.6 Russell Wright, bun warmer, USA, 1935
(courtesy of The Brooklyn Museum of Art)

forms created by designers who embraced the modern ethos. Other modern aluminium forms followed afterwards. The classic aluminium chair, the 'Landi', created by the Swiss designer, Hans Coray, for the Swiss National Exhibition held in Zurich in 1938, acquired a high level of iconic significance, not just because of its physical lightness but also, more significantly, as a result of Coray's introduction of small round holes punched repeatedly into the metal to express that sense of lightness. The symbolism and function of aluminium were also combined in the bodies of BMW's racing cars of the 1940s. By 1945, through the intervention of design, the 'light, shiny metal, had become one of the most symbolically potent of all the materials of modernity.

New materials played a crucial role in many of the modern designed forms that emerged from the USA in the 1930s and the imagery designers created for them was often strikingly innovative. As Donald Dohner, the designer employed by the Westinghouse company, explained, 'Imitating other materials may be an interesting technical stunt for some engineers but it robs the new material of its birthright, destroys its identity and natural beauty, thereby degrading it'.[30] That strong commitment to the idea that new materials carried their own modern identity within them was echoed widely by many other designers who chose to work with them. Donald Deskey's interior work in New York's Radio City Music Hall has frequently been cited as an example of modern materials at their best. In his book,

Depression Modern: The Thirties Style in America, the writer Martin Grief has provided a long list of synthetic substances used in that era. They included Pyralin, Fiberloid, Nixonoid, Tenite, Ameroid, Durite, Textolite, Makalot, Micarta, and Insurok.[31] Increasingly, consumers sought new materials in their everyday goods as a mark of their love affair with modernity.

The 1933 'Century of Progress' exhibition, held in Chicago, at which an all-aluminium Pullman coach was on display, was seen as a shrine to new materials. The central theme was described as, 'the dramatization of the achievements of mankind, made possible through the application of science to industry'.[32] The temporary buildings were made of plywood, light steel, asbestos and gypsum board and the 'Homes and Industrial Arts' section consisted of eight model houses, each one fabricated in a different material, among them steel, Masonite and glass.

Chromed steel also took on a modern significance in the inter-war years. The presence of a shiny, reflective surface appealed to the increasingly visually conscious consumers of modernity. Within modernism artifice, seen as the marker of a progressive, democratic and benevolent technology, was valued above nature and the idea that technology could create its own objects, which, in turn, became the material manifestations of the powerful role it played in the modern world, became widespread. At the same time, however, there was a limit to how far people would go to let technology enter their homes and, in Europe, chromed steel tube furniture only penetrated the most avant-garde of interiors.

The development of the new materials was driven by large-scale American corporations and they were given forms by American designers who employed their visual imaginations to that end. Progressive European architect–designers also experimented with new materials, especially in the area of furniture design. Through the efforts of Marcel Breuer and Mies van der Rohe, in particular, Germany's achievements in tubular steel have been widely documented, as have those of the French architect, Le Corbusier.[33] Steel tube, a discovery of the nineteenth century, and, because of its combination of low weight and strength, used for the frames of bicycles, suggested itself as a structural material for furniture design. In the hands of Breuer, Mies, Le Corbusier and the Dutchman, Mart Stam, among others, it facilitated a fundamental shift from the solid upholstered chair to a new skeletal seating object that emphasized space over mass.

In Finland, the architect, Alvar Aalto, produced furniture designs made from sheets of bent, laminated plywood that could be used to perform a similar role to tubular steel. Through the use of new bending and bonding processes, wood could be made to work in new ways. Unlike their American equivalents, those experiments in new materials were led by designers and were less dependent, in the first instance, upon industrial manufacture. Quite quickly, however, given the nature of consumer demand, the industrial production of furniture made from those materials was realized. Examples included the tubular steel chairs manufactured by the British company, Pel. Aalto's furniture, produced by the Korhonen family firm in Finland, was imported into Britain in significant numbers in the 1930s by Finmar.[34]

New materials did not constitute technology's only contribution to the forms and images of modern design, however. Production engineers also played a key role in making new forms possible. In steel manufacturing, for example, the challenge was to create ever larger pieces that could form product casings with a minimum amount of seams. The modern look had left nature far behind, suggesting, rather, that the new artefacts had fallen out of the sky. A seamless casing gave the impression of a magic object, the product of science and technology, untouched, seemingly, by the human hand. Much effort went into the creation of an all-steel car body in the period. Early cars, the 'Model T' among them, had been basic assemblages of components put together with little regard for the visual effect of the end results. That gradually changed as steel bodies were developed and the aesthetic of streamlining began to unify the car's form. The all-steel, mass manufactured automobile body eventually emerged in the 1910s in the USA, while the French company, Citroën, was the first to achieve the same result in Europe a little later. Efforts were also made to make the refrigerator look as if it had been made from a single piece of steel. By the middle of the 1930s, the body of the refrigerator could (with the exception of the door) be made from a single piece of steel. The inability, at that time, to bend steel with small radii, however, meant that fridges boasted dramatic swollen forms that guaranteed them pride of place in kitchens and helped them to replace furniture as the home's most important status symbols.

While the inter-war years saw a huge expansion in the industries that focused on automobiles and domestic appliances (Figure 2.7), the manufacturers of more traditional goods, such as ceramics and glass, also sought to modernize their production techniques. The home also underwent a number of technological transformations that helped nudge it into the modern arena. Innovations in that sphere included the use of linoleum in bathrooms, of aluminium pots and pans in kitchens, of laminated plastics on kitchen surfaces, of the introduction of modern-style, mass-produced furniture items into living rooms, of moulded glass and ceramic ornaments on mantelpieces and of plastic-handled knives and forks on dining-tables. All these items, and many more besides, represented an engagement with modernity and an acknowledgement of the impact of technology and design in everyday life. The world of fashion was also dramatically transformed by the advent of rayon, the new artificial silk and, a little later, by that of nylon (Figure 2.8).[35]

The cultural impact of new materials, aided and abetted by design, was a highly significant contribution to the modernization of the lives of many people in the inter-war years. Both the materiality of the new way of life and the way in which these new seamless, non-natural products were catapulted into everyday life, apparently untouched by the human hand, provided consumers with a new view of the world. That new view was determined by culture rather than by nature and it helped to take people one step further away from the world they had inhabited before industrialization had changed things for ever.

Figure 2.7 Walter Dorwin Teague Gas range for the Floyd Wells Company, USA, 1935
(© Walter Dorwin Teague Associates)

Figure 2.8 Advertisement for 'Balcora' velvets and rayons, USA, 1940s
(courtesy of the author)

3 The designer for industry

Art and industry

The years leading up to 1914 witnessed the emergence of a new generation of visually trained individuals who applied their skills to the formation of modern images, objects and spaces. Their role was to provide the aesthetic options on the basis of which consumer decisions could be made. In that context, the need to clarify the design process, and the tasks of designers, became increasingly imperative. No single model for designing presented itself, however, and the activity continued to evolve in an ad hoc manner, largely dependent on the way things had happened in the decorative art industries in the past, the new requirements of industrial production and the vagaries of the marketplace. It remained the task of a wide range of diverse individuals – fine artists to teams of anonymous art workers to architects to engineers to craftsmen to decorative artists and a new breed of visualizers referred to as commercial artists – to contribute, in different ways, to the visual face of the everyday modern world. Different areas of production – the traditional decorative arts, new consumer products, fashion items, two-dimensional designs of various kinds and interior spaces and environments within the private and the public spheres – embraced design in different ways developing models of practice that suited their industries and their markets. At the same time, art and industry began to develop a strategic alliance with each other, with the aim of creating products, images and spaces that would appeal to the expanding body of consumers and which communicated the required sociocultural messages.

The decorative arts industries that had targeted élite markets had employed fine artists to make their products look appealing. In the creation of the early mass-produced goods aimed at larger scale audiences, however, the art content was frequently borrowed from elsewhere and adapted to the mechanical processes involved in industrial manufacturing. A number of studies have focused on the changing nature of the design process in the shift from craft manufacture to industrial production and on the new tasks developed for individuals engaged in the creation of the aesthetic component of goods such as textiles and ceramics. In particular, they have documented the ways in which the division of labour transformed traditional practices. From the eighteenth century up until the twentieth century and beyond, different means of providing goods with their design content have existed in different industries. In the nineteenth-century British calico-printing industry, for example, as Hazel Clark has explained, freelance painters sometimes supplied prints to manufacturers, while in-house art workers were responsible for transferring them on to the calico.[1] In Manchester, where there was a high concentration of textile manufacturing, the local design school frequently supplied trained individuals to local firms.

In the early mass production ceramics industry, as Adrian Forty has demonstrated, another group of art workers emerged to make the manufacture of decorative wares for the mass market possible.[2] At the other end of the market for ceramic goods, Doulton continued to create its artefacts, in a more traditional manner, in its Lambeth Studio, employing fine artists to both model and decorate its wares. At the other end of the spectrum, however, the same firm mass produced stoneware drainpipes, the forms of which were also designed without any input from fine artists. Without that more mundane area of production, however, the creation of the fine art ware would not have been financially viable.[3] The example of designing at Doulton highlights the coexistence of two models of design practice: that of the in-house, usually anonymous, art worker/designer and of the external, consultant fine artist/designer, whose name was frequently used to sell goods. The independent artists often operated across a number of different industries, while the workers remained in house, developing the required specialist technical expertise.

In the production of new goods dependent upon new technologies – such as items of transportation and the new household machines – it was left to engineers to determine their appearance. In the early automobile industry, engineers were responsible for the creation of the chassis and the product's working parts. Those components were subsequently combined with the body that had been created by traditional carriage builders who had transferred their skills into that new context. The extension of craft practices, such as that of the carriage builder, into the new engineering industries, often determined not only the appearance but also the symbolic meanings of the products in question. For that reason, early cars were frequently referred as 'horseless carriages'. It was to be some time before the car was considered to be an object of taste fulfilment like a ceramic teapot. Later, in the 1920s, when differentiation between mass production models became important to consumers, artistic design, known as styling, entered into the world of automotive manufacture.

Other mass-produced, engineered goods also revealed the hand of the artisan – metalworkers in particular – their crude forms openly reflecting the nature of the manufacturing process. The application of the art nouveau scrollwork, mentioned earlier, painted in purple on a pink background, on to the surface of Hoover's first electric suction sweeper, for example, was an attempt to transform that essentially utilitarian artefact into an art object (see Figure 2.3). As has been explained, the addition of beauty was crucial to any machine that played a role in domestic display. One American electric iron, produced in 1912, was even named the 'American Beauty' in an attempt to bridge the gap between art and industry in the eyes of its potential consumer.[4] Aluminium pots and pans, as we have seen, remained primarily utilitarian artefacts into the early twentieth century, their appearance reflecting their process of manufacture, their functional requirements and their place in the kitchen. The anonymity of their design and the lack of visual self-consciousness displayed by products such as these provided an important source of inspiration for the later modernist architects and designers who sought to develop an aesthetic that was rooted in utility rather than conspicuous display. Ironically, though, the very self-consciousness involved in the selection of such utilitarian forms as visual sources transformed the modernists' designs into art objects.

As the nineteenth century progressed, architects and decorative artists of repute gradually began to add goods produced by the new manufacturing industries to their lists of achievements. The contribution of the English Arts and Crafts metalworker, W. A. S. Benson, to lighting design was a case in point. His objects ranged from oil lamps, designed in a simplified style, to bronze and copper candelabras to electric light fittings. Benson had wanted to be an engineer but had turned to architecture instead. His work bridged the gap between the rarefied world of the craftsman-maker and that of the metalworker creating low-priced artefacts for the domestic sphere. As his obituary pointed out, 'he preferred to approach his subject as an engineer rather than as a hand-worker; to produce his beautiful forms by machinery on a commercial scale rather than single works of art'.[5] A number of other late nineteenth-century British decorative artists, many of them from architectural backgrounds, were also attracted by the idea of utility that was associated with mass manufacture. The English designer, Christopher Dresser, for example, who had trained as a botanist, worked across a wide spectrum of artefacts that embraced élite, handmade products at one end, and, at the other, collaborations with mass manufacturers of metal goods.[6]

Through the second half of the nineteenth century, architects took the reins as the designers of many everyday goods and spaces. Not only did they create buildings and their interiors but they also began to venture into other arenas, among them the applied arts and industrial production. Right up until the late 1920s, they continued to dominate the world of product design, seeing the creation of the forms and decoration of the banal goods that made up the everyday environment as an extension of their work in the built environment. Sometimes, as in the cases of William Morris in England, C. R. Mackintosh in Scotland, Henry van de Velde in Belgium, Frank Lloyd Wright in the USA and Eliel Saarinen in Finland, among others, because they were unable to find appropriate goods and furnishings in the marketplace for their own personal domestic environments, they created fully furnished homes for themselves and their families, designing everything they needed themselves – from textiles to knives and forks. Theirs was a holistic approach to designing that derived from a belief in the *Gesamtunstwerk* (the total work of art), a concept that dominated progressive design from the 1860s up to the 1930s. The vast majority of designers discussed by Nikolaus Pevsner in his groundbreaking study, *The Pioneers of Modern Design*, first published in 1936, were architects first and foremost. So powerful was architecture as a model for design practice in the early decades of the twentieth century, in fact, that the philosophical and aesthetic ideals underpinning it were applied directly to furniture and to products created for use in interior spaces. Arguably, that colonization of design by architects had the effect of stifling the emergence of a theory of modern design for industry that went beyond commercial pragmatism or technological rationalism.

The German designer, Peter Behrens, went further than most of his contemporaries in applying his creative skills to the products of the new industries. From a background in art nouveau poster design and the decorative arts he went on to create an entire visual identity for the German AEG company that was applied to its factories, its canteen cutlery and its publicity material, in addition to all its electrical products (Figure 3.1). Like William Morris and Henri van de Velde before him, Behrens also created his

Figure 3.1 Peter Behrens' kettles for AEG, Germany, 1909
(© AEG Hausgeräte GmBH)

own family home and all its contents. He adopted the same holistic approach to the design of the electrical company's corporate identity. The electrical products he worked on for AEG – fans and kettles in particular – combined a traditional decorative arts approach with more utilitarian ideas emanating from engineering. The positioning of the products, either in different areas within the home or in the private sphere, influenced the degree of decoration applied to the products. While the kettles, destined for domestic environments, boasted textured surfaces, the fans, intended for offices and factories, had an overtly engineered appearance.[7]

New designers also emerged in the world of two-dimensional design at that time. By the turn of the century, the development of the American advertising profession was fairly advanced and agencies, such as that of J. Walter Thompson, acted as middlemen between manufacturers and artists. Often, the latter were simply required to draw decorative borders around press advertisements. The craft skills of wood engraving and lithography provided the primary means by which advertisements were created a little later. The graphic designer, defined as 'someone who would receive instructions from a client, devise drawings and plans and then instruct technicians, typesetters and printers to realise the designs' followed on the heels of the commercial artist, who had dominated the picture in the early years of the century (Figure 3.2).[8] As in factory production, the advertising industry witnessed the emergence of a new generation of visually literate professionals whose task was to create a much-needed bridge between art and manufacturing.

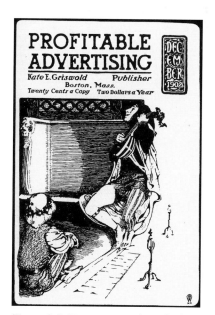

Figure 3.2 Front cover of *Profitable Advertising*, USA, 1902
(from the Library of Congress)

Packaging design also expanded in those years. In the late nineteenth century in the USA, packaging, branding and advertising transformed commodities into popular products.[9] The process of creating product packaging brought together visual artists, copywriters and can and package manufacturers. The identities they created were strongly dependent on visual images. The decision to opt for a particular image or range of colours could be arrived at in an ad hoc manner. The red and white used on the, now famous, Campbell's soup can were, for example, suggested by someone who had just attended a football game where the Cornell University team had worn those same colours.[10]

Making an impact with assemblages of packaged goods was the responsibility of the store designer or shop-window display artist, who could be retail proprietors themselves or, in the case of department stores, visually trained practitioners brought in to undertake that task. In his study of early shop display, William Leach has provided a fascinating account of the professionalization of that area of work.[11] Through the case study of L. Frank Baum, he has described how, alongside the spectacle created by coloured advertisements, electric sign advertising and mail-order catalogues, the shop window became a key aspect of urban visual culture and modern display. Specialist magazines, aimed at the store window artist, appeared at that time, magazines were launched and national associations formed. Baum founded the National Association of Window Trimmers in 1989), for example, to help professionalize the activities of the skilled artists working in that expanding field.

The fashion couturier also emerged in the years before 1914 and operated in an overtly commercial context. Although he was catering for élite customers and his dresses were one-offs rather than serial productions, the Englishman, Charles Frederick Worth, based in Paris, initiated the idea of using live models on catwalks and was among the first to use his name as a brand (Figure 3.3). As a system that depended upon continual stylistic change, fashion provided a model for emulation by a number of industries which needed to provide added value in their products and images. The application of art to many areas of commerce was a mark of manufacturers' growing awareness of the importance of eye appeal in their goods and of the growing importance of taste in consumption choices.

Many of the designers who made an impact in those years were men. A few women were trained in the subject but the application of their aesthetic skills was restricted, for the most part, to domestic embroidery and to other delicate crafts, such as jewellery making and enamel work. In line with their special relationship with domesticity, women were considered to have a natural capacity for interior decoration. Although a few women set themselves up as house decorators in Britain as early as the 1870s, it was in the first decade of the twentieth century that they began to dominate that visual field.[12] The first female interior decorators emerged at a moment when many nouveau-riche clients, who did not trust their own taste, were seeking

Figure 3.3 Worth evening dress, c. 1896
(© Musée Galliera)

others to decorate their home interiors. Only a couple of decades earlier they would, if they could have afforded to, have used the services of architects, or those of an upmarket decorating and furnishing firm, such as that of the Herter Brothers.[13] By 1897, Candace Wheeler, a decorator herself, was advocating interior decoration as an appropriate profession for women.[14] Women's amateur work undertaken in their own private spaces was, of course, unpaid. As a result, the issue of professionalization did not have the same urgency as it did for men. In addition, it had become a truism that women's work was aesthetic in nature and it was their duty to create beauty in the home. In the early twentieth century, the American actress, Elsie de Wolfe, became first an amateur and subsequently a professional (albeit untrained) interior decorator (Figure 3.4). By 1914, a number of other women had joined her in the same activity.[15] In contrast to the

Figure 3.4 Elsie de Wolfe, interior decorator, USA, 1920s
(courtesy of the author)

European male architects, who were also venturing into furniture and interior design, developing a new aesthetic appropriate to the modern, rational age in which they found themselves, the new American female decorators adopted what looked to be a more traditional approach, advocating a return to historical styles, especially those of eighteenth-century France, albeit realized with a new modern sensibility. At most levels of society, however, interior decoration remained the responsibility of the unpaid housewife.[16]

If design was to be the harmonizing force between a society that wanted to express itself through taste and a manufacturing industry that aspired to ultimate rationality and efficiency, designers, who could understand both sides of the equation, needed to be educated to undertake that subtle bridging task. In the years leading up to 1914, design education expanded significantly in a number of countries. In Britain, there had been much discussion at government level, in the first half of the nineteenth century, about taste and the importance of the addition of art to industrial production as a means of improving the quality of British goods. The Victoria and

Albert Museum, with its accompanying design educational institute, the Normal School, had been founded in 1837 to set about meeting that deficit. The school was the first of a vast number of others that were established in the key manufacturing areas. Their graduates were employed by local industries to inject a level of art into their otherwise engineered products. Students were encouraged to copy from models and to develop drafting skills that could be applied to architectural and product decoration. In the late nineteenth century, other countries also expanded their design education systems along the lines of the British model. In the USA, for example, the Cincinnati school was among the first to emerge, while, in early twentieth-century Germany, the traditional academies of art were transformed in the early twentieth century by Herman Muthesius, the Superintendent of the Prussian Board of Trade for Schools of Arts and Crafts, into schools that could train artists for industry.[17]

Unlike architecture, which was far removed from the marketplace and operated according to a set of elevated principles, product, fashion and advertising designers were essentially governed by the requirements of the market. Its expanded taste requirements and its need for increased product differentiation necessitated their very existence. Their task was to determine what was fashionable, to both reflect and form public taste and to keep the public informed about the multiple products and services available to them. By 1914, designing remained a diverse and ill-defined activity comprising a range of parallel but diverse practices based on different philosophies and with different professional and trade bodies encompassing them. Designers could be humble factory workers, engineers, decorative artist, architects, couturiers and commercial artists, among others. Some signs existed, however, of an emerging conflict between those who saw themselves as operating within the commercial system and those (mostly architects) who had a more idealistic view of their relationship with industry and society and of their cultural roles and responsibilities. By the inter-war years, the two approaches were openly vying with each other, the former openly embracing the commercial face of design and the latter sheltering under the banner of progressive architecture and design reform.

The consultant designer

> The modern industrial designer has both a technical and a cultural background and a sense of the public into the bargain and it is these three things which qualify him to perform his job of creating sales.[18]

In the years before 1914, the activity of designing – even if it had not been overtly named as such – had been firmly established in a range of manufacturing industries and commercial contexts. Indeed, it had become a fundamental aspect of the creation of images, goods and environments, as well as of marketing and the creation of corporate identities. As an individual with a distinct job description, however, a broadly understood concept of the designer did not yet exist.

In the years between the two World Wars, the concept of the consultant designer for industry came of age. It was partly as a solution to economic challenges and partly a means of bringing together the expanding numbers of tasks needed to link production and consumption in a way that met the needs of industry, the commercial sector and the general public. The role required both a high level of specialist skills in the areas of visualizing and conceptualizing, but also a broad approach that enabled practitioners to look across a wide range of industries.

Building on the work of men such as Peter Behrens in Germany, the first consultant industrial designers to be recognized as such by the public emerged in the USA at the end of the 1920s, at a time when consumer practices were being dramatically transformed. The financial crisis that had led Henry Ford to close his River Rouge factory for a year in 1926, in the face of the competition provided by the General Motors Company, marked an important moment in the emergence of the designer for industry. As we have seen, in response to changing consumer demands, General Motors had rejected product standardization in favour of a more flexible manufacturing system and, in the same year, Alfred P. Sloan, the Vice President of General Motors, had hired the coachbuilder, Harley Earl, to make his automobiles look more appealing.[19] The formation, in 1927, of the Styling Section at General Motors represented the first attempt to introduce an aesthetic element into the mass-produced automobile. Although that practice had long been normal in the decorative arts industries, it was unprecedented in automobile production, where the engineer had reigned supreme. As Sloan later explained, Earl's contribution to the commercial success of the Cadillac La Salle, his first GM project had been highly significant, 'The car made a sensational debut in March 1927, and proved itself a milestone in American automotive history by being the first stylist's car to achieve success in mass production'.[20]

The experience of the automobile industry was rapidly emulated by other manufacturers of new technological goods – refrigerators and other domestic appliances, office machines, telephones and radio sets among them. Challenged by the economic depression of the inter-war years, they decided to inject artistic styling into their products in an attempt to fight off their competitors. American industrial design, as it emerged in the late 1920s and 1930s, has been documented by a number of historians. Jeffrey Meikle's 1979 *Twentieth Century Limited: Industrial Design in America, 1925–1939*, for example, set out to understand the way in which the industrial design profession emerged in the USA.[21] His analysis has focused on the fact that 'technological innovation and mass production brought former luxury items to people at lower income levels' and on the aspirations of industrial designers to inject a level of modern luxury into new goods, as well as a level of attractiveness into the commercial context of advertisements and retail outlets that helped to sell them.[22] It was no coincidence that several of the leading industrial designers of the day had begun their careers in graphic advertising and department stores which, in emulation of French models, had been quick to embrace the modern style. Raymond Loewy worked for Saks of Fifth Avenue for a period of time while Norman Bel Geddes created modernistic window displays for the Franklyn Simon store in New York (Figure 3.5). Loewy's later move into refrigerator design reflected the growing requirement to make the industrial product itself desirable, rather than by stimulating desire through the commercial frame that surrounded it.[23]

Figure 3.5 Norman Bel Geddes, window display for Franklyn Simon department store, New York, USA, 1928
(courtesy of the Norman Bel Geddes Collection, the Performing Arts Collection, Harry Ransom Humanities Research Center, the University of Texas at Austin)

In his book, *All Consuming Images: The Politics of Style in Contemporary Culture*, Stewart Ewen has also approached the emergence of American industrial design from a cultural perspective.[24] He claimed that industrialization had 'displaced the customary fabric of culture' and that the marriage between art and commerce, which, he has noted, had commenced with Walter Rathenau's employment of Peter Behrens at the German AEG company, had offset that displacement by bridging the gap between production and consumption. His description of the work of one of the advertising pioneers of the early twentieth century, Earnest Elmo Calkins, as being focused on the effort 'to construct an unbroken, imagistic corridor between the product being sold and the consciousness (and unconsciousness) of the consumer', reinforced the close link between consumer culture and the American consultant design profession of the inter-war years.[25]

The best known industrial designers of the day – Norman Bel Geddes, Raymond Loewy, Walter Dorwin Teague and Henry Dreyfuss among them – penned their own accounts of their careers, in which they stressed their perceptions of themselves as idealistic modernists. Linking themselves to the modern European architectural movement provided them with a means of separating themselves from the commercial context and of elevating the status of their contributions. In his 1940 text, *Design This Day: The Technique of Order in the Machine Age*, Teague, for example, made repeated references to Le Corbusier, Walter Gropius and Mies van der Rohe, suggesting, perhaps, that his name should be added to the list.[26] In his autobiography, *Horizons*, published in 1932, Norman Bel Geddes also referenced European modernism, in his case the abstract paintings of the artists Pablo Picasso and Paul Cezanne, making claim to them as his artistic roots.[27] Their pretensions served to reinforce their claims to be adding artistic value to the products of industry.

Although most accounts of the work of the American consultant designers of the 1930s have concentrated on their advocacy of dramatic streamlined forms for the future, the majority of their time was, in reality, devoted to redesign projects. Also, they worked for conservative markets as well as more adventurous ones. The accounts of their work have tended to play down their market-oriented pragmatism and present them as the celebrities that they were heralded as by the press of the day. *Time* and *Life* magazines celebrated their work on several occasions and reported on the details of their daily lives as if they were Hollywood stars. While their celebrity status was undoubtedly important to them as individuals, it was even more crucial for the manufacturers who employed them, bestowing, as it did, on their creations an instant added value. The designers became branded entities and their names were used as a form of product endorsement. In turn, the products became their own advertisements.

The consultant designers quickly became intrinsic components of the American commercial system that had engendered them and an extension of the face of the commercial context in which goods were bought and sold. In an attempt to demonstrate that designers were, however, mere products of their environment and that they should not be given too much credit for design change, the historian, Adrian Forty, has undertaken an analysis of Raymond Loewy's redesign of the Lucky Strike cigarette pack, in which he has claimed that the decision to change the colour of the pack from green to white was not, in fact, an individual creative act but rather a reflection of the era's obsession with hygiene and cleanliness.[28] While Forty's argument probably granted the social and cultural context rather more agency than was actually the case, it provided, nonetheless, an important balance to the accounts of their achievements that those men had claimed for themselves.

Two significant things can be learned from the American consultant designers of the 1930s. Firstly, they demonstrated the way in which the commercial design profession was dependent on earlier visualizing work undertaken in the contexts of commerce and spectacle. The aestheticization of the marketplace, one of the defining characteristics of modernity, had begun before the emergence of the industrial designer. It had been achieved by countless artists who had created shop-window displays, exhibition stands and many types of advertising material. Indeed, the most prominent consultant designers for industry came to their profession, as we have seen, from backgrounds in advertising and store-window display. Bel Geddes's first career had been in stage design, an experience in creating dramatic effects that had led logically on to his work for shop windows and products. Teague had created decorative borders for advertisements for the Calkins and Holden agency in the early years of the century. While the designers claimed purist European backgrounds for themselves, they were, in fact, much more steeped in American commercial pragmatism and the irrational world of consumer desire.

Secondly, the arrival of the American consultant designers represented the moment when designer culture – the attribution, that is, of added value to an object, image or environment as a result of the fact it had a well-known designer's name attached to it – came into being. Such was the power of the first-generation American consultant designers that the application of their names to a railroad train or of a biscuit bestowed instant added value to those artefacts. A number of explanations have been offered for this phenomenon. The most persuasive has suggested that it represented the need for consumers to construct their identities through the acquisition of commodities that were associated with the name of an individual known to possess a high level of taste. This explanation builds on the fact that, in the years before industrialization and the rupture between production and consumption, the upper classes had been guaranteed identity and social status through the acquisition of custom-made, crafted artefacts. What the French social scientist, Pierre Bourdieu, has described as 'cultural capital' could be consumed, in the 1930s, through a material artefact, the visual appearance of which could be attributed to an industrial designer of note.[29] The cultural capital in question was hugely enhanced by its links with modernity, a concept that could, it was suggested, be appreciated by only the most discerning consumers. The association of a name with otherwise anonymous products could be seen to restore individualism to mass-manufactured goods by personalizing anonymous products. As the numbers of accessible standardized products increased, the need to inject individualism into them became paramount. The consultant designers were acutely aware of the diversity of consumer tastes in the marketplace. Bel Geddes, for example, acquired his knowledge of the market by undertaking extensive consumer questionnaires and proposed four different radio designs to the Philco Radio Company – the 'Highboy', the 'Lowboy', the 'Lazy-boy' and a radio-phonograph combination – each of which was styled with a different market in mind.[30]

While the automotive industry preferred to keep its stylists in house, maintaining their anonymity for the most part, many other new industries engaged in producing consumer machines, including domestic appliances and office machinery, benefited from bringing in generalist consultant designers who had an overview of the industry as a whole. The model of consultant design that emerged in the USA from the late 1920s onwards was rapidly emulated by other countries, as they also began to look for ways of embedding design into their emerging industries and of creating enhanced levels of consumer desire. In the years after 1945, the dissemination of its design model constituted one of the USA's strategies of cultural imperialism.

In Great Britain, the Design Research Unit was formed in 1942 along American lines; in Sweden, the industrial designer, Sixten Sason, worked with the Electrolux and Hasselblad companies; in Italy, the graphic designer, Marcello Nizzoli, collaborated with the Olivetti company and the Necchi sewing machine manufacturer.[31] In their different ways, they and many other designers and design groups, extended the professional model of commercial consultant design that had been developed in the USA between the wars.

Although the consultant designers focused most of their attention on the products of the new industries, the traditional decorative art industries also began to employ consultant designers, many of them calling on architects to perform that role. By the inter-war years, they tended to work either in a modern style, influenced by the progressive work being undertaken in Germany, or in the *moderne* style, influenced by the French decorative artists who had shown their work at the 1925 *Exposition Internationale des Arts Décoratifs et Industriels Modernes*, held in Paris. The New Zealand-born architect, Keith Murray, working in Great Britain, for example, created some striking ceramic designs for Wedgwood and cut-glass designs for Stevens and Williams, while Marcel Breuer, a graduate of the German Bauhaus school, came to Britain for a short period and collaborated with the furniture producer, Isokon, while he was there.[32] In Finland, Göran Hongell worked with the Karhula Glassworks, while in Sweden the graphic designer, Wilhelm Kåge, (Figure 3.6) modernized the products of the ceramics company, Gustavsberg. In Germany, Wilhelm Wagenfeld, a graduate of the Bauhaus metal workshop, worked with a number of glass and metal manufacturers, while Herman Gretsch collaborated with the Arzberg ceramic manufacturing company.

The graphic and fashion design professions also consolidated their modern roles in those years. In Europe, the modern graphic designer was

Figure 3.6 Wilhelm Kåge, designer, Gustavsberg ceramic company, Sweden
Photographer: Riwkin (courtesy of the Nationalmuseum, Stockholm, Sweden)

rooted in the British nineteenth-century reform movement (Figure 3.7). The poster movement of the same century had also been enormously influential. As Jeremy Aynsley has explained in his book, *A Century of Graphic Design: Graphic Design Pioneers of the 20th Century*, by 1914, 'the book and poster arts were about to be subsumed into a greater whole: graphic design', a concept which was to emerge fully in the 1920s.[33] Fashion designers or couturiers had existed for many years. Located in Paris for the most part, they had supplied a global wealthy clientèle with custom-made, hand-made clothing. With the advent of the sewing-machine and factory production, however, ready-to-wear clothing, aimed at large markets, made its impact in the first decades of the twentieth-century, providing an alternative to its up-market equivalent that was marketed through the name of the couturier in whose house it had been produced. It was the branded individualism of the fashion designer that had inspired manufacturing industry more generally to sell its goods through designers' names (Figure 3.8). Surprisingly perhaps, given that designer-branding had been invented in the world of fashion, industry was relatively slow to use it at its mass-production end. The couture trade remained very influential in the inter-war years, however, with names like those of Chanel, Lanvin and Schiaparelli dominating world fashion from their Parisian base.

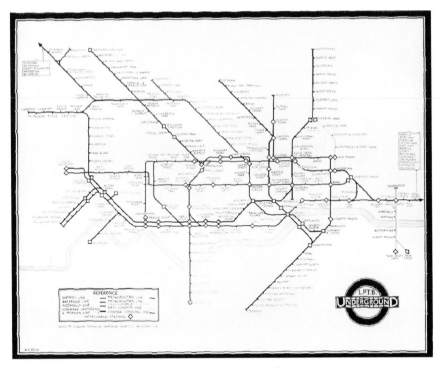

Figure 3.7 Henry Beck's 1933 London Underground map
(courtesy of London's Transport Museum)

Increasing opportunities existed for women to become professional designers in those years but they were not spread evenly across all design areas. While male designers tended to work with the new, technology-led industries, women could only be commonly found working in the areas of ceramic and textile design.[34] Suzette Worden and Jill Seddon's survey of women who worked as designers in Britain in the inter-war years has shown that, while many female designers had existed, most of their names had been lost to history and, predictably, they had been most successful in the areas of craft, textiles and graphic design (especially illustration).[35] Most of the work undertaken on the subject of female designers in this period has focused on a handful of modernists – Eileen Gray, Charlotte Perriand and Lilly Reich in particular – on the small number of women who were successful working either in the private sphere or in the decorative arts industries – Elsie de Wolfe, Ruby Ross Wood, Nancy McClelland and Syrie Maugham in interior decoration, for example, Susie Cooper and Clarice Cliff in ceramics and Marion Dorn in rug design – or on the anonymous women who either worked in the art production industries – the paintresses within ceramics manufacturing, for example – or those who

Figure 3.8 Coco Chanel, sketch for evening dress, 1930s
(© *Musée de la mode et du textile, de la collection*: UFAC)

worked as amateurs in, say, the fields of home dressmaking or embroidery. While the 'hidden from history' approach, which has characterized so much work in the area of women's studies, continues to uncover forgotten names, the broad picture is clear. Design in the new, technologically oriented industries was male-dominated and the most aggressively modernist end of the aesthetic spectrum was inhabited by male architects for the most part. In general terms women embraced a more conservative model of modernity and did not participate, on a large scale, in the world of professional design practice.[36]

By 1939, the professional designer for industry had emerged, although still in a variety of guises and not always overtly named as such. Perhaps more significantly, however, designer culture – the idea that designers encapsulated within their very beings the spirit of modernity and were thereby able to inject into manufactured images and objects the added value that comes from having an association with art – had also become widely visible. Arguably, those designers whose names were used to promote goods were themselves also consumed in the process. Through a perceived access to knowledge and power that was denied to others, they became mythological figures whose names alone could add value to the products, images and spaces with which they were associated. Their artistic skills and their privileged position at the interface of the worlds of production and consumption granted them a cultural role that was considerably more powerful than their everyday tasks might suggest. At the same time, they also performed a real role within industry, bridging the worlds of production and consumption, enabling the products of industry to fulfil the needs and desires of consumers and, most importantly, perhaps, ensuring that manufacturers were able to remain in business.

4   Modernism and design

Theory and design at the turn of the century

> We realised that the product made by machines could possess an
> 'aesthetic' properly derived from a confrontation between function and
> form.[1]

The transition from the nineteenth to the twentieth century witnessed a new
approach towards the design of the visual, material and spatial world. The
growing dissatisfaction with conspicuous consumption on the part of an
international group of progressive architects and designers, and their belief
that the rationalism of engineering provided a better basis on which to
move forward than the commercial pragmatism of the capitalist marketplace, underpinned a sudden and dramatic revision of the principles that
had long determined the role of the decorative arts. The group increasingly
disassociated itself from the concept of decorum that had governed social
and cultural life in the west for several centuries and, in a search for a new
language of design, many of them rejected the idea of decoration.

Much has been written about the development of architectural and
design modernism and the ideas that underpinned the search for an
aesthetic to represent the machine occurred at the end of the nineteenth
century and the early years of the twentieth century. Much design historical
writing has focused on the writings of architects and highlighted the work
of those designers who developed a theoretical relationship with the
modern world.[2] In 1936, Nikolaus Pevsner pinpointed those architects and
designers that he believed to be the key protagonists in the transformation
from historicism to modernism, charting a path from William Morris and
his Arts and Crafts followers to Walter Gropius at the Bauhaus (Figure 4.1).
Along the way he embraced, among many others, the thoughts of A.W.N.
Pugin, John Ruskin, Isambard Kingdom Brunel and the modern engineers,
as well as French architects, such as Auguste Perret, who used steel and
concrete in their innovative architectural structures. The American architects, Louis Sullivan and Frank Lloyd Wright, were also included, as were
the protagonists of rectilinear and curvilinear Art Nouveau and the early

Figure 4.1 Morris & Company's workshops at Merton Abbey, Surrey, England, c. 1900
(courtesy of the London Borough of Waltham Forest, William Morris Gallery)

machine style – Charles Rennie Mackintosh, Otto Wagner, Josef Hoffmann, Henri Van de Velde, Hector Guimard and others. The members of the German Werkbund – Peter Behrens and Richard Riemerschmid among them – were also marked out for attention. In describing the dominant design ideas of the years following the First World War, Pevsner also focused on the work of the Russian, Dutch, French and German modernists, who aligned their search for modern design with developments in fine art.

In creating his famous lineage, Pevsner created a stable of pioneer modernists who have remained important historical figures to this day. In his seminal text of 1960, *Theory and Design in the First Machine Age*, Reyner Banham, a doctoral student of Pevsner, modified the list slightly, adding the work and ideas of a sequence of artists and architects from the Italian Futurists to the German Expressionists who, although undoubtedly modern in outlook, had not been included in Pevsner's account and who did not conform naturally with the aesthetic journey that he had chosen to describe.[3] Banham's narrative built on Pevsner's, however. He sought to isolate the forces that had caused so many architects and designers to review the philosophical and aesthetic bases on which they practised, focusing on what he believed to be three underlying causes of change – a growing sense of social responsibility (as epitomized by the work and ideas of the followers of William Morris and finding its full realization in the activities of the German Werkbund), the structural approach to architecture (as implemented by Viollet-le-Duc) and the tradition of academic instruction.[4]

Like that of Pevsner, Banham's account privileged the architect as the prime mover within modernism and also acknowledged the role of the fine artist. He also established an important link between architecture and industrial design.[5] The role of engineered artefacts as an inspiration for modernist architectural thinking lay, he claimed, at the heart of the ideas of the British architect, W. R. Lethaby, who, he explained, 'frequently turns to objects like railway viaducts and bicycles whose value . . . lay "in their nearness to need"'.[6] The growing association of architect–designers with industrial production was also noted as an agent of change; the work of Peter Behrens for the German company, AEG, from 1907, and the emergence of the German Werkbund, both being highlighted as powerful influences upon the direction that was subsequently taken by architecture and design.

To date, the accounts of early modernist theory and design provided by Pevsner and Banham have not been seriously challenged, although they have been supplemented by new narratives and more detailed research. They still provide a useful account of one face of architectural and design practice in the early twentieth century, one that was rooted in modernist ideology and which went on to underpin the ideas and policies of many important twentieth-century design institutions, among them educational establishments, museums and governmental bodies. Neither account provides a complete picture of modern design's cultural role and impact through the twentieth century, however, which was, in reality, much more diverse. Ideological modernism focused primarily on the public sphere and on the arena of high culture. It was politically driven and rejected values emanating from the commercial arena and the private sphere. As a result, neither Pevsner's nor Banham's account fully represents the multiple stylistic variations that could be found in twentieth-century visual, material and spatial culture. They both privileged architecture as the unquestioned queen of the arts and only referred to interior design, furniture design and graphic design inasmuch as it was practised by pioneer modernists. They excluded most of the other areas of material culture from the period, including fashion design, commercial graphic design, interior decoration, the design of luxury goods, product design, car styling and other specialist areas such as theatre set design and shop-window display. Nor did their accounts make any attempt to look beyond the metropolis or the Western industrialized world.[7] Most importantly, neither account takes us beyond the inter-war years. Modernism's long-term significance lay in the fact that it became a hegemonic ideology underpinning the aspirations of many different cultural groups and nations through the twentieth and into the twenty-first century. Many developing countries have felt the need, at one time or another, to embrace modernism as a sign that they have entered the modern world. In

2011, for example, China's Academy of Art in Hangzhou invested a huge sum of money in purchasing a collection of early twentieth-century designed objects with an emphasis on designs emanating from the German Bauhaus.

As both Pevsner and Banham acknowledged, the roots of modernist thinking lay within the reformist ideas that were first expressed in the writings of A. W. N. Pugin and John Ruskin and which re-emerged in the thoughts of William Morris and others allied to the British Arts and Crafts Movement. Central to their ideas was a feeling of unease with what they felt to be the over-embellished, inauthentic products of the factory. For them, an escape from that cul-de-sac involved a return to Christian values of the medieval past and a sideways look at the natural world.[8] By the end of the nineteenth century, a new design vocabulary had emerged in Britain. It addressed what was seen by many to be the mindless products that had simply sought to placate consumer desire. It had been helped on its way by Gottfried Semper, a German resident in London in the 1850s, who had proposed a classification of objects based on function. In his attempt to find a system that would sidestep the problem of what was, or was not, appropriate ornament, he had linked together objects with common functions, such as 'pouring out' or 'containing'.[9] In the same spirit of rationalization, Owen Jones and, later, Christopher Dresser had also attempted to control what they believed to be arbitrary ornamentation.[10]

Some of the theoretical underpinnings of design modernism were documented in 1970 by Herwin Schaefer. In defining what could be called 'the vernacular tradition', Schaefer usefully pointed out that, in addition to the status objects produced for nineteenth-century middle-class consumers, another level of production for everyday life had also existed that had emphasized utilitarian values. It was to the honest, simple qualities of those vernacular products that many design reformers had begun to look, according to Schaefer.[11] Indeed, within early European modernist writings, a strong sense of awe was expressed in discussions about the simple products of early American mass production. Clocks, keys, bicycles, farm machinery and standardized bookcases, for example, were widely revered as functional, visually unselfconscious products of the machine (Figure 4.2). That romantic idolatry was highly selective, however. Most significantly it failed to take into account the full picture of American mass production. While it did include many goods that simply reflected their means of manufacture in their appearance, it was also responsible for a plethora of artefacts that, through their high levels of elaboration and stylishness, were linked more closely to social status that to everyday utility.[12] Those latter qualities were features of many of the goods created for the sophisticated, urban society that the USA was rapidly becoming. The myth of utilitarianism, expressed in a number of modernist writings, including Siegfried Giedion's influential text of 1948, *Mechanisation Takes Command*, was based, therefore, on a short-lived moment during which a body of new consumers were coming to

Figure 4.2 Singer sewing machine. First patent model, 1851
(courtesy of the Singer Sewing Company, Lavergne, Tennessee)

term with the world of goods and their complex meanings.[13] The modernists' shared nostalgic longing for that age of innocence was a response to their deeply felt anxieties about the commercial context of design.

Whether a myth or not, the potency of early functionalist theory was undeniable. The strong sense of rationalism that underpinned it was embedded in many areas of American life in the first years of the twentieth century. The influence of Taylorism on factory and office practice, for example, represented a widespread belief that the future would be defined through the application of scientific method to everyday life. The extensive measuring and calculating that went into the recommendations made to managers as to how to reorganize their work areas, was part of a shared belief in the rules of science. The subsequent infiltration of Taylorism into the domestic sphere reinforced its ideological dominance. The need for an economical use of space in the kitchens in Pullman trains and ocean liners also offered a lesson to modernist architects as they sought to define the spaces within the kitchens in their designs for minimal dwellings, a concept to which they were deeply committed.

By the early twentieth century, the theoretical basis of design modernism had moved from Britain to the USA and to the Continent. It converged with parallel ideas, emerging in the USA, exemplified by the writings of the sculptor, Henry Greenough. In his short treatise, *Form and Function*, he praised the simple aesthetic achieved by engineers.[14] Like so many of his fellow proto-modernists, he evolved his ideas partly as a response to his anxieties about design as social display. 'Fashion', he proclaimed, 'has lived too long, and exercised an influence too potent for us either to deny or to escape it...I regard Fashion as the instinctive effort of the stationary to pass itself off for progress'.[15] The famous words of the Chicago architect, Louis Sullivan, 'form ever follows function, that is the law', reinforced that American search for a rational methodology for architecture and design.

In mainland Europe, similar thoughts were being expressed by members of the German and Austrian Werkbunds of the early century. One of the most powerful and influential texts in that context was the Austrian, Adolf Loos's, *Ornament and Crime*. In that study, the author took the need to repudiate decoration to a new level of intensity and fervour. Loos proposed that, through its rejection of ornament, mankind had become increasingly civilized. The most mature society, he maintained, was represented by the most simple of forms and it was the responsibility of the modern architect–designer to develop that principle. 'The modern man who tattoos himself', he wrote,' is either a criminal or a degenerate...Ornament is wasted labour power and hence wasted health. It has always been so.'[16] Loos's work has been the subject of study by the feminist architectural historian, Beatriz Colomina, who has shown that his own interior designs did not conform to his own rhetoric but were more complex and sensorial than one might have expected from his writings.[17]

As the twentieth century came into being, architects and designers abandoned the natural world and the focus on individualism and sought a more objective formula that took the rationalism of machine production as a starting point. The contrast between those two approaches was reflected in the two faces of the Art Nouveau movement.[18] While, in its curvilinear manifestations, the movement looked to the sinuous shapes of nature in its raw, state its rectilinear designs built on a neoplatonic, essentialist approach that combined the fundamental forms underpinning nature with the essence of, for example, 'chairness'. Although that approach to design did not reach a peak until the Dutchman, Gerrit Rietveld, created his famous 'Red-Blue' chair in 1917, the work of Josef Hoffmann, C. R. Mackintosh, Otto Wagner and others represented a step in that direction. Wagner had already shown his commitment to the functionalist approach when he penned the words that, 'all modern forms must correspond to new materials and the requirements of our time if they are to fit modern mankind'.[19]

The collision between nineteenth-century individualism and twentieth-century collectivism reached a head in 1914, in the form of a confrontation that took place between the Belgian architect–designer, Henri Van de Velde and the German diplomat, Hermann Muthesius. Van de Velde had already articulated a number of ideas that were in tune with the protofunctionalist face of Art Nouveau. 'Utility can generate beauty' he had proclaimed, while also maintaining that, 'ornament should be structural and dynamographic' and that, 'ornament and form should appear so intimate that the ornament seems to have determined the form'.[20] Rejecting nature as a source of form, he had developed a theory of object symbolism that focused on the expression of the object's own inner structure.

Muthesius was strongly committed to an abstract aesthetic of the kind Van de Velde described but, unlike the Belgian architect, he believed in the principles underpinning industrial standardization and the sacrifice of the individual to the mass. There was no room in his thinking for the individual artist. He sought instead the availability of well-designed mass-produced goods for everyone. The lively debate between the two men pinpointed what was to remain a fundamental dilemma for the supporters of design modernism for some time: whether, that is, it represented an attempt to develop a modern aesthetic using the idea of the machine as a key metaphor or to design for machine production and facilitate the widespread availability of goods such that everybody had the possibility of engaging with modernity.

By 1914, modernism's architecturally derived ideas were fully formed and their implications for design clearly expressed. They had not, at that date, however, penetrated the commercial design arena. That is not to say that ideas were not being expressed in that context but that they were much more area specific. In the field of interior decoration, for example, ideas were being formulated about the relationship between the domestic interior and the development of personal identity but they were being directed exclusively at the readers of women's popular magazines, for the most part. Early graphic designers were also beginning to look for a science-based theory that would provide them with a set of rules with which to work (Figure 4.3). Fashion designers had a strong, intuitive sense of the workings of the marketplace but did not enter into theoretical debates for the most part. Within other specialist areas – stage-set design and store-window display for example – ideas were also developed that related just to those areas of practice. None of those sector-specific ideas, however, were able to compete with the dominant design discourse of the twentieth century that emanated from architectural modernism.

Figure 4.3 Lucian Bernhard, poster for Stiller shoes, 1907–8
(courtesy of the Poster Collection, Zurich Museum of Design)

The hegemony of modernism

> Where the De Stijl movement was original, as regards furniture design,
> was in creating the first chair deliberately designed, not for comfort, not
> for dignity, not for elegance, nor for rational assembly according to
> commonly accepted principles of woodwork, but simply 'designed'.[21]

The inter-war years witnessed an intensification of the theoretical debates
that had underpinned modernist architecture and design in the early
century. In the 1920s, in particular, many progressive architects, craftsmen
and decorative artists, based in several important centres, discussed their
work in the context of cultural modernity and technological change. Most
of those discussions took place in Europe, where the avant-garde movements in painting and sculpture had joined hands with the rationalist ideas
emerging from modern architectural theory to form a single movement –
referred to here as 'modernism' – that was to dominate design through the
rest of the twentieth century and up to the present. As we have already seen,
it took its inspiration from the early material manifestations of modernity –
railway stations, bridges, aeroplanes and automobiles among them – and
from the rationalism believed to underpin industrial production. Above all

it celebrated the concepts of objectivity, collectivity, universality and utility. Modernism operated within the context of the political, the social, the technological and the aesthetic and its advocates were united in their rejection of what they believed to be the irrational, feminized, commercial culture that represented the unacceptable face of material modernity.

Architectural and design modernism has been widely documented. In his introduction to his edited book, *Modernism and Design*, Paul Greenhalgh has explained that modernism had two main historical phases: 1914–1929 and the 1930s; claiming that 'the first phase was essentially a set of ideas, a vision of how the designed world could transform human consciousness and improve material conditions' while 'the second phase was less an idea than a style'.[22] The 1930s can be seen as the period of the international dissemination of the machine aesthetic that entered into environments and interior spaces worldwide. It was also the moment when modernism was used by political regimes, including those of Germany and Italy, to embrace ideologies that stood in opposition to the democratic beliefs that had originally engendered it. Its clearly delineated rules made it an effective tool of authoritarian control, whichever ideology underpinned it.

In the tradition of William Morris, one face of design modernism remained closely linked to social and political idealism. From the early twentieth century, visual, material and spatial culture had played an important part in the radical political activities that were spreading across Europe. In the years following the Russian Revolution of 1917, for example, graphic designers participated in the propaganda campaign led by the Bolsheviks. In the wake of the Revolution, architecture, dress and products became key agents of change in the hands of committed artists and designers such as Vladimir Tatlin, Alexander Rodchenko and Kasimir Malevich (Figure 4.4). Many Russian avant-garde artists, designers and architects saw within the world of material culture an opportunity to inject modernity into a previously backward-looking society and of defining design as an ideological concept with transformative powers. The propagandist role of graphic design was especially powerful in that context and artists such as El Lissitzky were highly articulate in expressing their radical ideas. Committed to industrial printing and the potency of typographical composition, he developed a sophisticated approach that involved building up a page of type with attention to shape, size, proportion and composition. His constructivist approach to building imagery and form from basic elements could as easily be applied to design and architecture, as it could, metaphorically, to the idea of a new society.[23]

A belief in design as an agent of social and political transformation remained a constant within the articulation of a set of modern design principles that also developed in, among other countries, Germany, France, Holland and the Scandinavian countries in the inter-war years. Their commitment to the idea that design could contribute to social democracy explains the hostility frequently expressed by modernist architects towards

Figure 4.4 Alexander Rodchenko's design for the interior of the Worker's Club in the Soviet Pavilion, Paris Exhibition of Decorative Arts, 1925
(courtesy of the Society for Co-operation in Russian and Soviet Studies)

the middle-class interior. It also makes sense of the strong commitment manifested in all those countries to social housing, to the concept of the minimum dwelling and its furnishings and to the role of standardization in making cheap, functional goods available to everyone.

The Dutch *De Stijl* movement embraced fine art, architecture and design, refusing to accept hierarchical distinctions between them. It represented the shared ideas of a group of painters, architects and designers – Piet Mondrian, Theo Van Doesburg, Vilmos Huszar, Bart van der Leck, J. J. P. Oud, Robert Van't Hoff, and Gerrit Rietveld among them – who were united by their belief that the styles of the past were outmoded and that architecture and design had an important social role to play. That role was performed, they believed, through the aesthetic function of images, artefacts and environments, which, they maintained, had the power to transform lives. As Nancy Troy has explained, '...the *De Stijl* artists sought to preserve the primacy of aesthetic principles as agents of social reform in their own right'.[24] The cleansing process that underpinned the modernists' rejection of conspicuous consumption, and which resulted in the simplified geometry and minimal colours of *De Stijl* creations, was essentially a social process which, it was believed, brought about liberation from commodities.

The glue holding the group together was the magazine, *De Stijl*, which ran from 1917 through to 1931, and which communicated the theoretical ideas articulated by the *De Stijl* protagonists. They included a belief in a relationship between the individual and the universal, a faith in the role of technology and a commitment to the agency of art, architecture and design to influence the future of social and cultural life.[25]

Although its outlook was international, *De Stijl* was born of specifically Dutch conditions. Holland had adopted a position of neutrality in the First World War and the *De Stijl* protagonists were all keen to erode distinctions between classes and to provide environments that encouraged a lifestyle that could be shared across classes. Paul Overy has shown how Gerrit Rietveld's interior of the house he built for Truus Schroeder was intended to be a 'model for the future, a symbol of a new way of living which, it was hoped, would later be transferred to the public realm'.[26] Paralleling that high level of social idealism and commitment to materiality that characterized one face of modernism, several members of the De Stijl group, notably Mondrian and Van Doesburg, embraced a more spiritually oriented approach to material culture that drew them to theosophy and the ideas of Rudolf Steiner. Their spirituality was shared by a number of inter-war modernists, including the work of Wassily Kandinsky and Johannes Itten, both teachers at the Bauhaus who saw the role of technology as inspiring as much irrational thinking as it did rationally-based ideas.

Swedish architects and designers also understood the power of the links between modern design and social democratic reform. The roots of a modern design movement in that country lay in its nineteenth-century craft traditions and their relevance in a modern democracy. While the indigenous decorative arts industries took a while to move away from their luxury backgrounds, such was the impact of the German *Werkbund* on Sweden that, in the years following the First World War, the Swedish Society of Craft and Industrial Design (*Svenska Slöjdforeningen*) organized an exhibition in Stockholm on the subject of social housing. In 1919, its President, Gregor Paulsson, published a hugely influential book entitled, 'More Beautiful Everyday Things'.[27] It wasn't until 1930, however, that the full blossoming of Swedish modernism was revealed to the rest of the world. The Stockholm exhibition of that year, conceived by a group of architects that included Paulsson as well as Gunnar Asplund, Eskil Sundahl, Sven Markelius and Uno Ahren, was modelled on the Stuttgart Weissenhof exhibition of three years earlier. The German functionalist aesthetic was embraced and slogans such as 'the functional is beautiful' became the battle cry for the Swedish architects involved in that event.[28] The 1930s saw a battle enacted between the 'Funkis' (the functionalists) and the 'Tradis' (traditionalists), with the latter ultimately winning the day.

As well as being linked to real social and political change, the twin qualities of rationalism and idealism that underpinned modernism were apparent in the education of designers in the inter-war years. Nowhere was it more visible than at the German Bauhaus, where a new language of design was created through the introduction of a highly systematized pedagogical model which was to provide the basis for design educational programmes in many other countries in the years following the Second World War. In *The New Architecture and the Bauhaus*, Walter Gropius, the director of the school, explained that the dual principles of standardization and rationalization underpinned everything that went on within its walls. 'A breach has been made with the past', he proclaimed, 'which allows us to envisage a new aspect of architecture corresponding to the technical civilization of the age we live in.'[29] Like the *De Stijl* artists and designers before him, Gropius saw the development of type-forms as a fundamental prerequisite for an egalitarian society. Like that earlier movement, he also promoted 'a fundamental unity underlying all branches of design' as a means of achieving a non-hierarchical society that valued all the arts equally.[30]

The painters Wassily Kandinsky and Paul Klee taught students basic principles during their first year at the Bauhaus. They worked in a *tabula rasa* way that required students to bring nothing with them from the past but, rather, to build up their work through a series of creative strategies which involved them developing abstract images from the raw materials of line, colour and form.[31] That systematic cleansing process was used to enable students to find new solutions for new problems. As Gropius explained later, 'The first task was to liberate the pupil's individuality from the dead weight of conventions and allow him to acquire that personal experience and self-taught knowledge which are the only means of realizing the natural limitations of our creative powers'.[32] Students from the preliminary course went on to work in one of the craft workshops – focusing on stone, metal, wood, clay, glass and textiles – which were conceived as laboratories for mass production. There they applied the knowledge and skills they had acquired in the preliminary course and created designed artefacts, such as chairs, teapots, electric lights and woven wall hangings, which addressed their basic functional and structural elements. Inasmuch as all the objects were hand-made, a craft approach was espoused but, because they were built up from basic components and demonstrated that fact in their simplified, undecorated aesthetic forms, the students' creations were both metaphors for mass production as well as potential prototypes for it. A number of Bauhaus objects were put into mass production after its closure by the National Socialists in 1933.

The Bauhaus celebrated the aesthetic of functionalism – the idea, that is, that the form of an object should reflect its inner structure – and injected it into the production of objects. As a theory, functionalism had been in existence within architectural circles for some time but its application to mass-produced goods had lagged behind. Ironically, while it suited objects rooted in craft, when attempts were made, a little later, to apply functionalist principles to the design of complex consumer machines, it proved inadequate. Such was the complexity of industrially created mechanical and electrical goods that they could not replicate the craft-based ideas embraced at the Bauhaus. As a set of constructional principles, the machine aesthetic and the theory of functionalism were more easily and appropriately applied to a simple wooden chair and a silver teapot than to the bodies of a vacuum cleaner or a radio which, while the objects ended up looking simple, were achieved by concealing, rather than revealing, their inner structure.

In 1957, Edward Robert De Zurko published *Origins of Functionalist Theory*, in which he outlined the diverse roots of the idealist aesthetic methodology that had underpinned design modernism. He showed that the attempt to relate utility to beauty had classical, medieval, renaissance, eighteenth-century and nineteenth-century foundations.[33] In his analysis of functionalism, expounded in his book, *Changing Ideals in Modern Architecture*, Peter Collins has also shown that the theory had a number of analogies – biological, mechanical, gastronomic and linguistic.[34] Although, in the inter-war years, functionalism was still relevant to architecture, as well as for the manufacture of craft-based artefacts, its application, as explained above, to the world of industrial design proved more problematic. In the end, rather than a set of rules that could inform practice, it became a post hoc justification for the simple, undecorated geometric style favoured by most modernist designers.

The engineer was a recurrent point of reference within modernism. The description, articulated by the influential French modernist architect, Le Corbusier, of the engineer as a noble savage was an encouragement for others to follow him (Figure 4.5). As he explained, 'The Engineer, inspired by the law of Economy and governed by mathematical calculation, puts us in accord with universal laws. He achieves harmony'.[35] While the progressive European architects and designers saw themselves working in a continuum with contemporary avant-garde fine artists in terms of their development of a geometric aesthetic, they also saw in engineering products a model for their own aesthetic preferences and, more importantly, perhaps, for their working processes, which pursued the logical path of problem solving. Their recourse to reason protected them from what they believed to be the illogicality and the dangers of conspicuous consumption. Le Corbusier developed his ideas about the engineer later in the same text, claiming that engineering principles were essentially innovative, whereas those of the architect, who was dependent on past styles and upon taste, were moving backwards rather than forwards. The idea that taste should not enter into the equation was an indication of the modernists' shared fear that subjectivity and market values would undermine the power of rationality to bring about change. At times, it seemed as if that fear was almost pathological, a suggestion that was evidenced, perhaps, by the strength of the language that Le Corbusier used to describe his anxieties about conspicuous consumption – 'rooms too small, a conglomeration of useless and disparate objects, and a sickening spirit reigning over so many shams – Aubusson, *Salon d'Automne*, styles of all sorts and absurd bric-a-brac'.[36]

Figure 4.5 Interior of Le Corbusier's pavilion of '*L'Esprit Nouveau*', Paris
Exhibition of Decorative Arts, 1925
(© FLC/ADAGP, Paris, and DACS, London, 2003)

Modernism circumvented the world of commerce for the most part and remained, instead, within the gallery, the design school, the manifesto, the art journal and the craft workshop. When projects were realized they were usually for wealthy clients, such as Truus Schroeder for Gerrit Rietveld and Madame Savoie for Le Corbusier, who were happy to act as open-minded patrons to the artists, architects and designers who sought to express their progressive ideas in material and spatial form.[37] Commissions such as these did not impose the same market constraints as those experienced by designers working with manufacturing industry. Inevitably, however, much designing went on in those years that would not have been accepted by the small group of purists who delineated modernism's theoretical parameters.

The practice of interior decoration, for example, operated almost completely outside the limits of modernism. Rooted in historicism, comfortable with the idea of domesticity and aimed at an élite and aspirational audience, it betrayed most of modernism's rules and was looked upon with disdain by many purists. A rare sign of the influence of rationalism on the domestic interior came, however, in the form of the application of Christine Frederick's ideas about scientific management to kitchen design. Although she was a domestic advisor rather than a designer, her approach was visible in the small kitchens created by Grete Schütte-Lihotsky for the apartments in Ernst May's Frankfurt housing development of the 1920s. That influential urban rehousing project contained small galley kitchens featuring standardized storage units and items of equipment.[38]

The two areas of design that also lay outside the highly theorized and idealized world of modernist architecture and product design – advertising graphics and fashion design – did show some signs of coming under its influence at their margins, however. Conscious that it worked on the emotions rather than on the rational mind, the former sought to make its activities appear scientific by appealing to the laws of psychology.[39] Ellen Mazur Thomson has documented a number of experiments that were undertaken from the 1890s onwards to measure the effects of advertisements. Dress also had its own reform movement in those years (Figure 4.6). The Men's Dress Reform Party, for example, was founded in Britain in 1929. It emphasized healthy dress and a diversity of dress types for different needs. Physical comfort also played a key role, with open-necked shirts being favoured, while sandals were preferred to shoes. New materials, such as artificial silk, were promoted to remove the unnecessary weight from men's traditional clothing.[40]

Figure 4.6 Aesthetic dress design from *Le Journal des modes*, London, 1881
(reproduced in *Journal of Design History* vol.7, no. 2, 1994, by permission of Oxford University Press)

Modernist design reform had its roots in the nineteenth century but it continued unabated through the first half of the twentieth century. It sought not only to improve the quality of the material environment but also to develop a new aesthetic that would both embody and express a new relationship between society and the visual, material and spatial world. The strong moral imperative that underpinned the modernist campaign was, perhaps, its overriding characteristic. It was inherent in the post-Second World War concept of 'good design' that was undoubtedly its heritage. The avoidance of decoration within the modernist aesthetic was believed to engender a sense of morality and truth. The way an object was made, the modernists contended, should be apparent through the visibility of its inner structure. As Paul Greenhalgh has explained, 'illusion or disguise of any kind...was synonymous with a lie'.[41]

As we have seen, in spite of its heroic ideals, modernism had its limitations when applied to the design of complex objects. In spite of its determination to move beyond style and its belief that it should penetrate society as a whole, its protagonists underestimated the fact that, in the end, it had a relatively small international audience and that, from the perspective of the marketplace, it was quickly reduced to just another style (Figure 4.7). In spite of Gropius' determination to avoid that fate, expressed in his words, 'A "Bauhaus Style" would have been a confession of failure and a return to that very stagnation and devitalizing that I had called it into being to combat' – the objects that emerged from the Bauhaus were all characterized by a strong, shared visual language that soon became synonymous with the stylistic epithet, 'modern'.[42]

Figure 4.7 Walter Gropius' Bauhaus building, Dessau, Germany, 1925/6
Photographer: Walter Funkat (© Bauhaus-Archiv, Berlin)

The limitations of modernism in design resided, ultimately, in its failure to achieve the level of universality to which it aspired. As the present author has explained in her study, *As Long As It's Pink: The Sexual Politics of Taste*, inasmuch as it rooted its theory in the public sphere, emphasized the rational over the irrational, ignored the arena of consumption that was a strongly feminine site of activity and minimized the role of the domestic interior and the private sphere in favour of the public arena of work, modernism was gender specific.[43] In the author's words:

> Architectural modernism implied an end to the rule of women's tastes in the domestic arena and a clean sweep of the slate such that their influence was eradicated once and for all. In their place it substituted the controlling hand of the professional (male) architect and designer, working in tune with modernity, defined in masculine terms, and with a renewed architectural language which aimed to minimise the possibility of a resurgence of feminine values in the formation of the material environment.[44]

The gendered bias of modernism was not its only limitation, however. In terms of other cultural categories, ethnicity and class among them, it was also myopic. In the 1930s, the appeal of modernist architecture and design was limited to an audience of white, middle-class intelligentsia who appreciated its subtle message. In its application to social housing, it represented the imposition of one class on another. Generally speaking, it had a limited market appeal, especially in the context of domesticity.

In spite of the limited audience for modernist designs in the period of their production, the impact of modernist ideology upon design theory and practice was, and remains, unequalled. It has penetrated the global design education system and numerous design-focused institutions to the extent that it became the overriding philosophy of twentieth-century design. As such, its influence was, and remains, subtly pervasive and it continues to dominate many discussions about design's relationship with society and culture in the contemporary world.

5   Designing identities

Representing the nation

By 1914, a sophisticated understanding of the ways in which design could be used by individuals, groups, institutions and countries to form identities had emerged. Groups of all sizes, keen to persuade others of their status and authority, began to use designed artefacts and images as a means of persuading others of their economic, political, technological or cultural authority. Nowhere was that phenomenon more apparent than in the way existing and emerging nations used design as a means of forming, expressing and promoting their identities both to their indigenous populations and to the world at large.

The strategies employed to link design with national identity at that time were essentially two-fold. They either involved looking back to craft traditions and readdressing them in the light of contemporary preoccupations or taking a leap of faith into the future and developing an art into industry programme that proposed the development of new forms appropriate to the age of the machine. Inevitably, the two strategies frequently overlapped and the edges between them became blurred.

The consolidation of the strong nation states and of their empires is one of the dominant themes in the history of the Western industrialized world in the first years of the twentieth century. The desire to emphasize the nation as a political and economic unit above all others, the vying for hegemonic power that led to the international crisis of 1914 and the strong sense of cultural identity that flowed from those preoccupations, were, for the majority of the populations that inhabited those nations, both reflected in and formed by the visual, material and spatial culture of their daily lives. The story of design's alliance with national programmes of reform and international competition has been widely documented and flavours the most familiar accounts of twentieth century design. Nikolaus Pevsner's *Pioneers of Modern Design* stressed the relationship between design and nationhood and many other design historical texts, such as Fiona McCarthy's *A History of British Design 1830–1970*, have focused on the design achievements of a single nation.[1] McCarthy's text has documented the way in which national identity was inseparable from the visual, material and spatial culture that accompanied it. The research underpinning her study derived from official records for the most part and it inevitably prioritized, therefore, an official account of design.

John Heskett's *Design in Germany 1870–1918* has also focused on the theme of national identity and the search for a national style and design ideology through which to express it. The late unification of Germany in the late nineteenth century was accompanied by a highly strategic programme of design reform that involved establishing museums and schools of applied art; looking to other countries – the United Kingdom and France in particular – for models to emulate; holding exhibitions (the German Art and Industry Exhibition, for example, was held in Munich in 1876); launching specialist magazines (*Innendekoration*, for instance, was established in Darmstadt in 1891, two years before Britain's highly influential *Studio* magazine); and involving governmental agencies in a number of different ways.[2] A Standing Exhibition Commission for German Industry was, for example, set up within the Ministry of the Interior.[3] In the form of domestic interiors created by Bruno Paul and Bernard Pankok, the country's presence at the huge Paris Universal Exhibition of 1900 was a mark of the German government's proactive agenda at that international event where the imperial powers of England and France were also on public display. Interestingly, the most intimate of designed spaces – the domestic interior – was used to demonstrate to visitors that Germany had a private, as well as a public, face.

Ideologically driven presentations of visual, material and spatial culture characterized the numerous exhibitions that were held all over the industrialized world through the nineteenth century and which continued into the twentieth century and up to the present. Beginning with the first major international exhibition held in London's Hyde Park in 1851, Britain, France, the USA and a host of other countries, organized a series of events – universal exhibitions (the French term) and world's fairs (the American term) among them. Each had a different agenda to fulfil – including the improvement of taste in the home market, the enhancement of trade with competing nations and the establishment of national and, in some cases, imperial identities that would serve to unify populations under a single banner or brand. In *Ephemeral Vistas: the Expositions Universelles, Great Exhibitions and World's Fairs, 1851–1939*, Paul Greenhalgh has provided an overview of many of those extraordinary events, showing how they focused on a cluster of themes – new technologies, raw materials and manufactured goods among them – that were thought to display the prowess of the nation in question.[4] Design played a key role, represented by the presence of decorative art objects, the products of the new industries and the achievements of engineers.

Great Britain was among the first nations to exhibit the visual, material and spatial achievements of its industrial transformation. The Great

Exhibition of 1851 has been widely documented and it set a precedent that other nations felt obliged to follow, the USA in 1853, 1876 and 1893; Paris in 1867 and subsequently in 1889 and 1900; Vienna in 1973; and Italy in 1902, among many others. The event set out to show the rest of the world that Britain led the way in both the quality and the volume of its manufacture. By the end of the century, Britain had become associated in the minds of many other countries as the home of the Arts and Crafts movement, a number of exhibitions held in the last years of the nineteenth century conveyed to the rest of the world the strong commitment to design reform that characterized British design's message.[5] Although the Arts and Crafts movement was perceived as being synonymous with Britishness, it provided a model for a number of other countries which, in search of their own modern national identities through design, began, in turn, to look to their own indigenous craft roots for inspiration.[6]

The lasting significance of the British Arts and Crafts movement was, ultimately, less in Britain than on the Continent and in the USA, where it stimulated the emergence of a number of nationally conceived design movements. Ironically, in spite of Prince Albert's efforts to promote design in the mid century – which had included the establishment of the Victoria and Albert Museum and of a system of design schools located throughout the country – Britain failed, ultimately, to achieve an influential modern design movement with which to promote itself as a nation. However, the Arts and Crafts movement played a key role in the formation of the German Werkbund, while Austria's Wiener Werkstätte were modelled directly on C. R. Ashbee's Guild of Handicraft. Founded by Josef Hoffmann and Koloman Moser in 1903, the Austrians openly acknowledged their debt to British achievements, as Hoffmann explained, 'We have founded our workshop ... it should become a centre of gravity surrounded by the happy noise of the handicraft production and welcomed by everybody who truly believes in RUSKIN and MORRIS'.[7]

The question of nationhood was extremely important to the countries associated with the Austro-Hungarian Empire. Walter Crane travelled extensively in Hungary and was recognized by that nation when it came to evolve a national design identity for itself. The Gödöllö Workshops, formed in Hungary in the last years of the nineteenth century, also set themselves up on the basis of Arts and Crafts idealism, although the emphasis was primarily upon reviving the craft of weaving.[8] Hungary established its Museum of Applied Arts in 1872 and its Applied Arts Society in 1885 as part of its attempt to unite its traditional material culture with its modern national identity.[9] The new museum was opened by Franz Joseph, the Kaiser of Austro-Hungary. The Society focused on organizing exhibitions and publishing professional journals. In line with several others, the country pursued its own art in industry programme, inspired by the British model.[10]

Czechoslovakia also responded to the need to represent its national identity through design. Three international exhibitions were staged in Prague, in 1891, 1985 and 1898, and the country moved fast to catch up with its neighbours in embracing design as part of its modern national identity. Like Hungary, it also looked back to its own folk traditions but projected itself forward as well, inspired by the urban modernity that was in its midst. In the area of glass manufacture, for example, leading artistic figures, such as Jan Kótera, created strikingly modern forms. Following the spirit of the Gesamtkunstwerk that was very much in the air in Europe at that time, Kótera worked on interior decoration as well on textiles, metalwork, lighting fixtures, wallpaper and linoleum. To demonstrate his commitment to the modern age, he also even designed a saloon tram for Prague and a railway carriage for the Ringhoffer Company.[11]

The most influential and effective efforts to define national identity by applying art to industry were made in Germany, however. The work of the German Werkbund has been documented by a number of historians, notably Joan Campbell and Lucius Burckhardt.[12] Indeed, it was recognized by Nikolaus Pevsner as a key catalyst in his account of the birth of modern design. The main significance of the Werkbund to an understanding of the evolution of twentieth-century design was the fact that it directed its efforts at industry rather than supporting the handicrafts. Set up in Munich in 1907, its aim was simply to 'improve the design and quality of German goods'.[13] The wider aim, however, was to restore unity and national identity to Germany through the medium of improved industrial manufacture and to assert the nation's pre-eminence in the international marketplace. It was an ambition that closely resembled that of Britain half a century earlier. The difference in time, however, meant that Germany could ally its programme to the context of turn-of-the-century modernity and seek a product aesthetic that was in tune with the progressivism of that era.

The Werkbund acted as a forum bringing together industrialists, artists, architects, craftsmen and any other individuals interested in the possible links between the artistic and economic aspects of mass production. It was highly supportive of the collaboration between the architect, Peter Behrens and the AEG, which it held up as a model for others to follow. Frederick Schwartz's in-depth analysis of Behrens' work for the AEG has demonstrated how innovative his work was at this time and how far ahead AEG was of comparable companies in the USA and Britain, where engineers sang the tune and artists followed.[14] During its early years, the Werkbund supported a number of activities – lectures, exhibitions and publications among them. It focused on the products of the modern industries – mechanical and electrical products and objects of transport – with the aim of applying the rationalism of mass production to the design of products. A number of Werkbund-linked designers, Richard Riemerschmid among them, set out to apply the new principle of standardization to the more traditional area of furniture, developing the idea of the *Typenmöbel*. It was, however, most at home within the public sphere where rationality and neoplatonic ideas about form were deemed most appropriate. No attention was given to the problematic areas of fashion, nor to market demand or consumer desire. The concept of the minimal dwelling was a primary concern, however, especially for the architects who made up a large part of the membership. It was at the more functional end of the built environment spectrum – railway stations and factories – where the Werkbund had its greatest successes. When it sent its travelling exhibition to Newark in 1912, the culture of design that it brought with it had an enormous impact on the USA which, dominated as it was by commercial preoccupations and competition in the internal marketplace, was struggling to integrate design into its own national programme at that time.

In 1914, at the height of its influence, the Werkbund organized an enormous exhibition in Cologne. Inevitably, the events of subsequent years rapidly overtook it and, although it continued its activities into the 1920s and beyond, it never quite picked up the momentum that it had had in the early century. As a propaganda machine for modern design understood as an aspect of a national economy and culture, however, the Werkbund had made its mark. It was emulated by many similar groups that were subsequently established in a number of other countries, among them the Austrian *Werkbund* founded in 1910, the Swiss Werkbund established three years later and the Design and Industries Association set up in Britain in 1915. Its unrelenting commitment to a highly rational model of design, with an accompanying aesthetic that took the metaphor of the machine as a starting point, provided *the* model for a philosophy of modern design that was to dominate design education and reform through the middle years of the twentieth century and beyond.

In the years leading up to 1914, the Nordic countries also moved towards a model of modern design with a craft basis to it. Accounts of events and strategies employed by those countries have been articulated by David McFadden in his overview of twentieth-century design in Scandinavia. McFadden has provided an account of official intervention into the formation of the national identities of Sweden, Denmark and Finland and their strong relationships with visual, material and spatial culture, as well as the tactics employed by the craft industries in those countries to transform their traditional production and embrace the concept of modern design.[15] The Swedish Design Society (*Svenska Sljödföreningen*) had been in existence for sixty years at the time of the German Werkbund's formation. That Nordic body focused exclusively upon handicrafts rather than machine production. However, knowledge of German design reform came to Sweden through a visit by Gregor Paulsson, soon to be the Society's director, to Berlin in 1912. He returned enthused by the ideas he had heard discussed there by Werkbund members. In 1917, as we have seen, the Swedish Society organized an Art and Industry Exhibition in Stockholm that emphasized, in the same spirit of social democracy that existed in Germany, the design of worker's and one-family housing. The exhibition stimulated a discussion about the Society's future role and it was reorganized, seven years later, along Werkbund lines.

The Swedish Society took on the role of an employment agency, putting fine artists and manufacturers in touch with each other. As a direct result of that scheme, the ceramics company, Gustavsberg, employed the artist Wilhelm Kåge in 1916 (Figure 5.1), while the glass manufacturer, Orrefors, took on board the artists Simon Gate and Edward Hald a little later. Although trained as fine artists, all three men were quick to learn craft techniques and were soon all working on mass-produced wares in close collaboration with other members of the production teams. That initiative represented an important transitional moment for twentieth-century Swedish design. It stood for the marriage of art and industry that was to become increasingly important to Sweden's identity on the world stage as the century progressed. Although Sweden's manufacturers were traditional applied-art industries, they pursued a programme of innovative practice where the aesthetics of their products were concerned. They rejected the relentless rationalism and geometry of Germany developing, in its place, a softer, more humanistic, decorative modern style in the years following the First World War. The Swedish home market was amenable to the idea of modernity being expressed through design and the country's strongly middle-class population embraced a modern, democratic approach towards it from a relatively early date.

Figure 5.1 Plate-making at the Gustavsberg ceramics works, Stockholm, 1895
(courtesy of the Nationalmuseum, Stockholm, Sweden)

Denmark and Finland also developed heightened senses of their own national identities and of the role that visual, material and spatial culture could play within them. Jennifer Opie has explained that Finland reacted against Germanic classicism in the 1890s and embraced a more romantic ethos in its search for a national style.[16] Like many other countries, Finland created a pavilion for the Paris 1900 Universal Exhibition demonstrating its unique, national identity that looked both backward and forward at the same time. Designed by Gesellius, Lindgren and Saarinen, it espoused a language of form that owed much to the Karelian traditions that infused Finland's national identity at that time. The team's commitment to creating an image for their homeland, which hovered between its indigenous background and the need to relate to international modernity, was recognized when, in the following year, they won the competition to build the National Museum, a monument to Finnish culture.

Denmark allied itself more openly with Germany and defined its national identity as being strongly linked to the neoclassical idiom. Like its Scandinavian neighbours, it also looked to its own indigenous craft traditions and devoted its energies to furniture and ceramic manufacture. 1888 saw the Nordic Industrial Exhibition held in Copenhagen, an attempt to rival events held in Paris and London. It was characterized by the awareness that a renewal of style, with which to express Danish modernity in an international setting, was badly needed. Like so many other countries, the Danes looked to the British Arts and Crafts for inspiration. Several designers, such as the metalworker Georg Jenson, owed much to that movement.[17]

The northern European countries set out on a programme of design reform, linked to a search for national identity, that was predicated upon the achievements of the mass-production industries and which oriented itself towards the population as a whole. In a similar manner, France also sought a means of using its achievements within the area of visual, material and spatial culture as a basis upon which to grow a homogenous cultural image and identity that would make it a player on the international stage. However, it focused less on the concept of a modern democracy than on the traditional luxury trades. The art historian, Debora L. Silverman, has provided an account of the ways in which the various craft organizations in turn-of-the-century France developed a programme of reform and activity that allowed them to move forward without sacrificing their past achievements.[18] The exhibitions of 1889 and 1900 were crucial showplaces for the French nation to show its wares to the rest of the world (Figure 5.2). Lisa Tiersten has shown that, while the manufacture of decorative arts was an important aspect of French culture at that time, France was a heavily mercantile country and the developments in retailing of the late nineteenth century created a strong consumer culture that also proved a strong influence on the direction that design was to take.[19] The *Bon Marché* store exhibited an interior at the 1900 Universal Exhibition and it was clear at that event that French culture was determined to maintain its links with its

PARADIS DES DAMES
8 et 10, Rue de Rivoli — PARIS

EXPOSITION UNIVELLE DE 1900 — L'ÉLECTRICITÉ

Figure 5.2 The Pavilion of Electricity at the Paris Universal Exhibition, 1900
(courtesy of Paul Greenhalgh)

traditional luxury trades – fine furniture making in particular – and to build a modern consumer culture on the basis of that established identity. France's was a much more evolutionary approach towards the development of design as a representation of modernity than that of other countries. Ironically, however, it was to have a greater impact upon popular taste than the democratic machine aesthetic promoted by Germany. Indeed, France was among the first countries to understand the way in which individual and national identities needed to come together and the importance of targeting female consumers in an attempt to instil a sense of modern nationhood into its citizens.

The USA's national identity of those years was highly eclectic, dependent upon the many cultures it had absorbed through the waves of immigration over the years. Like its European counterparts, the USA also exhibited designed wares in a number of large exhibitions in the second half of the nineteenth century. The 1853 New York exhibition was its version of the 1851 British event at the Crystal Palace, at which the USA had shown its latest technologies, the Yale lock and the Colt revolver among them. The 1876 Centennial Exhibition, held in Philadelphia, focused on the nation's technological virtuosity. However, by the time of the Columbian Exhibition, hosted by Chicago in 1893, it was clear that the USA was looking for a national style and that it had found it in a form of classicism, referred to as the Colonial Revival (Figure 5.3). Unlike Germany, and more in line with

Figure 5.3 The Columbian Exhibition, Chicago, 1893
(Photographer C.D. Arnold, courtesy of the Chicago Historical Society)

France, the USA evolved its national style from its past rather than from its present and its future. The arrival of the German Werkbund exhibition in Newark in 1912, however, stimulated a response from a handful of individuals who were keen to take the USA down a similar route. A new American identity was also emerging linked to the idea of a modern, technology-enabled lifestyle free from the weight of European traditions. Specifically American movements in material culture emerged, among them that of Mission furniture – a heavy wooden idiom that was linked, so it was claimed, to an indigenous vernacular style. Those forays apart, in the years around the turn of the century the USA's national identity was essentially linked to the development of a consumer society. All the accoutrements of the culture of consumption of those years – mass circulation magazines, department stores, shop windows, and advertisements among them – could all be seen as part of the 'American way' helping to make its consumers 'Americans'.

By 1914, it was clear that design had played a large part in forming and communicating a large number of national identities, especially the contested ones in Europe. It was an important means through which governments and corporations could define their citizens and its consumers and, just as importantly, through which citizens and consumers could define themselves.

Corporate culture and the state

> National identification in this era acquired new means of expressing
> itself in modern, urbanised, high technology societies.[20]

In his chapter on nationalism between the two World Wars, the historian,
Eric Hobsbawm, explained that two crucial factors had to be remembered
in that period. Firstly, the rise of the modern mass media – the press, the
cinema and the radio among them – had, he maintained, the power to
'standardize, homogenize and transform popular ideologies as well as
exploiting them for the purposes of deliberate propaganda by private interests and states'.[21] Although Hobsbawm omitted 'design' from his list, by
those years, through the agency of industrial mass production and other
forms of reproduction (photography and printing among them), designed
objects images and spaces had come to constitute an important component
of the mass media. Indeed, arguably, through its multiple manifestations as
representations, images, physical artefacts and environments, it was more
capable than other faces of the mass media of communicating values and
ideas in a persuasive way.

In the inter-war years, modernist design became a powerful cultural force
to reckon with within the arena of international high culture. This reached a
peak at the International Style exhibition held at New York's Museum of
Modern Art in 1932.[22] Simultaneously, however, design developed a day-to-
day relationship with the commercial context of the industries and consumers
it served and, as a result, took on a rather different demeanour. Increasingly,
individual nations chose to define and represent themselves through the
commercial face of design, seeing it as a means of establishing cultural and
trading identities for themselves and of appealing to the popular audiences to
which they addressed themselves. As a result of design looking simultaneously in two directions, two modern design styles emerged. They have been
described as 'modernist' and 'modernistic'.[23] While the former reflected a
complete break with history and adopted an international perspective, the
latter maintained a level of continuity with the past through the development
of a language of decoration that took its inspiration from the contemporary
world and which took on different guises in different countries.

The commercial face of French modern design was in evidence at the
Paris International Exhibition of Decorative Arts of 1925, where the leading department stores of the day (the *Magasins du Louvre*, the *Galeries
Lafayettes*, the *Magasins de la Place Clichy*, the *Magasins du Printemps* and
the *Magasins du Bon Marché*) created extravagant pavilions (Figure 5.4).
As has already been demonstrated, in 1900 France's self-image was largely
dependent upon its luxury manufactures and its strong retail culture.[24]
Although the 1925 exhibition was international in scope and contained a
number of modernist displays (the pavilions designed by the Russian
architect, Konstantin Melnikov, and Le Corbusier's *Pavillon de L'Esprit*

Figure 5.4 Edgar Brandt's Gate of Honour at the Exhibition of Decorative Arts, Paris, 1925
(courtesy of the author)

Nouveau were the most prominent), the event was dominated by the department stores' pavilions, which contained the work of France's leading decorators and craftsmen of the day – among them Süe et Mare, Jean Dunand, Andre Groult and Maurice Dufrène. Those practitioners chose to work with rare woods, animal skins and precious materials, reflecting France's empire and its decorative artists' interest in exoticism. The exhibition as a whole reflected an image of a country that was home both to design modernism at the margins but which also embraced a softer modern idiom. The latter proved the more popular style and, by the 1930s, under the name of 'Art Deco', it had penetrated the mass environment on a significant scale, visible on shop fronts, factory and cinema facades and interiors, American skyscrapers and a wide range of mass-produced fashion accessories and decorative objects.

National identity and commerce went hand in glove at France's event. As Tag Gronberg has explained, although the exhibition had the word *industriels* in its title, 'it included none of the spectacular displays of industrial manufacture that had characterised other French exhibitions'.[25] Instead, the nation, or at least the city, a microcosm of the nation, was presented as a shop window. The strong emphasis on consumption was matched by the dominance of femininity. Indeed, the city of Paris itself was characterized at the event as a centre for women's luxury shopping – the home of haute couture – and it was through that aspect of its material culture that France chose to represent itself, rather than through its modernist achievements.

Design was used in 1925 to evoke a world in which luxury, interior décor, commerce, couture and the decorative coexisted. As Tag Gronberg has pointed out, 'An identification with *haute couture* was an important means of promoting Paris as the centre of modernity and consequently France is "in advance" of other nations'.[26] The interior displays within the pavilions offered a level of bourgeois distinction to the consuming public that visited them. Simon Dell has argued that it was identity itself, rather than objects, that was on display and that 1925 marked the important moment when the both individual and national identities were formed, not through production but through consumption.[27]

Although architectural and design modernism made an impact in the USA, that nation's indigenous industrial design movement adopted a very different form of self-presentation characterized less by a set of philosophical beliefs than by a pragmatic negotiation with the marketplace.[28] Stylistically and ideologically, the achievements of the Europeans set a gold standard against which many projects were judged. Many American designers took off from a different starting point, however, preferring to let the right solution arise from the problem at hand. A number of European émigrés – including Paul Frankl, Joseph Urban and Frederick Kiesler – came to the USA in the inter-war years bringing with them ideas that had originated in the old world.[29] Quite quickly, however, their approaches were absorbed into the commercial setting in which they found themselves and their work became integrated into the USA's highly commercialized modern design movement. Indeed, the origins of that movement within advertising, marketing and consumer culture continued to determine its progress through the inter-war years. The USA was one of the few countries that did not exhibit at the 1925 Paris exhibition, the reason given being that it was not yet ready to show itself to the rest of the world.

The USA's relationship with marketing, however, was growing in strength. A number of individuals played a key role in that development. In the 1920s, Edward Bernays, a nephew of Sigmund Freud, for example, explained his uncle's ideas about the irrational self to the world of business and, in so doing, helped to develop a number of the fundamental strategies that have underpinned mass marketing and mass propaganda since that time. One of Bernays' marketing successes was to persuade women that smoking in public was an act of liberation.[30] The literary historian, Rachel Bowlby, has described how, in the 1930s department store, salesmen were trained to penetrate customers' subconscious minds and to utilise strategic selling techniques.[31] A text from the period, Christine Frederick's *Selling Mrs. Consumer* of 1929, validated that fact. It focused on the gendered role of consumption and showed how the appeal to the irrational mind of woman was a fundamental part of the process.[32] In 1932, Roy Sheldon and Egmont Arens published their book, *Consumer Engineering*, in which they outlined a number of ways in which manufacturers could ascertain consumer needs and desires and attempt to fulfil them through their products. One chapter, entitled 'The Artist Comes in the Back Door', explained how art had come to be at the service of industry. In the authors' words, 'This unobtrusive artist was a realist of the machine. He simplified as he worked, discarding geegaws and flourishes. Convenience, fitness, cleanliness were uppermost in his mind. To these qualities he added beauty, good taste'.[33]

The artists in question were collaborating with manufacturers in the economic context of Roosevelt's 'New Deal'. The national identity and the future of the country were linked to the fortunes of manufacturing industry and to the large corporations that developed in those years. In turn, they depended upon design. Nowhere was that more apparent than at the 1939 New York World's Fair, at which the spotlight focused on the USA's large corporations – General Motors, Ford, Chrysler, Dupont, the National Cash Register Company, AT & T, Westinghouse, Lucky Strike Cigarettes, Firestone, the National Dairy Products Corporation and others (Figure 5.5). Collectively, they *were* the nation and, in 1939, they used design and the industrial design profession to communicate their values to the visiting public.

Figure 5.5 Poster for the New York World's Fair, 1939
(© Queens Museum of Art, New York)

The event has been well documented, with an emphasis upon the work of the leading designers of the day – Norman Bel Geddes (who created the General Motors 'Highway and Horizons' exhibit), Walter Dorwin Teague (who masterminded the event, designed the Ford Motor Company's exhibit, the United States Steel exhibit and the State Reception Room of the United

States Government Building, among others) and Raymond Loewy (who worked on Chrysler's contribution). The reason for asking the designers to stage-manage the event was provided by the event's organizers, when they explained that, 'because the industrial designers are supposed to understand public taste and be able to speak in the popular tongue, and because as a profession they are bound to disregard traditional forms and solutions and think in terms of today and tomorrow it was natural that the Board of Design should turn to them for the planning of the major exhibits in which the theme of the Fair is to be expressed'.[34]

The aesthetic idiom used on all the USA's exhibits was that of streamlining, a style that had its origins in automobile styling but which had rapidly been transferred into domestic and office machines and finally into architecture. It evoked an image of futurity, of technological confidence and of control over the material world. Its seamless, undecorated forms were redolent of a progressive model of modernity that was materialized through a collaboration of art with industry. The very theme of the fair – 'Building the World of Tomorrow' – indicated the forward-looking thrust of the event which set out to show the rest of the world that the USA was the most technologically, economically and socially advanced nation in the world. Above all, it sought to address its own consuming public as a unified, undifferentiated emotional mass. In the words of Warren I. Susman, the intention was to both to educate and dazzle but most importantly, 'to cut through divisions of class, ethnicity and ideological distinctions of left and right to form a basic sentiment on which a national culture might be founded'.[35] Modern design was used as a means not only of representing but also of helping to create what has subsequently been called 'the American way of life'.[36]

The striking evocation of a future made possible by technology that epitomized the USA's self-image in 1939 was absent from Great Britain's self-presentation at that event, through an exhibit that featured the 'pageantry of the past.' Its display of heraldry marked Britain's determination to keep one foot firmly in the past and to present a conservative identity to the rest of the world. Britain hosted and participated in a number of exhibitions during the inter-war years, all of them dominated by the theme of its colonies. At the British Empire exhibition of 1924, for example, which like so many other exhibitions of the same era placed a strong emphasis on trade, a variety of African arts and crafts were displayed.[37] It was suggested at the time that such artefacts might provide an alternative inspiration for modern designers to that of international modernism.[38] In general terms, Britain adopted an ambivalent approach to modernism and only a relatively few private residences and social housing schemes embraced the radical modernist style that was emerging on the Continent.[39] Instead, when it represented itself as a nation through exhibitions, Britain called much more frequently on its indigenous traditions, both mythical in nature and otherwise. In her study of the *Daily Mail* Ideal Home Exhibitions, Deborah S. Ryan has shown that progressive ideas about efficiency in housework coexisted alongside the display of Georgian- and Tudor-style housing.[40] The influences of the French Art Deco style and of American streamlining were also in evidence in the displays, which were aimed at an audience of female consumers.

Such was the power of consumer culture in the inter-war years that no nation that saw itself as advanced, and that wanted to present itself to its own population as such, could avoid presenting an image of itself through its manufactured goods. In the creation of those identities, therefore, design and its richly nuanced meanings played a key role. The Ideal Home Exhibition combined an educational with a commercial agenda and promoted a model of domestic Englishness that hovered between the modern and the nostalgically traditional.

Two countries that used design effectively in exhibitions to represent themselves as nations in the 1930s, were the Fascist states of Germany and Italy. Like Britain, both countries embraced a mix of the international modern and the traditional with which to create their respective national identities. While Germany combined the *volk* ethos with a modern industrial aesthetic in its production of cars, ceramics and metal ware, Italy looked to its craft traditions, its neoclassical past and international modernism all at the same time to convey the idea of a nation characterized both by its strong past and its progressive approach towards the future (Figures 5.6 and 5.7).

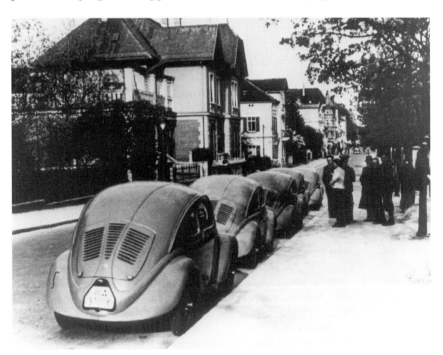

Figure 5.6 Ferdinand Porsche's design for the Volkswagen, 1936–7
(© Volkswagen AG)

Figure 5.7 Palazzo dell'Arte, Triennale building, Milan, 1933
(© Archivo Fotografico, La Triennale di Milano)

Many other nations became increasingly sophisticated in their use of exhibition displays as means of presenting themselves both to their own populations and to the rest of the world. Inasmuch as no industrialized nation could afford to appear insular, the international message of modernism played a key role in the ways in which nations promoted themselves but a careful balancing act was needed if countries were to also retain their distinctive characteristics. Countries, such as the newly formed Czechoslovakia, created in 1919 as a democratic state formed of Bohemia, Moravia, Slovakia and Ruthenia, for example, embraced modernism as part of its bid to enter the international arena and to create a modern national identity for itself and its people. To make that identity distinctive, it flavoured the international style with some local inflections. 'The aspirations of the young republic', David Elliott explained, 'were reflected in a desire for new styles of art, architecture and design which were accessible to the people and which drew inspiration from the vernacular language of the village and the city street'.[41] Although it drew on a wide range of contemporary European avant-garde tendencies – from Futurism to Dada, to Constructivism to Surrealism – it also developed its own modern design movement. *Devetsil*, as the Czech movement was called, embraced the cubist ceramics of Josef Havlicek and Antonin Heythum and the typographic experiments of Karel Teige. Although *Devetsil* did not enter the world of mass production, its potency lay in its attempt to bring Czechoslovakia into the modern world through the creation of a progressive design movement that represented modernity. Inevitably, another face of the country represented by folk production and cut glass continued to be shown at international exhibits, expressing quite a different identity for the new republic. When the country succumbed to Stalinist rule in 1948 Czech modernism came to an abrupt end.

By 1939, the USA had moved the furthest in integrating design into its private corporations, rather than, as in more centrally controlled countries and totalitarian states, maintaining it as a tool of ideological control. However, there were signs in other countries as well that corporate design was becoming very powerful. In Britain, for example, the Shell Company was using poster design to promote its services very effectively, while in Italy the Olivetti Typewriter Company understood, as the AEG had before it, the way to use designers to create a forceful, high-quality company image. Although Italy had a regime of autarchy in the 1930s, Camillo Olivetti operated in an international arena. He had visited the USA and met Henry Ford and implemented American manufacturing techniques in his typewriter and office machine factory in Ivrea. In 1933, he produced fifteen million office machines and nine thousand portable typewriters.[42] Design was soon added to his successful commercial formula. The initiative to implement a design strategy, in the form of modernist buildings, graphics and product design, was taken by Camillo's son, Adriano, who employed a number of Bauhaus graduates, including Xanti Schawinsky, as well as a leading Italian architect of the day, Eduardo Persico. Finally he brought the modernist graphic designer, Marcello Nizzoli, into the group to work on product design. The result was a totally modern corporate identity that was to make a strong impact internationally in the post-war years.

By the end of the 1930s, design had become a tool available for use both by private enterprises and by nations to persuade others to consume their goods or to recognize their authority. As a medium for propaganda, both economic and political, it had enormous potency. It was capable of transmitting values that satisfied consumer desire and of stimulating a level of aspiration that encouraged consumers to embrace goods and images as forms of identity formation. The same powers of persuasion and offers of identity could be used by political regimes to encourage national loyalty. Unlike the radio broadcasts and the other forms of the mass media, design could function in a multi-layered way such that the meanings of commodities and images, already coded by designers, could be re-presented, by other designers, within the doubly coded context of an exhibition, a shop window, a printed page or an advertising campaign. By the inter-war years, many nations and corporations had come to depend on design for their various commercial or ideological ends, fully aware of its power to persuade.

Part 2

Design and postmodernity, 1940 to the present

6 Consuming postmodernity

The dream of modernity

> The conditions were present for the arrival in Britain of that complex
> and pervasive phenomenon to which J. B. Priestley, returning in 1954
> from a visit to the USA, affixed, by a happy stroke, the name of
> 'Admass'.[1]

In the years following 1945, design, as a messenger of modernity, penetrated the lives of increasing numbers of people across the globe. Inevitably,
the war years had seen a temporary reduction in mass consumption and
more emphasis upon making do and mending. However, by the late 1940s
and '50s, consumption was becoming the main form of self and group identification for people across a broad social spectrum. The result was a further
democratization of the expression of taste in the marketplace manifested in
a flurry of purchasing, especially of homes, furnishings, consumer gadgets,
clothing and cars. New levels of earning motivated people to improve their
material conditions and their social positions. In turn, those new expectations were part of the drive, on the part of many of the countries in Europe,
to establish new national identities for themselves. Although the new
lifestyles on offer in the marketplace were expressed through individual
consumption, they also helped to define the new nations as modern, liberal
democracies.

Several studies of Britain and Europe have described the new phenomenon that hit their shores in the 1940s and 1950s as 'Americanization'.[2] It
brought with it a new model of consumption that, as conditions varied from
place to place, was inevitably affected by, in the words of Victoria de
Grazia, 'very different relationships between state and market, varying
modalities of class stratification and different notions of the rights and
duties and citizens'.[3] For countries such as the USSR and those in, what was
at that time, the Eastern bloc, for example, consumption had a strong needs
component within it and the range of goods on offer was severely restricted.
Nonetheless, the American model was highly influential in Europe. Even in
the German Democratic Republic (GDR), as Ina Merkel has demonstrated,

it eventually took a hold. Merkel has described the conflict that took place in East Germany as ideas from the West gradually infiltrated that country – 'One the one hand, in the East, the idea of socialist equality with its holy trinity of work, bread and housing was paramount... On the other hand, social and cultural differentiation in the West had developed and deepened deriving from experiences of upward mobility and post-war economic successes'.[4]

In the more affluent, capitalistic European countries, however – Britain, Germany and Italy among them – consumption played an increasingly large part in everyday life. Countries with a strong tradition of social democracy behind them – the Scandinavian countries for example – and others which had a cultural antipathy to the 'American Way – France in particular – attempted to resist the impact of US-style conspicuous consumption but were only partially successful. To a significant degree, the model of consumer modernity that had begun to make an impact on ordinary American citizens before the Second World War was felt as a wave engulfing Europe after 1945.

Americanization was accompanied by new levels of materialism.[5] In his 1958 study, *The Affluent Society*, the economist, J. K. Galbraith, described the new consumerism as it affected the USA. While more recently, historians such as Erica Carter in her account of 1950s German consumerism, have looked at its influence on European countries.[6] Mass consumerism was heavily criticized at the time by a number of writers. In Britain, for example, Raymond Williams, wrote in *Culture and Society* of 1958, of the dangers inherent in emulating the American experience.[7] In many ways, he was echoing the pre-war anxieties of the members of the Frankfurt School who had expressed serious doubts about the benefits of mass culture.[8]

Along with Richard Hoggart, Williams was one of the founders of what, by the 1970s, had become, in Britain, the academic discipline known as cultural studies. He was fearful of a wholesale embrace of the mass media, including the products of the mass production industries, concerned that it would mean a loss of traditional culture and an erosion of standards. 'Isn't the real threat of mass culture', he wrote, 'of things like television rather than things like football, or the circus – that it reduces us to an endlessly mixed, undiscriminating, fundamentally bored reaction?'[9] He highlighted advertising as playing a very special role within the mass media. 'In a sense', he explained, 'the product has become irrelevant: the advertiser is working directly on image and dreams... all ordinary values are temporarily overridden by a kind of bastard art, not clarifying experience but deliberately confusing it'.[10]

The mass media – film, television, magazines, advertising and massmanufactured products themselves – were instrumental in disseminating a number of lifestyle models that could be appropriated through consumption.[11] Many of them encouraged aspirations that had implications for design. The ideal of the modern, or as it was referred to at this time, the 'contemporary' home, was communicated widely through the mass media and, especially for new married couples who had not hitherto had the opportunity to own their home and consume on such a scale, it significantly displaced the traditional home as an aspiration (Figure 6.1).

Figure 6.1 Advertisement for Kenwood's 'Steam-o-Matic' iron, 1950s
(© Kenwood Ltd)

The American version of the contemporary home was disseminated through popular television programmes, such as *I Love Lucy*, which was also broadcast in Europe. In Britain, the style featured in the sets designed for television programmes.[12] Above all, they filled the pages of popular women's magazines on both sides of the Atlantic. Elizabeth Wilson has described the way in which Mary Grieve, the, then, editor of *Woman* magazine, understood the close link between consumption and women's engagement with modern life.[13] For new consumers, buying a house for the first time and equipping it with contemporary furniture, a kitchen filled with new gadgets, a large refrigerator (in a range of new colours with exotic names) and a new car in the driveway represented their primary means of proclaiming their engagement with the post-war world and of defining themselves. However, as the American writer, David Riesman, has explained in his influential text, *The Lonely Crowd*, first published in 1950, as mass society expanded, so individuals became increasingly isolated.[14] Inevitably, the mass media, of which mass-produced visual, material and spatial culture was a part, played a role in that process.

The consumer-oriented *Do-It-Yourself* magazine succeeded the much more technically oriented *Practical Mechanics* of the pre-war era, its front covers showing couples working together to build cupboards and strip walls. Often, wives were pictured holding their husbands' ladders, while the latter precariously drilled holes in the wall. The myth of wedded together-ness was widely disseminated, helping to confirm the importance of the close-knit, post-war nuclear family. It also served to consolidate the isolation of such units and the loss of a traditional sense of community. Increasingly, self-identification was formed through consumption and participation in the fashion cycle. In Britain, the importance of design to that process and its strategic role within the nation's desire to build a new post-war society and identity was explicit in the words of a government report on the subject of education written by John Newson:

> Our standards of design, and therefore, our very continuance as a great commercial nation, will depend on our education of the consumer to the point where she rejects the functionally futile and aesthetically inept and demands what is fitting and beautiful...Woman as purchaser holds the future standard of living of this country in her hands...If she buys in ignorance then our national standards will degenerate.[15]

It was clear that consumption was seen as the key to Britain's future and that it required educated taste, which, at that time, meant a preference for the contemporary style. As Newson made clear, the main responsibility for consumption fell to women. Believing that if the home market for good modern design expanded then trade with other nations would improve, the British Council of Industrial Design, formed by the Board of Trade of the Coalition Government in 1944, focused on the education of consumer taste. Men were also consuming in those years, however. In his study of the consumption of menswear in Britain, Frank Mort has outlined the ways in which a particular image of modern masculinity manifested itself in dress, lifestyle accessories and a commitment to popular culture. Work under-taken on the emergence of the concept of the teenager in those years has also demonstrated that the consumption of certain key items provided entry to a range of young male sub-cultural groups – those of Teddy Boys, and later of Mods and Rockers, in particular.[16] Older men undoubtedly consumed as well, although rather more silently.

For new consumers in particular, the emphasis was upon the consumption of modern goods and images and it was generally acknowledged that designers had the necessary visualizing skills to create appropriate forms. Several texts, notable among them Thomas Hine's *Populuxe*, have provided detailed accounts of the exuberance of contemporary American material culture in those years.[17] It was undoubtedly an era that pushed imaginations to the limit in the search for ever new and evocative forms with which to entice consumers, especially in the areas of domestic goods and automobiles, which accounted for the vast majority of private consumption choices.

While, at the level of high culture, the visual and ideological language of modernism remained in place, such was the expansion of the market for designed goods and images that a multiplicity of modern forms rapidly began to appear in the marketplace. A concept of popular modernism emerged that sat alongside other contemporary manifestations of popular culture, represented by Hollywood films, advertisements, pulp novels and popular music. The disparity between what have been called 'highbrow' and 'lowbrow' cultures was widely discussed by cultural critics and, what Theodor Adorno and Max Horkheimer had described as 'safe standardised products geared to the large demands of the capitalist economy' were seen, by many, as regrettable manifestations of modern society.[18] For others, however, among them the members of the Independent Group which met at London's Institute of Contemporary Arts through the early 1950s, the emergence of popular culture brought with it a new energy and an aesthetic exuberance that pointed the way forward towards a new postmodern sensibility that would openly embrace the values of the marketplace.

Not all the accounts of 1950s consumption and design have claimed that the impact of modernity upon people's lives was always accompanied by optimism, however. In her case study essay, 'Inside Pramtown: A Study of Harlow House Interiors, 1951–1961', the design historian, Judy Attfield, for example, took a cooler look at the way in which the vision of modernity affected consumers. She described how the working-class women housed in Harlow suffered a severe loss of community and found that their kitchens were intolerable to be in because they were located at the front of their houses and were permanently overlooked.[20] While Attfield's case study focused on social housing, other studies have looked at the consumption of clothing items, where more choice was exercised and where the possibilities of experiencing pleasure were, potentially at least, greater. Such was the case in the consumption of stiletto-heeled shoes, Lee Wright has claimed. They could, she suggested, be seen as a means through which many women engaged with the world of modernity for the first time. 'Expressions of femaleness', she maintained, 'can signify power'.[21] Although many feminist writings of the 1970s criticized women's passivity in the marketplace, Wright looked back at 1950s with a more sympathetic approach to women's consumption.[22] The debate between the views of the earlier generation of feminists and Wright's post-feminist ideas hinged upon the different ways in which designed artefacts carried meanings. Were they simply non-negotiable symbols of the ideological status quo, the question was asked, or could they act as bearers of power, giving meaning to women's lives? While 1970s feminism adopted a neo-Marxist view of historical change, attributing to objects a single ideological role as commodities, Wright's view was more pluralistic and non-ideological in its understanding of the ways in which visual, material and spatial culture have the potential to interface with society and culture.

A similar argument about designed artefacts' ability to act, in semiotic terms, as floating signifiers and to change their meaning according to their context, has been presented by the cultural theorist, Dick Hebdige. In his article on the Vespa motor-scooter he has described the way in which that small object of transport underwent a transformation from a mainstream cultural artefact, developed to replace the bicycle in Italy in the 1940s and 1950s, to become, in the 1960s, a customized, cult object that played a key iconic role in the visual identity of the British subcultural group, the 'Mods' (Figure 6.2).[23] The identities that were formed by the consumption of material goods in the early post-war years were highly gendered. Following

Figure 6.2 Vespa motor scooter, designed by Corradino D'Ascanio for Piaggio, Italy, 1946
(courtesy of Piaggio)

women's experiences of liberation during the Second World War, when they had had to take on a number of roles that were almost indistinguishable from those of their male counterparts, the post-war period saw a rapid re-gendering of women and men and a reversion to the ideology of the separate spheres. In Britain, the overriding motivations underpinning that volte-face were linked to the need to rebuild the population and to construct a nation state made up of settled, committed citizens. On another level, it was a means of facilitating the expansion of individual consumption, part of a larger strategy to increase profitability and to improve the status of British international trade.

In the idealized imagery of advertisements and films, the 1950s were frequently depicted as a highly feminized decade in which housewives looked like glamorous hostesses and products were decorated with a range of colours that emphasized their role as aestheticized lifestyle signs rather than functional tools. In the area of women's dress, for example, Christian's Dior's 'New Look', presented in Paris fashion in 1948, was widely repre-sented in the mass media and energetically copied. An overtly feminine, full-skirted, longer length, extravagant image of the ideal female, complete with pinched waist was offered to female consumers in an era in which they were encouraged to return to the home to become wives and mothers. It was also an era in which the door-to-door sales of cosmetics and food-container home-selling parties became highly popular. The latter strategy of getting women to combine their social life with economic exchange was a subtle one. It served to overcome the isolation of suburban life and to link the idea of consumption with the concepts of pleasure, beauty and house-wifely efficiency.[24] An image of exaggerated femininity was reinforced by the emergence of numerous new consumer goods. The overtly feminized pastel colours of items of plastic kitchen equipment – washing up bowls and drinking beakers among them – played a key part in the new visual land-scape, encouraging women's sense of belonging in the domestic sphere.

The strong emphasis upon gendered and youth identities of those years did not escape either the marketing man or the designer and was, to a considerable extent, a result of their collaborative efforts. The need to reach ever larger audiences for their products led manufacturers to increase the size of their marketing and design departments. Men, women and young people were frequently targeted separately. In the area of radios, for exam-ple, large, table-bound models were offered to men, while lighter, portable models were created for women so that they could carry them to and from the kitchen as they undertook their domestic duties. By the end of the 1950s, the miniature transistor radio, which teenagers could secrete under their bedclothes, had also been launched. Styling decisions were based upon assumptions about gendered consumption patterns, although, of course, they played a significant role in determining them as well. The Detroit aesthetic of American automobiles, for example, featuring chromed features and complex instrument panels, was introduced into a range of products aimed at men, from hi-fi equipment to razors. Increasingly, designers responded to what they saw as the cultural needs of the marketplace and differentiated their products to suit them.

Many new developments also took place in the field of retailing. The department store, for example, underwent yet another incarnation in the post-war years. While it continued to meet the needs of middle-class consumers, less well-off customers were also welcomed and encouraged to use credit facilities. In Britain many retailers put much effort into displaying the modern character of their goods, often in collaboration with bodies such as the Council of Industrial Design in Britain. Consumers were increasingly introduced to the concept not merely of modern design but, more particularly, of good modern design, the equivalent of what they were encouraged to use when shopping: in other words, good taste. On one level, that spirit of design reform, at its strongest since the mid nineteenth century, was a response to the rapidly expanded picture of consumption. The fear of being overrun by bad taste, associated with an uncontrolled marketplace that threatened an ordered society, was experienced internationally. In the USA, the Museum of Modern Art in New York ran a series of exhibitions, entitled 'Good Design', which aimed to educate the consumer. In Great Britain, the Council of Industrial Design worked with the mass media to promote its message, while in Denmark, *Den Permanente*, that country's design reform body, opened a retail outlet in an attempt to educate the public into an understanding of the craft-based model of good design that had come to represent that country's engagement with modernity.[25]

Advertising took on a new face in that context of expanded consumption, with American techniques of persuasion moving rapidly across the Atlantic. American agencies, such as J. Walter Thompson, became active in Britain and several British graphic designers – Alan Fletcher, a founder member of the Pentagram design group among them – spent time in the USA, learning the 'American Way', before setting up their businesses back on British soil. The American industrial designer, Raymond Loewy, who maintained one foot in graphic design, set up an offshoot of his US-based company in Paris in the 1950s.

The 1960s saw a dramatic shift in the picture of consumption and design that had dominated its evolution in the USA and Europe since 1945. Design's link with high culture was challenged by the growing force of mass culture at that time. The result was a widespread crisis of modernist values. Age took over from gender as the dominant cultural category defined by consumption (Figure 6.3). With those shifts came the first fundamental revision of modernism and a growing awareness that design's relationship with the culture of consumption had become its dominant face. As a consequence, many design-related institutions had to come to terms with the implications of that fact and to review the values that underpinned their activities.

Figure 6.3 Mary Quant dress designs, 1960s
(courtesy of the author)

Consumer culture and postmodernity

The crisis in modernist design values that occurred in the 1960s initiated a
new phase in the relationship between design and culture that has lasted to
the present day. Indeed, culture itself was redefined as it embraced different
social and cultural groupings and sought to represent their values and atti-
tudes. Within that new definition of culture, design was forced to move
beyond the limits of modernism and to embrace a more pragmatic, market-
oriented approach. What came to be called 'postmodernism' was predicated
upon that significant shift.[26] In the words of the architect, Robert Venturi,
one of the new movement's earliest advocates, 'I prefer "both-and" to
"either-or", black and white, and sometimes gray, to black or white'.[27]
Postmodernism questioned the line that had hitherto separated high culture
from its popular equivalent, sought ways of bringing marginal voices –

those defined by gender, sexuality and race – to the centre and rejected value judgements based on what were seen as limited and out-dated criteria. For some, there was a serious danger that in embracing an all-inclusive definition of culture, all values would be overthrown.[28] Many of the theorists of postmodernity and the cultural manifestations that it brought in its wake saw it as a threat and their efforts to define it exposed the dangers that they felt it brought with it.[29]

By the 1970s it began to look as if the idealistic, politically motivated, production-oriented concept of design that had been formed as a by-product of architectural modernism had been replaced by a new emphasis on its links to consumption, advertising, marketing, branding and identity creation. That shift was manifested in a number of ways, among them the move, on the part of a number of radical Italian architectural groups – Superstudio, Archizoom and others – to conceptual work that lacked a material outcome, sub-cultural dress taking its inspiration from the street rather than from the Parisian fashion houses and by the widespread expansion of a popular interest in the past, manifested in the emergence of stylistic revivals and the growth of the heritage industry. The Craft Revival – a movement characterized by groups of makers in Europe and the USA choosing to work outside the confines of mass-production industry – also surfaced at that moment of rampant eclecticism.

In the domestic arena, pinewood replaced the chromed steel, sci-fi-inspired objects and spaces of the 1960s ideal home, while a spiral of stylistic revivals – from Art Nouveau, to Art Deco to 1950s popular styling – reversed the earlier commitment to an aesthetic that had represented the future. In the context of the early twenty-first-century economic recession that interest in stylistic revivalism has remained in place encouraging many consumers to revisit the styles and the austerity/boom mentality of the early post-Second World War years. However, in that new context, retro-style sits alongside a continued attachment to the minimal interior, although black leather and chrome sofas have become markers of refined living rather than of social idealism.

Back in the 1960s, the shift away from the modernist paradigm towards one in which consumers had already begun to see modernism as just one of the stylistic options in the marketplace was already underway. Indeed, from one perspective, modernism can be seen as an interlude in the history of modern design, a cul-de-sac that interrupted design's mission to democratize taste and luxury and to disseminate the concept of modernity to the widest possible audience. By the 1970s, however, the influence of postmodernity seemed to have displaced modernity from its position of dominance.

In that shift, the media inevitably played an enhanced role, disseminating more information to increasingly large numbers of consumers. While, on the one hand, increased interaction with the media resulted in a breakdown of traditional modes of social communication, on the other it gave consumers access to a wider range of possible lifestyles. More than ever before, design and designers aligned themselves with the mass media and played a central role within the construction of the numerous lifestyles that were on offer. Increasingly, design looked less to its early roots within manufacturing as goods, images and spaces increasingly communicated instant messages and became closely aligned to marketing and brand creation. At the same time, the democratization of design helped to create multiple, fragmented markets for goods, including one for products that depended heavily on the signatures and identities of the designers who had conceived them. Such was the power of brand selling that designers themselves were transformed into brands and their names were increasingly used to inject individualism into otherwise bland, mass-produced goods. By the '80s and '90s, designer jeans had been badged with the names of Gloria Vanderbilt, Giorgio Armani, Gianni Versace, Calvin Klein and Donna Karan, among many others, as a means of adding value and commanding a high price. The message that standardization and individualization could coexist become a commonplace in a world in which consumer choices had become dominated by emotions and instant responses. Among others, the German critic of postmodern culture, W. F. Haug, expressed an anxiety about, 'the domination over people that is effected through their fascination with technically produced artificial appearances'.[30] In his view, designer culture represented just another face of advanced economic capitalism.

Through the 1980s and '90s, the culture of consumption, with design at its centre, affected many areas of everyday life, from shopping to tourism, and embraced a wide range of leisure activities, from visiting heritage sites, museums and theme parks to buying branded fashion items. As town centres emulated theme parks and shopping malls were transformed into fantasy environments, it became increasingly difficult to separate the real from the designed experience. Within the shopping mall, for example, design not only determined its spatial shell but all its contents, from the general interior and directional signage to the individual shop interiors to the objects displayed within them, together with their packaging and their brand identities (Figure 6.4).[31] A realization about the omnipresence and enormous power of designed visual, material and spatial culture inspired many cultural theorists to express views on the subject, among them Jean Baudrillard and Umberto Eco, who sought to understand the ever complex nature and workings of postmodern consumer culture.[32] While they did not always openly acknowledge the concept of design, their ideas were largely stimulated by its effects.

Through the 1970s, '80s and '90s, the activity of shopping as a core postmodern experience came to the fore. It inspired a body of literature that was forced to acknowledge the important role played by visual, material and spatial culture in everyday life. A body of writing relating to the department stores of the late nineteenth and early twentieth centuries also emerged, emphasizing shopping as a primarily feminine activity. By the '90s, a series

Figure 6.4 The Bluewater shopping mall, Kent, 1999
(© Peter Durant/arcblue.com)

of books on the subject of masculinity began to balance that picture. As we have seen, Frank Mort's 1996 book focused on the way in which men created their identities through consumption in 1980s Britain. He directly addressed the agency of designers, positioning the graphic designer, Neville Brody, and the fashion stylist, Ray Petri, alongside journalists – Julie Burchill and Robert Elms among them – and advertisers and marketing professionals. For Mort, they all played key roles as creators of the young male identities available in the marketplace.[33]

A number of other studies of consumption published in the period also addressed design's important role within identity formation. Joanne Entwistle's essay '"Power Dressing" and the Construction of the Career Woman', for example, focused on the fashion designers, Ralph Lauren and Donna Karan, explaining that it was the mediation of their clothes and of clothes like them in television programmes such as *Dallas*, rather than the clothes themselves that rendered them capable of identity creation.[34] Although the physical details of the clothes themselves – their heavy padded shoulders, for example – provided them with a set of potential meanings, it was only in the context of mediation that those meanings were able to confer unambiguous identities on their wearers. To use a linguistic analogy, words have to be contained in sentences before they acquired fixed meanings. This work built on the studies of Dick Hebdige, written a decade earlier, which had explained that artefacts could work on two levels.

By the '80s and '90s, design had come to be understood as part of a process that also depended on advertising and marketing, as well as the mass media. In close conjunction with them, it was able to create specific identities that could be consumed, along with the goods, images and spaces it defined visually and functionally. It was not a static process, however, but one that was perpetually in flux, as consumers sought to continually redefine themselves. Once one set of unsatisfied desires were met they were simply replaced by others. Although the process built on the socioeconomic system described by Thorstein Veblen at the end of the nineteenth century, his idea of trickle down emulation was rendered more complicated by the increasingly complex shape of society and the multiplicity of markets that characterized the postmodern era.

In the early 1990s, social psychologists also began to address the issue of commodity culture and the formation of personal identities.[35] The assumption made by Peter K. Lunt and Sonia M. Livingstone, following in the wake of those anthropologists, Mary Douglas and Baron Isherwood, for example, was that people needed goods, 'for making visible and stable the categories of culture'.[36] Through the '90s, analysts of contemporary culture sought to understand design as a distinct subject of study in the context of other, related, commercial practices. On one level, as it merged into the umbrella arena of the mass mediation and the representation of images and identities, the concept of design became hard to isolate. Paul du Gay's work on the Sony Walkman (Figure 6.5) and Celia Lurie's on Nike trainers, among others, have positioned the concept of design as a component of branding and defined the material commodity as a manifestation of the process, but only at the margins.[37] Another perspective on the relationship between consumption and design was articulated in the writings of Zygmunt Bauman, who claimed that the expertise acquired by consumers through the art of shopping acted as a compensation for the fact that they had no understanding of the complex technologies and materials upon which everyday commodities depended. 'What is being sold', he explained, 'is not just the direct use value of the product itself, but its symbolic significance as a building-block of a particular cohesive lifestyle – as its indispensable ingredient'.[38] Inasmuch as they created the visual language that attracted the consumer in the first instance, his argument implied, designers provided a key interface between the commodities and consumers.

Although the idea of the brand had been in existence for nearly a century, the 1980s saw a revitalization of the concept on a global scale.[39] It was especially apparent in the areas of clothing and fashion accessories, where the logos of such manufacturers as Nike, Rebok, Benetton and Swatch came to stand for the items themselves and the lifestyles they denoted. The brand had long played an important role in designer fashion and, following the model that Coco Chanel established in the 1920s, Giorgio Armani, Ralph Lauren, Calvin Klein, Issey Miyake and others gave their names to the perfumes and other lifestyle accessories developed to reinforce their

Figure 6.5 Advertisement for Sony Walkman, Japan, 1979
(© Sony United Kingdom Ltd)

marketing identities. As Naomi Klein explained in her best-selling 2001 book on the subject of global branding, when describing the operations of new kind of corporations – Microsoft, Tommy Hilfiger and Intel among them – 'What these companies produced primarily were not things ... but images of their brands. Their real work lay not in manufacturing but in marketing'.[40]

One of the most successful design-related branding exercises of the late twentieth century was one undertaken by the household electronic goods inventor and manufacturer, James Dyson. His work was heavily dependent upon the 1930s idea of the cultural potency of product design to suggest advanced and efficient technology and to create its own unique selling point and product brand.[41] Dyson took that idea several stages further, however, combining visually desirable artefacts with a very strong brand. Perhaps the most sophisticated of all the branding exercises of the 1990s, however, was undertaken by the Japanese company, Muji, which adopted a 'no name' policy as its mark of distinction and good taste. The strategy involved creating an extra layer of desirability for its products. The absence of a brand created a sense that Muji objects had been removed from the commercialism of the marketplace. It was a sophisticated idea that cleverly responded to a growing popular anxiety about conspicuous consumption.

While perfume, clothing, foodstuffs and products had all been branded for some time, the 1980s, 1990s and early 2000s saw the idea being extended to places, especially leisure sites, offered for consumption by tourists. Pioneered by Disneyland, the American theme-park, many decades earlier, place-branding became an increasingly widespread phenomenon (Figure 6.6). In that early example, the use of Disney's name had been applied to what was, in effect, an elaborate fairground, immediately evoking a particular kind of experience, familiar to watchers of Disney cartoons, that was characterized by charm, magic, humour, fun, childish innocence and pleasure. That brand image was carefully maintained through the realization, in real space, of that imagined, two-dimensional world. Disneyland

Figure 6.6 Sleeping Beauty's Castle in Disneyland Park, Paris
(© Disney Enterprises, Inc.)

was both a branding and a design exercise of huge proportions and it has had an enormous influence on design for leisure experiences up to the present day.

The Disneyland phenomenon represented the possibility of recreating the real out of the imaginary, the material from the merely visual. As such, it reversed the usual process of culture, which had been to create fantasy out of reality. That inversion of what had happened in the past – of, that is, the traditional practice of stage sets emulating real spaces and settings – became a key characteristic of postmodern place-branding. It featured in the construction of numerous leisure environments of the late twentieth and early twenty-first centuries, from the casinos of Las Vegas to reconstructions of English country house interiors to the regenerated areas of cities to large hotel complexes, complete with pools surrounded by palm trees, constructed in a range of exotic locations. Moving, as many of these constructed spaces did, from the imagined to the real, they were not dependent on the specificity of their locations except, that is, when the local climate was a precondition of the experience. Visitors to postmodern leisure sites could be almost anywhere in the world. That new sense of geographical flexibility of experience was facilitated by the worldwide web, which enabled vast numbers of people to access a wide range of simulated experiences, either in two dimensions, or, with the help of multi-media technologies, in virtual space. As a result of the increasing popularity of branded real or virtual spaces, the 'experienced designer' emerged at that time, demonstrating that designers need not be rational 'problem solvers', as modernism would have claimed, but rather practitioners with the capacity to empathize with users and create experiences for them.

Some of the most strikingly designed and eagerly consumed experiences of the last three decades of the twentieth century, and of the first decade of the twenty-first century, were created for the heritage industry. As had been the case with Disneyland, the roots of the phenomenon lay in the mass media, not this time in the child's cartoon but, rather, in the adult television and film costume drama. The heritage industry was the subject of studies by Robert Hewison, by Patrick Wright, in *On Living in an Old Country*, and more recently by Raphael Samuel, in his *Theatres of Memory* volumes.[42] All three texts focused on the strong tendency – exhibited especially strongly in Britain but also in the USA, Europe and the Far East – towards a nostalgic invocation of the past. It was, for the most part, a romanticized vision, as conveyed, for example, in the televised version of Evelyn Waugh's *Brideshead Revisited*, of John Galsworthy's *The Forsyte Saga*, set in suburban West London and, more recently, of Julian Fellowes' *Downton Abbey*. Spurred on by the public's enthusiastic reception of those nostalgic offerings and the need, as the old industrial infrastructure went into decline, to create a new image of nation, Britain put much effort into recreating the past. From the refurbishment of the stately home, an activity that had begun in the 1950s through the work of the interior decorator, John Fowler, working with the National Trust, to the recreation of industrial centres for the tourist gaze, Britain underwent a reconstruction of selected aspects of its past.[43] From the Jorvik Viking Centre in York to the Ironbridge Gorge Museum, to the refurbishment of Liverpool's Albert Dock and the National Trust's reconstruction of Paul McCartney's and John Lennon's Liverpool childhood homes, Britain set out on a path of memory evocation. It was a long way from the modernist vision of design but it had no less significance. Both Hewison and Wright understood the phenomenon as a mark of a nation in decline and the latter pointed to what he called 'the cultural manipulation (which) pervades British society'.[44] For many architects and designers, however, it represented a new challenge; one that could result in the construction of new neo-buildings in the neoclassical style, exemplified by Quinlan Terry's scheme for Richmond-upon-Thames, which came complete with landscaping and public areas, or an extension of nature itself, as in the recreation of the terraces located above Lake Rotomahana in New Zealand.[45]

The need for designers and architects to use their imaginative skills in the creation of theatres of memory represented an important aspect of their cultural role in the last decades of the twentieth and the first decade of the twenty-first centuries. Exhibition designers, including the London-based firm of Casson/Mann, which created new display areas in both London's Science Museum and Victoria and Albert Museum, were in hot demand. The Millennium celebrations also brought work to vast numbers of designers worldwide (Figure 6.7). The emphasis upon design for experience had come to overshadow many of designers' other roles, thereby linking the design process firmly to the condition of postmodernity. Ultimately, the emphasis on design for experience served to bring about a cultural shift such that it became increasingly difficult to differentiate between the worlds of the real and the artificial. The landscapes of Disneyland and Las Vegas permeated the environments of shopping malls and city centres worldwide, to the extent that it became impossible for consumers to know whether they were going shopping or out for a leisure trip. Umberto Eco's concept of 'hyperreality' became, for many, the *sine qua non* of everyday life in the postmodern world and design played a complicit role within it.[46]

Rooted, as it was, within the early years of mass consumption and moving, as it had done, from advertising and shop-window display to the physical manipulation of the product itself to the creation of real and virtual experiences, design was easily assimilated into the consumer culture of postmodernity. Indeed, arguably, it lay at the core of the new condition. Its strategies were intrinsically aligned to its ends. Whereas, within modernism, the product had been generated by architects (Le Corbusier designed his chairs to fit within the spaces of his houses, for example), within postmodernism, that process was transformed and products emanated, as indeed did buildings, from the desires and identity requirements of consumers rather from the whims of architects. In Disneyland and the shopping mall, for

Figure 6.7 The Millennium Dome, Greenwich, London, 2000
(© Finbar Good)

example, meaning was generated less by the individual components of the environment itself than by the promise of the stimulation and fulfilment of desire.[47] Arguably, this could be seen as a reworking of the *Gesamtkunstwerk* that had inspired the early modernists to envisage a range of complete environments.

Within the context of postmodernity and beyond, design provided back-cloths for experiences and many of the designers who came to the fore in that area were skilled in the art of display, image making, spatial design and online interaction. The product and furniture designers – the heroes of modernism – were displaced, surviving only as the creators of high-cultural icons that acted as the legacy of that early twentieth-century design movement. Only within that elevated level of culture could modernism survive. Through the pages of upmarket lifestyle magazines, such as the British

Wallpaper* magazine and Sunday newspaper supplements, it continued to provide the idealistic, aspirational face of visual, material and spatial culture. Manufacturers continued to market to niche groups but, increasingly, markets came to be defined less by geographical identities, class, gender or age, than by global taste cultures, lifestyle values and personality types. As brands and experiences took over from individual products, so design became part of every experiences, from tourism to shopping. By the end of the twentieth century, as the creators of the visual, material, spatial and experiential environments through which the mass of the world's population formulated both their group and their individual identities, designers had found an important role for themselves.

In the early twenty-first century, that market demand for designed goods did not vanish, nor did the desire, on the part of consumers, to establish their social positions and identities through consumption. However, an imperative to make design a tool for social and environmental improvements and change, rather than merely a capitalist tool, became increasingly visible. In that new context, a new rational, responsible consumer came into being who adopted a more critical attitude towards the consumption of visual, material and spatial culture. While, on one level, that new approach could be seen as a reincarnation of the modernist project, on another it emerged through the opening up that was made possible by postmodernism. In the early 1970s, the publication of Victor Papanek's book, *Design for the Real World*, had established the idea that designers should develop a sense of social responsibility and distinguish between people's wants and needs.[48] Papanek had also proposed that they should turn their attention to the needs of the Third World. By the early twenty-first century, his ideas had acquired a new resonance and, worldwide, design projects were undertaken that were underpinned by social ideals rather than by a desire for economic profit. In many cases, the new approach focused more on the design input into networks and systems than, as hitherto, on the creation of images, objects and spaces. From 2002 onwards, for example, Ezio Manzini and Francois Jégou worked, on a project entitled 'Emerging User Demands for Sustainable Solutions'. It involved working with local creative communities – that is, mutual support groups, groups creating communal gardens out of waste land, others providing services for each without any financial exchange and direct access networks based on cutting out the middle man between producers and users, etc. In all those cases, the designer's task was to create 'enabling systems...designed to consolidate the social innovation and to make it easier to promote to a wider audience'.[49] The project represented an important new application of the designer's skills; one that required innovative thinking combined with sensitivity towards users, without the necessity for a visual, material or spatial outcome. Rather, social sustainability and local identity were the ends in sight.

Some examples of social design did engage with visual and material products, however. The work supported by Britain's Design Council to enhance the dignity of hospital patients, for instance, resulted in a group of products that included a new hospital gown, a retractable fabric screen that was halfway between a curtain and a wall, a pre-manufactured washroom that provided a high level of privacy and a table mat with patient information printed on to it. A significant amount of research into patients' problems and needs underpinned the project and informed its outcomes.[50] The same principle inspired a project undertaken at London's Central St Martins College of Art and Design entitled 'Design Against Crime'. In that instance, the aim was to think about ways in which design could be used to minimize crime through practical interventions in urban spaces, such as housing blocks and car parks. One project focused on the redesign of city bicycle racks to help prevent theft.[51]

The concept of 'inclusive design' also emerged at that time. Rooted in similar ideals to those underpinning social design, it worked on the assumption that nothing should be created that does not take account of the needs of users with exceptional needs, whether the elderly, the disabled or people who were socially marginalized for a number of reasons. The work was based on the assumption that whatever supported exceptional needs would also work for more standard requirements.

In the recession-defined years of the first decade of the twenty-first century, however, the crisis of consumption really took a hold. A young generation, reacting against its parents' desire to buy lifestyles and identities in the open marketplace, developed strategies to enable them to recycle goods and prevent waste. Clothing swapping parties became commonplace, while e-Bay, car boot sales, charity shops and suppliers of vintage clothes and goods challenged conventional forms of retail (Figure 6.8). Many manufacturers responded to the widespread fears of eco-disaster and marketed their products under a 'green' label. That approach covered a multitude of possibilities – those of materials or product recycling or of artefacts being made from materials that would not damage the world's ecosystem, or ensuring that products took the idea of 'fair trade' into account. While much serious and important research went into these areas in the 1990s and there were signs that design had the capacity to play an important role in helping governments and manufacturers to address the issues of sustainability and ethical consumption, one immediate result was a new marketing opportunity for companies which cynically aligned themselves with current consumer sensibilities as a means of selling their goods.

There were many noncynical design-led responses to the challenge of sustainability as well, however, linked to the growing awareness that there was a need for designs for buildings, products and manufacturing systems that used energy and resources effectively and generated positive environmental, economic and social effects. 'Cradle-to-cradle' design emerged as a frequently discussed topic that advocated the idea that only materials that could be replenish the earth with biodegradable matter should be used for products. Many designers and manufacturers embraced that ideal. Herman

Figure 6.8 A vintage clothes shop, London, c. 2000

Miller, the American company that had manufactured Charles Eames's furniture designs from the 1930s onwards, for example, was particularly committed to sustainable design. That commitment represented more than just a way of designing their products, however, it also embraced the design of its buildings – among them its 'Greenhouse' building in Holland, Michigan, designed by architect William McDonough. In the area of designed products, the company focused on durability, innovation and quality and was proud to be able to claim that many of its classic designs had been on the market since the 1950s. It also stressed the need for energy saving, the reduction of packaging for its goods, disassembly and recyclability. As had been the case for the products of the early American arms manufacturers, the importance of ease of repair, repeated use and reassembly using standardized parts were paramount.[52]

Other designer goods manufacturers that embraced sustainability included the sports shoes and clothing producer, Nike.[53] Like Herman Miller, that company focused on reducing waste and making material choices that decreased the negative environmental impact of its work. For its 2010 football jerseys produced for South Africa, for example, Nike used one-hundred per cent recycled polyester, thereby, according to its own promotional material, diverting thirteen million plastic bottles from landfill.

Embracing sustainability went beyond the appearance or function of designed goods themselves to rethinking the entire system of production/consumption that had given design its meaning through the twentieth century. As such, there was a sense of *déjà vu*; of, that is, a return to the preoccupations of the early days of industrialization when changes in consumer tastes and awareness had fed directly back into the ways that manufacturers produced and marketed their goods. As early twenty-first century consumers became increasingly aware of the challenges presented by the world's depleting resources, so responsible manufacturers took that on board and rethought their operations as a totality, including design.

The sustainability agenda also played a role in refocusing ideas about production from a global to a local context. Indeed, the whole issue of localism as an antidote to globalism came sharply into focus in the early twenty-first century. The idea of social sustainability emphasized the need for the regeneration of local environments and communities. In turn, that new location-specific focus brought with it a new relationship between the manmade and the natural world and architects and designers began to embrace the latter in new ways. Landscaping took on a new significance in that context and the idea of blurring the boundaries between the insides and outsides of buildings was widely discussed. The 'green roof' became one common means of ensuring that buildings become more ecologically efficient. Whereas the modernists had divorced architecture from a specific notion of place, the new environmentally aware architects and designers sought to re-establish that link.

By the end of the first decade of the twenty-first century, both the consumer and designer had encountered many new challenges that had transformed them beyond recognition and redefined their relationship with production and consumption. That new relationship was less governed by social aspiration, taste and lifestyle than it had been in the past and more upon the recognition of the need for a shared understanding that the new challenges meant that production, consumption and design needed to move beyond the contradictions that had defined their past relationship and to work together in a new harmonious alliance. It represented the first radical challenge to design since its emergence within the division of labour introduced into the eighteenth-century factory.

7 Technology and design
A new alliance

The materials of abundance

In the years after the Second World War, consumer demand continued to set the pace for design innovation. However, the speed of technological change made it possible. New production technologies, emanating for the most part from the USA, dramatically influenced the way in which industry organized its manufacturing. Mass production, albeit modified to the tastes and desires of the marketplace, became the common means of ensuring that consumers had large numbers of goods available to them at prices that they could afford. In addition, technology joined with design in a hungry pursuit of new materials with which to meet consumers' enhanced desire for novelty and industry's demands for ever cheaper means of manufacturing goods. It continued to be the designer's task to ensure that those new materials acquired forms and meanings that were both appropriate and desirable.

The period after 1945 saw the beginning of a new phase of industrial expansion in the Western world and an intensification of the corporate globalism that was to become such a strong feature of late twentieth- and early twenty-first-century culture. It was characterized by the consolidation and expansion of the large-scale American corporations formed in the early century – General Motors, DuPont and General Electric, among many others – and their increasing presence in Europe and beyond. Many of the new technological breakthroughs had occurred during the war years. As an in-house Dupont publication explained, the changes made in that company built on wartime developments that had been put on hold but 'post-war America had new needs and made new demands. It was to satisfy those demands that the company now turned its attention. The program included modernizing plants and adding manufacturing facilities to fill expanded markets for pre-war product lines. Also it encompassed facilities to develop new processes and products which had been delayed by the war'.[1] After the War, Dupont moved into the development and manufacture of a range of new synthetic fabrics – among them 'Orlon' and 'Dacron', in addition to the already familiar 'Nylon' that had been launched back in 1941. Its experience was replicated by many other producer-goods industries, including the automobile producers, General Motors, Ford and Chrysler, as well as the large-scale manufacturers of household goods, among them the Tupperware Corporation and General Electric. Although they were all committed to the concept of standardized mass production, their growing orientation towards the consumer required them to become increasingly design-led and to offer the market a wide variety of goods. In 1957, one American furniture manufacturer offered 'twenty different styles of standard sofas...eighteen styles of love seats and thirty-nine upholstered chairs'.[2] Inevitably, they ranged from traditional to modern in style. The fact that several of the companies that directed their goods at the open marketplace – General Electric, Westinghouse and Chrysler among them – were also contracted to the military gave them an extra level of economic stability.[3]

The same period saw increasing numbers of American companies establish European subsidiaries, large-scale pre-war European companies flourish and the emergence of new, large-scale manufacturers in Europe. 1945 to 1950 saw a period of energetic industrial reconstruction in those countries that had been worst hit by the war – Germany, Italy and Great Britain among them. Much of the limited production that had been going on during those years had been focused on the war effort and the skills of designers had been utilised to military ends. Britain, for example, had employed many of its leading figures in its Ministry of Information, exploiting their graphic and narrative skills within their propaganda campaigns. Immediately after the War, therefore, a number of designers were ready to apply their newly honed skills in the context of peace.

The industrial reconstruction of Europe in the post-war years was largely made possible by the injection of American funding as part of the Marshall Plan.[4] Following the Plan, which was conceived as a means both of creating a trading partner and a defence against the Communist bloc, the USA poured huge sums of money into Europe to help restore its ailing industrial infrastructure. Inevitably, that financial imperialism had practical and ideological implications. The model of American corporatism led to the creation in Europe of a number of large, mass-production centres that utilised the manufacturing principles which had been established by Henry Ford and modified by Alfred J. Sloan earlier in the century. In Italy, for example, companies such as Fiat (Figure 7.1) and Olivetti modelled their factories on American lines, while the American giant corporations in the areas of electrical goods – General Electric and Westinghouse among them – continued to grow their European subsidiaries. In Holland, Phillips emerged, while in Germany AEG continued to develop and new corporations, such as Bosch, went from strength to strength.

The importation of American industrial and corporate models into Europe inevitably affected the way in which design was integrated into manufacturing and the type and nature of the goods that were directed at the expanding markets. In the areas of domestic machines and automobiles

Figure 7.1 Fiat production line, Turin, 1930s
(© Archivio Storico Fiat)

new production techniques, such as innovative methods of steel pressing, were shared. As a direct result, the aesthetic of streamlining was transferred to Europe. National cultural variants, dependent upon different class struc-tures and taste cultures, modified the stylistic imperialism of the USA, however. In Italy, for example, the exuberance of American pressed metal goods embellished with chromed surface detailing was tempered by a softer, less elaborate, more sculptural approach to product design. Battista Pininfarina's car designs for Ferrari and Marcello Nizzoli's design for a sewing machine for Necchi – the 'Mirella' – epitomized Italy's sophisticated version of streamform, which, in some ways, had more in common with contemporary sculpture than with bulbous automobiles.[5]

While, on one level, post-war Europe embraced American funds, support, technology and corporate culture, on another it continued to develop its indigenous, craft-based, small-scale industries. That phenome-non was especially apparent in Italy where the manufacture of textiles, furniture, ceramics, glass and metalwork was underpinned by deep craft roots. During the 1950s and 1960s, many small Italian companies were able to modernize their production, while still remaining small scale, to intro-duce design and to create high-cultural modern goods aimed at an international, niche market. That model of cultural production, which combined crafts skills with high-technology manufacturing and which put a strong emphasis upon design defined as an extension of art, was emulated by many other countries at a later date, Spain and Japan among them. Like Italy, those countries were confronted by the challenge of linking one level of their manufacturing industry with design to create goods with added value for their most discerning customers.[6]

In the 1950s, much of Europe's manufacturing was aimed at the American market. Both French and Italian haute couture and much of Italy's decorative goods – ceramics, in particular, were all targeted at US consumers.[7] An Italian exhibition of 1951, entitled 'Italy at Work', toured a number of American museums in an effort to attract consumers for Italian goods, while a large exhibition of Scandinavian design, motivated by a similar agenda, toured the USA between 1954 and 1957.[8] The European art and design industries filled a gap in the American marketplace, the majority of which was filled with cheap, mass-produced, indigenous ware. Italy's sophisticated luxury cars of the 1950s also found an enthusiastic, albeit niche, audience in the USA. For nearly a decade, North America remained a key market for those élite goods, thereby enabling Europe – Italy and the Scandinavian countries in particular – to develop a high-cultural, high-quality designs that depended upon craft-based manufacturing. French couture, the most luxurious of all Europe's production, also found an outlet in Canada.[9] As a fashion expert, Dora Miller, explained, it was 'as important to the economy of the nation [i.e. France] . . . as the automobile industry [was] to the United States'.[10] By the late 1950s, Europe had realized the economic potential of its modern decorative and luxury goods in the USA and had organized one level of its production, its design and its distribution accordingly. The following decade saw the emergence, following the establishment of the European Community, of a European home market for the same goods and the need to export to the USA became less urgent. The result was the emergence of a strong modern European design movement with strong centres in Italy (Milan in particular), Sweden, Denmark, Finland and Germany.

While one face of the relationship between technology and design in the years after 1945 related, therefore, to the export of American know-how to Europe, another related to the continual challenge presented by the emergence of new materials. The war years had seen many advances in that area, especially in the fields of plastics, metals, wood technology and, importantly, in the bonding together of those materials. In the USA, the work of the architect–designer, Charles Eames, was dependent on both new wood-processing techniques and bonding methods for the new ranges of furniture he created with the Finnish designer, Eero Saarinen, in the 1940s. During the war years Eames had experimented with moulding laminated wood while working on a commission from the US Navy to produce a series of leg splints. With Evans Products of Detroit, he went on to create a moulded plywood stretcher. In his book, *The American Design Adventure*, Arthur J.

Pulos has discussed the way in which plywood also moved into the area of temporary housing at that time of great need.[11] Eames developed his own experiments, at first with Evans Products and subsequently with Herman Miller, which reached a peak with the manufacture, in 1946, of his famous laminated wooden chair, which has been described as consisting of, 'shaped veneer laminates attached to a base of welded steel rods by means of rubber shock mounts'.[12] With Saarinen, Eames developed a highly innovative, modern furniture aesthetic that was widely emulated over the next decade in Scandinavia, Britain and Italy.[13] Through the use of the new moulding techniques the furniture could be mass-produced and it quickly moved into the public arena, filling school rooms, halls and lecture theatres.

Plastics also went through a transformation during the war and immediately afterwards. Polythene, PVC (polyvinyl chloride) and polystyrene, among countless other manifestations of that synthetic substance, were added to the already lengthy list of synthetics that had entered everyday life (Figure 7.2). Diverse cultural responses to the new possibilities were expressed. In Britain, for example, as Claire Catterall has explained, there was significant unease about the new materials, which was seen as being 'slick, streamlined and shiny'.[14] In Italy, there was more enthusiasm for the new synthetics and the late 1950s and early 1960s saw experiments on plastic chairs undertaken by the leading architect–designers of the day – Vico Magistretti, Marco Zanuso and Joe Colombo among them – with plastic chairs. They exploited the non-natural properties of materials, such as ABS (acrylonitrile butadiene styrene), and used a range of vibrant colours, including bright red, black and white (Figure 7.3). Several of the Italian designers linked with the Anti-Design movement of the late 1960s chose to employ a range of soft plastics, polyurethane foam among them, in their efforts to move beyond the hard, static forms of modernism.[15]

A number of design historical studies have focused on the effects of new materials and their cultural impact in the post-war years, emphasizing the role that they played in the construction of a popular image of modernity at that time. Judy Attfield's 1994 study of the emergence of the tufted carpet in Britain, for example, focused on the way in which an object can be seen as 'a material manifestation of cultural forces' – in that instance, of the reluctance of a conservative industry to embrace change and novelty.[16] Her work highlighted the slow take-up, by the carpet trade, of synthetic tufted carpets in Britain as opposed to the traditional ones made from woven wool.

A similar picture of British caution has been observed by Samantha Pile in her account of the response to latex foam in furniture design. Although, as she explained, it did not 'herald an immediate design revolution' in Great Britain, it was received more enthusiastically in Scandinavia and Italy, which were quick, after the War, to understand the way in which that new form of rubber could create a new aesthetic that depicted modern comfort. As Pile has pointed out, the ability of latex foam to reduce volume and

Figure 7.2 Plastics in the home, 1940s
(courtesy of the author)

weight was highly appealing to the Italian designers and manufacturers, who sought a new furniture aesthetic inspired by contemporary abstract sculpture, while it was also used by the Scandinavians, who favoured a softer version of domestic modernity.[17]

Figure 7.3 Vico Magistretti's 'Studio 80' table, 1967 and 'Selene' chairs, 1968,
Artemide, Italy
(© Vico Magistretti)

The complex ways in which materials, design, society and culture
negotiated each other in those years has been documented in Alison
Clarke's 1999 account of the development of the American polyethylene
food containers manufactured by the Tupperware Corporation. Clarke has
described the way in which the iconic meaning of that product could not be
understood by its design alone but, rather, by the way in which its advertising, marketing and distribution helped to construct a place for it within
a feminine model of domestic modernity.[18] In her words, Tupperware was
'an example of the historical specificity of material culture and the mediation of related social relations and cultural beliefs'.[19] As such, its material
novelty was only a part of the sociocultural context in which it was made
to play a meaningful role. Arguably, inasmuch as it denoted modernity and
efficiency, polyethylene's newness was an important component of
Tupperware's success but, as Clarke has pointed out, it was highly dependent on the manufacturer ensuring that, although the objects themselves
were transformed from rational products to emotional gifts, their material
meaning was consistent from production through to consumption. The
aesthetic of the Tupperware container was neutral enough for it to be able
to act as an empty vessel, capable of containing all the dreams and aspirations of 1950s American society, especially those of its female suburban
consumers. The same could be said of nylon stockings, which were almost

invisible. They carried within them, nevertheless, a high level of utopianism. Susannah Handley's *Nylon: the Man-made Fashion Revolution* of 1999, has focused on DuPont's successful foray into the manufacture of nylon in the post-war years (Figure 7.4). Stockings made from that new material brought with them a vision of modernity – defined less, by that date, by rational production than by glamour – to a mass audience of female consumers that had been deprived of self-expression during the Second World War.[20]

Figure 7.4 Bride in nylon dress in Dupont magazine, 1946
(© Hagley Museum and Library)

New materials had potent meanings in the early post-war years and the capacity to convey the optimism of that era. At the mass market level they were most successful when, through intensive marketing, marketing and inventive distribution systems, they could be made to represent consumer desire and aspiration. Thus, nylons and Tupperware food containers were embraced by female consumers as messengers of a modernity that was communicated through images of glamorous and efficient housewife-hostesses. Their new forms, defined by mass production techniques and bright colours, quickly became part of everyday environments. As they entered into everyday life, however, they became vulnerable to the gaze of the design reformers and were added to the marginalized world of material culture described as 'kitsch'.

Where the concept of good design was concerned new materials had to wait until they had a new, modern aesthetic provided for them by designers. In addition to the Italian chairs described above, the Kartell company (also Italian) worked with the designer Gino Colombini to create series of striking-looking plastic buckets and lemon squeezers which, by virtue of the way that they were presented as isolated objects on plinths in stylish magazines such as *Stile Industria*, came to be seen more as art objects than as mundane items of household equipment. That elevation of banal goods to a new level of significance was a mark of the added value bestowed upon them by modern design. Through aesthetic manipulation, the cheapest of goods could be transformed into new modern luxuries.[21]

In Scandinavia, stainless steel took over from silver. The Danish architect–designer, Arne Jacobsen, used that highly practical modern material for his stylish 'Cylinda Line' items, which were manufactured by Stelton. Other materials, such as glass, which had long-standing craft roots, were also transformed by technology in those years. Oven-to-tableware glass, created in the USA under the brand name of 'Pyrex', manufactured by Corning and first sold in 1921, for example, became widespread internationally in the 1950s. Like Tupperware and nylon stockings, Pyrex eventually found a mass market through its appeal to women, but only after a long period of time during which the manufacturer had sought numerous ways of making it desirable. Designers were brought in at several different stages in attempts to make it more appealing to housewives. However, according to the historian, Regina Lee Blaszczyk, it owed its success, in the end, to a female home economist, Lucy M. Maltby, who set up an experimental kitchen and managed to persuade housewives of Pyrex's superior qualities in the kitchen. As a result of her experiments, she redesigned several of the Pyrex products, although she was aiming for improved performance, rather than aesthetic appeal.[22] In her study of the batch-produced ceramic- and glassware created in the USA in the mid-twentieth century, which was sold to female consumers, Blaszczyk argued that, at that level of the market, products proved successful less as a result of the intervention of male industrial designers than by the input of a number of significant women who, 'empowered as consumers and linked to producers by fashion intermediaries...shaped the design of household accessories'.[23]

By 1970, many more new materials and manufacturing techniques had transformed the face of the everyday world. They spoke a language of modern utopianism to an audience that still trusted the power of technology to provide it with a better world, to improve the quality of everyday life and to empower them as consumers. Inevitably, the cultural response to change varied according to the level of investment that different people had in the past. Those with the least invested in it had less to lose. Design played an important role in ensuring that technology communicated appropriate messages. At different levels of the market, as we have seen, design interfaced differently with technology. Where the mass market was concerned, it existed alongside all the other activities that were part of the context of production. As democratization developed, however, designers, wearing high-cultural hats, sought to put in place a neo-modern form of added value, formulating a so-called authentic aesthetic for goods made from new materials that removed them from the category of kitsch. By 1970, however, that second wave of modernism, which sought to reinstate a level of taste into the materials of mass production, was also coming under scrutiny and its alliance with certain new materials – hard plastics and metals in particular – was being questioned.

Technology and lifestyles

The strong emphasis, through the 1970s, 1980s and 1990s, on the culture of consumption tended to eclipse the important relationship that design continued to have, nonetheless, with production and technological innovation. The concentration on lifestyle and on consumers' relationships with designed goods, brands, leisure environments and other experiences meant that their meaning was more market than technology focused. Nevertheless, by the end of the twentieth century, advanced technology had come to play a crucial part, once again, in the ways in which goods, images and spaces were made, as well as making an enormous contribution to their social and cultural meanings and to people's life experiences. Indeed, the myriad new electronic goods that emerged at the turn of the century owed their very being to technological innovations and, in the areas of information provision, communication and, increasingly, entertainment, generated a new faith in the power of technology to take society forward.

The 1970s witnessed the arrival of large numbers of high-technology Japanese consumer goods into Western markets. The manufacture of the sophisticated and highly complex electronic products – hi-fi equipment and cameras among them – manufactured by companies such as Sony, Sharp, Canon, Toshiba and Hitachi, were created by automated production systems. Not surprisingly, their appearance reflected that high-tech environment and, in spite of the fact that the new ranges of hi-fi equipment, for example, were destined for the living room, their complex control panels and multiple knobs and switches, redolent of the interiors of space shuttles, suggested high performance levels and technological virtuosity rather than comfortable domesticity.

The degree of technological utopianism represented by those overtly masculine artefacts, coloured black and silver, was expressed not only through their appearance, but also by their multiple and novel functionalities. No longer was a watch simply a timepiece, it was also a stopwatch and an alarm clock. That important move away from the idea of a single object performing a single function and, therefore, as modernism had decreed, of its form being determined by that function, accelerated dramatically in the last decades of the twentieth century and the first decade of the twenty-first century. By the end of that period, Apple's iPad – visually and materially speaking a simple, flat, neo-modern, rectangular plastic tablet with a fabric cover – had emerged, combining the functions of, among countless other things, a television, a radio, a telephone, a typewriter, a hi-fi system, a photo album and an address book. Through its link to the worldwide web, the entertainment, information and communication possibilities of that seemingly banal artefact were unprecedented. Most importantly, it was what it did rather than what it looked like that determined its popularity and which led to a redefinition of the designer who conceived its functionality.

Back in the 1970s, however, that shift was still to happen. The fact that the objects emanating from Japan expressed a faith in the power of technology was due to interventions by industrial designers in creating a look for them. Their high-tech aesthetic rapidly moved beyond the workplace to transform leisure environments and the private sphere as well. The modish, high-tech, neo-modern aesthetic of the '70s and '80s, immortalized in a book penned by the New York-based design writers, Joan Kron and Susanne Slesin, also characterized many architectural constructions of the era, from Renzo Piano's and Richard Roger's Beaubourg Centre to Norman Foster's Hong Kong and Shanghai Bank.[24] It became a self-conscious language characterized by the visibility of the structural components and services of buildings. The London-based furniture designer, Ron Arad, adopted the same language in a number of his furniture designs, among them a shelving system made out of scaffolding clamps. The transference of a language deriving from the workplace and the public sphere into the domestic arena brought technology into many peoples' daily lives and suggested a renewed commitment to the modernist idealism of the mid-twentieth century, albeit only on a stylistic level. The widespread faith in technology's ability to carry society through the politically and economically bleak years of the 1970s and on into the boom period of the 1980s, represented, at one level at least, an extension of the early modernists' belief that rationalism could provide an antidote to cultural complexity. By the 1980s, however, it was evident that high-tech, or what was also dubbed 'late modernism', was not an alternative to conspicuous consumption but rather yet another manifestation of it.

Japan's deep commitment to technology was expressed through a visual language of complexity, suggesting that technical knowledge had moved far beyond the capacity of society to keep up with it. It also created new behavioural patterns. Nowhere was that more apparent than in the effects of Sony's little 'Walkman' – a portable cassette-tape player launched on the market in 1982.[25] In use, its small components – a tape holder and linked earphones – became technological extensions of the body and the object's miniature size and portability allowed the user a freedom of movement that had not been either feasible or imaginable hitherto.

The combination of advanced technology and advanced consumer culture provided a challenge to designers, whose role was to package products such that the technology/culture interface was appropriately expressed. From the 1980s onwards, that challenge was presented many times over by a number of new gadgets that transformed conventional behaviour patterns in both the private and the public arenas. From the Walkman to the mobile phone (Figure 7.5) to the laptop computer to the digital camera to the portable compact disc player, the worlds of work and leisure were transformed by people's increasing ability to perform what had been room-bound activities in the street and other public spaces. The activities of music listening, of walking down an urban street and of sitting on a subway

Figure 7.5 Nokia mobile phone, Finland, early 2000s
(courtesy of Nokia UK)

train, were, as a result, transformed beyond recognition. The idea that there were spaces dedicated to specific activities – the domestic hallway for the telephone, the study or office for the typewriter, the living room or bedroom for the hi-hi system – also became increasingly redundant. By the early twenty-first century, numerous new behaviours had emerged as a result of the infiltration of the new technologies into everyday private and public life. Social networking, for example, meant that individuals could instantly send messages to large groups of people and immediately interact with them; people formed new relationships on screen; they could access instant information about anything, anywhere, at any time and read any books they wanted to wherever and whenever they wanted to. The result was a new form of public life, in which people engaging in travel and leisure activities focused more on the technological communication than what was happening through their mobile phones, Blackberries and iPads than on the immediate physical world around them. That behavioural change took to new levels the idea of the 'lonely crowd' that David Riesman had described half a century earlier.[26]

In *Technopoly: The Surrender of Culture to Technology*, published in 1993, Neil Postman expressed his anxiety about the supremacy of technology. Referring back to C. P. Snow's famous 1959 lecture, 'The Two Cultures and the Scientific Revolution', he claimed that, rather than existing in two different spheres, the two cultures that Snow had referred to – those, that is, of the humanities and the sciences – were fighting for supremacy. 'Once a technology is admitted', explained Postman, 'it plays out its hand: it does what it is designed to do. Our task is to understand what that design is – that is to say, when we admit a new technology to the culture, we must do so with our eyes wide open'.[27]

After 1970, Postman's warning grew in significance as the relationship between technology and culture became increasingly complex. It sounded a note of caution to a culture that, in its continuous search for novelty, needed to understand the consequences of that search. The challenge to the designer was to act as a bridge between technology and culture such that society could keep up with the rapid changes taking place in the former area. That took a number of forms. On the simplest level, it was manifested in the work undertaken by industrial designers to make machines, such as computers, look desirable and blend into the environments in which they were used.

Apple Computer Inc., based in California's Silicon Valley, went the furthest in realizing that aim, hiring first the German design consultancy, frogdesign, and later the British designer, Jonathan Ive, to make their machines user-friendly. On another level, being user-friendly applied not only to three-dimensional material artefacts – the hardware – but also to the immaterial programmes that operated in virtual space – the software – that provided the interfaces between the computer and its users. The huge advances in digital and internet engineering that took place from the 1980s onwards completely revolutionized users' relationships with artefacts. Just as back in the early years of the twentieth century, the designed body shell of a vacuum cleaner had disguised its inner workings, so, by the twenty-first century, a small, rectangular plastic pad with a fabric cover had the capacity to house myriad electronic software programmes offering its users multiple functions.

The designer's role in that context was transformed beyond all recognition. The visualizing and materializing skills of the past were replaced by the requirement to create virtual spatial or architectural systems and efficient, effective and pleasurable usability. From that need flowed the development of systems and interface designing, the former the preserve, for the most part, of engineers and the latter of human interface designers trained in anthropometrics and ergonomics. Most importantly, in addition to those technical skills the new designers needed to understand people's emotional relationship with complex machines.

As an activity, systems design grew rapidly in the early twenty-first century. Its influence was felt both by consumers, for whom products such as computer games became increasingly important, and by large corporations that depended, for the efficiency and effectiveness of their operations, upon their digital information and communication systems. Systems architecture, as it was often called, took its model from the world of three-dimensional spatial design, transferring it, metaphorically, into the world of virtual space. That process of dematerialization lay at the core of the significance of the digital revolution for design. It had already begun with the growing emphasis upon media design that had shifted the focus away from artefacts to screen-based activities but, with digital systems increasingly taking over from all other forms of information sharing and communicating, virtual reality became a force to be reckoned with by many people on a daily basis, both at work and at play.

In the early days of its development, systems design was mostly undertaken by engineers who tended, as had the early mass manufacturers, to focus on production rather than use. Quite quickly, however, it became clear that users – whether the players of computer games or employees engaged with computers in the workplace – needed to feel comfortable in their operations and even to discover a level of pleasure in those activities. Interaction design took the efficiency of systems design into the context of users and focused on the structure and behaviour of systems to create meaningful relationships with the people who used them. Inevitably, that activity drew on skills other than those of the engineer and, increasingly, psychologists, sociologists, human factors and ergonomics specialists, architects, product designers, set designers and fine artists, among many others, were drawn into its midst. Designers also worked with mobile devices, appliances and non-electronic products, as well as with services and events. The discipline acknowledged the complex relationship between the virtual and the physical worlds and prioritized the capacity of its practitioners to be able to create narratives and scenarios. That last requirement emphasized the skills of illustrators, animators and film makers who had the capacity to create story boards. Visualization remained important in that context, providing a means of seeing the unseeable. The continuing importance of the visual was joined by that of the virtual and the conceptual, while materiality and real space became increasingly marginalized.

As the twenty-first century progressed, more and more importance was given to the sensorial, the experiential and the emotional aspects of user interaction, both within the virtual world and on those of material artefacts and environments. The idea of designing with empathy was widely discussed, with a view to developing a deeper understanding of users' needs. One of the problems associated with the strong emphasis on consumer research that went with that approach, however, was that it tended to focus on the here and now rather than on the future. A balance was sought, therefore, between an empathetic, intuitive approach towards the needs of users (extensive research was undertaken to understand the nature of those needs) and one that depended upon designers' capacity to imagine the requirements of the future. A range of terms – 'participatory', 'experiential', 'interactive', 'open' and 'collaborative' among them – emerged to describe the new approach.[29]

Back in 1984, frogdesign's 'Snow White' computer for Apple had represented an early attempt to create a neat, visually pleasing little machine with a user-friendly appearance (Figure 7.6). Given the severe constraints of the brief to create a box to house a computer terminal's inner workings, attention was paid to the ways in which a designer could make a contribution to the radii of curves and the lines and colour of the body shell. Apple also paid attention to the user-friendly needs of the computer systems themselves, conscious that the feel of both the object and its performance were of equal importance in helping consumers to reach a purchasing decision. Later, in the 1990s, Apple pursued that line even further through its collaboration with Ive, which resulted in a series of designs for electronic objects that transformed them into lifestyle objects.[30] By the early twentieth century, the iPhone (2001), the iPod (2007) – a portable media player (Figure 7.7) – and the iPad (2010) – a tablet computer combining the function of a smartphone and a laptop computer – had joined the stable of Apple Inc. goods designed by Ive. By that time, the balance between the user-friendliness of the machines themselves and the functionalities they facilitated was such that the emphasis was firmly on the latter. While the physicality of Apple's sophisticated touch screens and the visual languages used to activate the machines' applications, were designed to minimize users' discomfort, it was the technological virtuosity of the machines' functionalities and the increasingly novel combinations of them that most impressed consumers. The iPad2, launched in 2011, came in a variety of colours, re-emphasizing the fact that the products were still lifestyle choices as well as providers of new forms of communication and entertainment. Increasingly, however, their

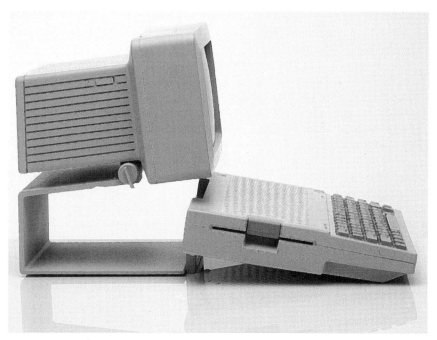

Figure 7.6 Apple Computer Inc.'s 'Snow White' IIc computer, 1984
(© frogdesign inc.)

Figure 7.7 Apple's iPod touch, designed by Jonathan Ive, 2005

traditional product design content was far outweighed by their sophisticated systems and interface design and it was the latter that ultimately determined their desirability.

The computer both made redundant and transformed many of the roles that had hitherto been performed by the graphic designer. On one level, the advent of software packages, such as Adobe Photoshop, made it possible for large numbers of people to undertake work that had previously been the preserve of the trained graphic designer. On another level, the rapid expansion of the internet opened up a new area of design expertise – web design – that was to become a widespread activity, especially in developing countries such as China and India. In addition, the arrival of CAD (computer-aided design) systems transformed the ways in which many designers – architects and product designers in particular – went about their daily work. In the early days, the look of many products and buildings owed much to the constraints of that process and numerous curved products and buildings emerged as a result. Gradually, however, CAD programmes became more sophisticated and less aesthetically constraining.

In addition to transforming the design process itself, the digital revolution of the late twentieth and early twenty-first centuries also transformed manufacturing. In particular, it enabled a greater diversity of goods to enter the global marketplace. The shift away from Fordist mass production to what David Hounshell has called 'flexible mass production' in the 1920s had reinforced the importance of design in ensuring product diversity and the niche marketing that flowed from it.[31] As a result of sociocultural change, the democratization of consumption and the move of manufacturers to large-scale batch production, the concept of the global niche market became increasingly visible later in the century. To appeal to their intended consumers, designers ensured that goods had distinctive identities and manufacturers increasingly modified their production systems to be able to produce enough goods with a sufficient level of diversity. Nowhere was that strategy more apparent, in the last years of the twentieth century, than in the example of the Swatch Company's watches. They were produced in large numbers, at low prices, but with a huge stylistic variety that was constantly being updated. The Swiss company exploited technological innovation and virtuosity – Swatch were slimmer than watches have ever been – but they also brought about a sociocultural transformation in which the watch ceased to be an expensive object bought to last but was transformed, instead, into a cheap fashion accessory to be discarded when its style became outdated.

From the 1980s onwards, Japan, followed quickly afterwards by Taiwan, Singapore, Indonesia, China and India, recognized the varied needs of world markets and set out to cater for local and national taste cultures. Where television sets were concerned, for example, discovering that Germany favoured black cabinets while Italy preferred white boxes and Britain wood-effect plastic casings, the Japanese electronics manufacturer,

Sharp, designed and marketed appropriate products for each country. Many Japanese manufacturers automated their production lines and used numerically controlled machines to make the necessary variants which it described as 'many versions in small lots'.[32]

At the luxury end of the market, variation was achieved by the system of small-scale flexible manufacturing that could be found in Italy, where traditional craft workshops brought in advanced electronic equipment to help them produce batches of high-quality goods. Describing the nature of what was referred to as 'the third Italy', the economic historian, Charles F. Sabel, has pinpointed the presence of what he called a 'high technology cottage industry' in that country explaining that, 'Most of the shops and factories...employ from 5 to 50 workers...the tools [are] the most advanced numerically controlled equipment of its type; the products, designed in the shop, sophisticated and distinctive enough to capture monopolies in world markets'.[33] In the second half of the twentieth century, both Japan and Italy contributed, in different ways, to developments in manufacturing techniques that reinforced the role of design in meeting the needs of niche markets through the creation of distinctive and diverse products.

Where the shifting relationship between design and manufacturing in those years was concerned, the most significant advance was in the area of rapid prototyping. First developed in the 1980s, the new production technology facilitated the automatic transformation of CAD-generated drawings into physical models and then into production-quality goods, manufactured singly or in small, medium or large quantities as required.[34] It represented a radical advance, as it brought about a new, direct and automated relationship between design and flexible manufacturing that helped to collapse the long-standing distinction between craft and design that had been in place since the advent of industrialization. As an example of the way in the technique could be used, in 2010, two Swedish student designers, Naim Josefi and Souzan Youssouf, showed how rapid prototyping could transform shoe design, manufacture and consumption. It was used to 'print' a shoe, made from recyclable nylon, and software was developed that enabled customers to visit a shop, have their feet scanned and have a personalized pair of shoes produced just for them.[35] Experiments such as this became increasingly widespread in those years, transforming the traditional relationship between design, production and consumption. It recalled the custom-made practices of élite consumption in the eighteenth century, while also allowing for large-scale manufacturing as required. It facilitated the proliferation of global taste cultures and linked the individual consumer more closely to the design and manufacturing processes.

The sense that craft and design sat at two ends of a spectrum, rather than, as hitherto, existing in opposition to each other, was manifested in many different ways in the last years of the twentieth and the first years of the twenty-first century. Many progressive designers showed a new interest in what had been understood up until that point as craft materials. Hella

Jongerius, for example, a member of the Dutch design group, Droog – which, in the 1990s, took on the mantle of radical design that had been pioneered by Italian designers in earlier decades – worked extensively with ceramic, creating objects that were both one-off examples and serially manufactured.[36] Her interest in making and in the value of materiality served as a counterpoint to the dematerialization that was occurring in the digital world.

While technological advances affected the way in which designers worked with manufacturers, they also influenced the way in which design was perceived by society at large. In her publication, *Feminism Confronts Technology*, the sociologist, Judy Wajcsman, has argued that 'the traditional conception of technology is heavily weighted against women...the very definition of technology has a male bias.'[37] One of the effects of the enhanced relationship between technology and design was the increased masculinization of both the material and the immaterial cultures that accompanied high technology.

That same gendered picture defined an area of product design that had always had a strong engineering orientation, namely automobile styling. Although women were frequently pinpointed as the consumers of cars, through the twentieth century, the design and meaning of automobiles was overridingly masculine. In the words of Virginia Scharff, 'American popular culture has treated the automobile as a phallic prosthesis, penetrating time and space with a speed and force surpassed only by the prophylactic image of the he-man test pilots pushing the inside of the Envelope'.[38]

The traditional exclusion of feminine values from that arena has only recently begun to be addressed as female designers, such as Anne Asensio, working for Renault and, subsequently, with General Motors, have begun to adopt a different design approach to automobiles that is based less on the objects' exterior form than on the comfort and functionality of their interior spaces (Figure 7.8). It was Asensio, for example, who introduced drinks holders for the back-seat passengers of the Renault Scenic. A little later, the Swedish firm, Volvo, undertook an experiment that involved getting a group of women to create a concept car – the YCC. The principle underpinning that project was not to create a feminine car but rather one that, by asking women to think about their needs, addressed the needs of both men and women. Space for shopping was given consideration, as was assistance with parking. Gullwing doors were added for easy access.[39]

The gendering of goods with high-technology content as masculine derives, not surprisingly, from the culture of the workplace. In *Boys and Their Toys*, a number of authors examined the labour situation in different parts of the automotive industry and discovered the existence of an overriding masculine culture.[40] While technological innovation led to the manufacture of a host of new goods that infiltrated everyday life in the years after 1970, it also resulted in advances in the development of new materials. In turn, they affected the cultural milieu in which goods were

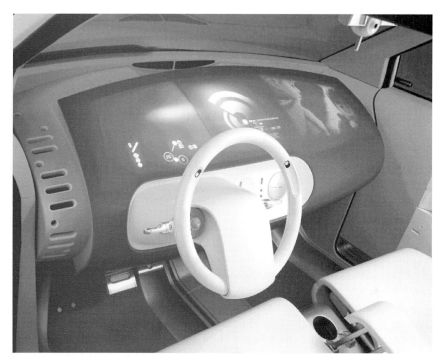

Figure 7.8 Ford's 24.7 Concept 22 car, 2000
(courtesy of the National Motor Museum)

consumed and used. The advances in materials technology that took place in these years were less, as they had been early in the twentieth century, the result of new discoveries but rather of the development of new combinations of known materials. So complex were the possibilities of combination, especially in the area of plastics, that, by the end of the twentieth century, an enormous gap had developed between the knowledge and understanding of, on the one hand, materials scientists and, on the other, of the consumers of products made of the new materials. There was little possibility, for example, of users knowing the names of the multiple synthetic materials that made up their running shoes or the ballpoint pens they used on a daily basis. Their understanding of the fabrics used to create their clothing was likely to be just as minimal. By the 1990s, the idea of smart materials – that is, shape-memory alloys which respond to temperature – was also being widely discussed in the context of monitoring health and working with the disabled.

In his influential book of 1986, *The Material of Invention*, Ezio Manzini outlined the way in which the innate flexibility of plastics had led to their becoming highly complex and unknowable. 'The word plastic' he explained, 'covers such a range of options that it tends to lose it meaning'.[41]

He demonstrated his point through a caption to an image of a shoe which, he pointed out, combined 'modified polybutylene terephthalate (PBT) with a strip of ethylene-propylene rubber'.[42] The cultural implications of that new level of complexity in the world of materials, much of it being led by research in the arenas of aerospace and the military, included a new relationship between object and user. The latter had to develop an understanding of the former that excluded knowledge of its fabrication process. Inevitably, this brought about a rupture between production and consumption. While the rift between man and making that William Morris had so regretted back in the nineteenth century was not new, it reached a greater level of intensity in the late twentieth and early twenty-first centuries. It presented designers with the challenge of providing objects with meanings that derived neither from the production process nor from the materials of which they were constituted but which related, rather, to the significance of the object in the context of consumption.

The new materials of the early twentieth century – concrete, steel and glass among them – had still been comprehensible to their audience of consumers, a fact that had provided designers with a starting point in their search for a meaningful aesthetic and a philosophy of design. However, by the end of the century, the loss of that comprehension, the use of automated production systems and the emergence of ever more complex materials and products combined in such a way that the golden rule of modernism – form follows function – had finally become completely redundant. As a result, designers had to look to the cultural, rather than the technological, context in which they found themselves.

By the end of the twentieth century, the modern materials from the early century had become part of history, capable of engendering a level of nostalgia for a period when consumers had had a reasonably close relationship with the materials of everyday life. Aluminium, for example, enjoyed a new popularity among designers in the 1990s, its shiny surfaces representing a simple modernity that had been lost. A number of innovative designers turned to that light metal for cultural solutions to the problem of identity loss (Figure 7.9).

While one aspect of materials research focused on the functionalities of new innovations – the need for lightness in sports equipment, for strength and resilience in materials for the automotive industry and for recyclability as part of the sustainability agenda – designers also set out to exploit their aesthetic and symbolic potential. An exhibition held at New York's Museum of Modern Art in the late 1990s, entitled *Mutant Materials*, set out to show the results of designers' interactions with the range of new possibilities. It emphasized the importance of providing an interface between users and the world of materials. Writing about the way in which designers were needed to perform that task and to make culture out of technology, Paolo Antonelli claimed that 'The best contemporary objects are those whose presence expresses history and contemporaneity; those that exude

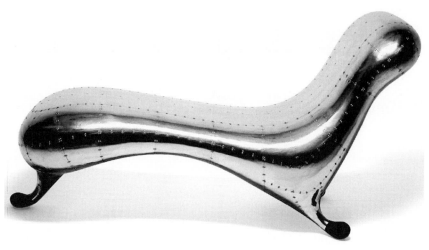

Figure 7.9 Marc Newson's 'Lockheed Lounge' chair, 1986
(courtesy of Marc Newson Ltd)

humors of the material culture that generated them, while at the same time speaking a global language; those that carry a memory and an intelligence of the future; those that are like great movies in that they speak a sense of belonging – in the world, in these times of cultural and technical possibilities – while they also manage to transport us to places we have never visited'.[43]

As the early twenty-first century progresses, the pace of technological innovation and change continues unabated and both culture and design are running to keep pace with it. It involves a constant process of imagining and translating such that the untamed and unarticulated developments of scientists and technologists are transformed into meaningful messages for everyday life.

8   Designer culture

International designers

As economic, social and technological forces combined to ensure that more and more people were able to define themselves through the consumption of designed images, objects and environments, so the need to provide levels of differentiation became increasingly imperative. Design was one of the ways in which that differentiation could be insured and, in the years after 1945, it increasingly operated in two modern worlds – those of modern mass culture and of a new élite, high culture, defined by its links with good taste. While the mass market could afford to consume the former, it increasingly desired the latter.

While all goods, services, images and spaces are designed, only some were understood by consumers as the direct result of a designer's hand. Through the 1950s, the existence of designers and the added value that resulted from their interventions were promoted through advertisements, magazines, exhibitions, television programmes and the work of a growing number of institutions briefed to encourage good design. A comparison of two texts, both written by Lesley Jackson, which focused on design in the 1950s and 1960s, respectively, with another study from the same period, Thomas Hine's *Populuxe: The Look and Life of America in the '50s and '60s, From Tailfins and TV Dinners to Barbie Dolls and Fallout Shelters*, serves to reinforce the difference between designed goods and environments and others that were seen to be part of popular culture.[1] Jackson's books focused on what in an earlier period would have been called decorative arts – ceramics, fashion, furniture, glass, lighting, metalwork, textiles and wallpaper – and the signature designers responsible for creating them. She stressed the influence of fine art on designed artefacts, highlighting Henry Moore's sculpture as a source of visual inspiration. Most of the designers selected for discussion by Jackson – from Arne Jacobsen to Tapio Wirkkala to Robin Day – were European male architects and craftsmen who had embraced product design. In sharp contrast, Hine's text focused on anonymous American goods that accompanied everyday life in the USA in the post-war years. Fewer designers' names were mentioned in his text and he emphasized popular interiors, automobiles, domestic machines and public spaces over decorative art objects. While as modern as the one inhabited by Jackson, Hine's world did not need references to fine art to validate it. Its meanings were confirmed, rather, by consumption and use.

The need for design to have a high-cultural face in those years stemmed from the desire on the part of the new middle classes to distinguish themselves from the consumers of mass culture. The purchasers of Hine's artefacts were more concerned to align themselves with particular lifestyle than to be defined by their good taste. Inevitably, however, in line with the dynamic created by aspiration and emulation, the desire for designer goods spread and the taste-conscious classes had to find new ways of distinguishing themselves from those just beneath them on the social ladder.

Designer culture spread across the globe in the 1950s. While the inter-war American pioneer consultant designers – Raymond Loewy, Walter Dorwin Teague and Henry Dreyfuss among them – had become highly visible in the media, the phenomenon was less widespread in Europe, where product design was still mostly undertaken by architects, engineers and craftsmen. When designer culture did eventually establish itself across the Atlantic, it tended to locate itself at the more traditional, decorative arts, end of the spectrum. Gradually, however, a new generation of European designers began to transform the look of the home, office and street and became increasingly visible as the decade progressed. Their faces and names were featured in both the specialist press and in popular household and women's magazines. Generally speaking the 1950s were years of great idealism and optimism for design and designers were seen as quasi-magicians with the power to improve the quality of everyday life.

The specialist Italian design magazines, *Domus* and *Stile Industria* in particular, promoted the work of a new generation of architect–designers; in Sweden, *Form* magazine performed a similar role for that country's design community; while in Great Britain, *Design* magazine, the mouthpiece of the newly formed Council of Industrial Design, promoted a new generation of designers. The weekly British magazine, *Woman*, dedicated an article to the home of the married couple – Robin and Lucienne Day (Figure 8.1). The same designers were also the subject of an article published in the Daily Mail's *Ideal Home Yearbook* of 1952–53, written by the Days themselves, in which they explained how they had created a modern domestic paradise for themselves.[2] An illustration used in the article depicted the room in which the couple worked. Drawings were carefully positioned on a table and Day's own furniture designs filled the space. The image recalled the reconstruction of Raymond Loewy's office that had been exhibited at the Metropolitan Museum of Modern Art in New York back in 1932. In turn, that installation recalled the way in which fine artists were frequently depicted in their studios. The *Ideal Home Yearbook* was careful to promote designers as authoritative, high-cultural individuals. Ernest Race's international credibility, for example, was confirmed by a reference to the fact that,

Punch, December 7 1955

When not actively engaged in designing highly individualistic furniture and textiles, ROBIN and LUCIENNE DAY are apt to be entertaining visitors from Europe or America. For this purpose they both agree that SMIRNOFF VODKA, either on its own, well iced, or as a base for long or short drinks, is an offering which is invariably accepted with alacrity.

In two strengths 65.5° and 80° proof. 34/- and 40/- a bottle.

Figure 8.1 British designers, Robin and Lucienne Day, in a Smirnoff Vodka
    advertisement, UK, 1950s
    (© Smirnoff)

'His work has been exhibited in many countries and he was awarded an honourable mention in the International Competition for Low Cost Furniture by the Museum of Modern Art, New York'.[3]

The enhanced level of popular interest in design and designers was partly a result of manufacturers' public relations exercises that promoted their stables of designers. In Italy and Scandinavia, in particular, small-scale manufacturers named their collaborating designers and marketed their products as if they were art objects. The design writer, Ulf Hard af Segerstad, explained in his 1961 account of Scandinavian design that, 'we must always keep in mind that it is first and foremost the individual designer who created and continues to create the good Scandinavian applied arts'.[4] The text of his book highlighted the work of numerous designers, including the Danish ceramists, Lisa Larsen for Gustavsberg and

Axel Salto for the Royal Copenhagen Porcelain Factory, the Finnish glass designer, Goran Hingell for Karhula-Iittala, the Swedish glass designer Eric Hoglund for Boda and the Danish furniture designer, Hans Wegner, for Johannes Hansen. A list at the back of the book attributed designers' names to manufacturers, revealing the fact that some firms employed a number of individuals while others, such as the Danish furniture manufacturer, E. Kold Christensen, worked exclusively with a single designer, in its case, Poul Kjaerholm.

The picture was similar in Italy, where many furniture and product manufacturers promoted their designs through the names of designers. In the 1950s, the furniture manufacturer, Cassina, abandoned its production of mass-produced, standardized furniture for the Italian navy and moved into the arena of designer furniture, firstly through collaboration with Franco Albini and subsequently with Gio Ponti and Vico Magistretti. There was a realization that the way forward for many, modestly sized Italian furniture firms was the batch-production of high-quality, designer-led, modern furnishings for an international, taste-conscious, élite market. The link with the designer worked in two ways. It insured innovative, modern work but it also allowed the product in question to be sold in the name of art (Figure 8.2). This was reinforced by developments in the infrastructure of design, which included the continuation of the *Triennale* exhibitions in Milan (the 1954 exhibition was subtitled 'The Production of Art'); the

Figure 8.2 Marcello Nizzoli's Lexicon 80 typewriter for Olivetti, Italy, 1948
(courtesy of Associazione Archivio Storico Olivetti, Ivrea, Italy)

instigation by the Rinascente department store of an annual design prize –
the *Compasso d'Oro* (Golden Compass) and the formation, in 1956, of the
ADI (the Association of Industrial Designers).[5] The 1950s saw many important manufacturer–consultant designer partnerships – among them those of
Achille Castiglioni with Flos and Brionvega and of Marco Zanuso with
Arflex and Kartell. The same model was adhered to by the large-scale
manufacturer, Olivetti. Working extensively with Ettore Sottsass on a
consultancy basis, the company understood the benefits of working with an
external designer in addition to its in-house team. While the former
provided a high level of innovation and cultural capital, the latter ensured
that the designs could be effectively realized.

A number of American manufacturing companies with a traditional,
decorative arts orientation also developed design strategies in those years.
The Grand Rapids-based Herman Miller furniture firm, which had
employed Gilbert Rhode and subsequently George Nelson to give advice
about design, had been working in that way since the 1930s. Through
Nelson, a link was established between Herman Miller and the architect,
Charles Eames. Together, they went on to create one of the most well-
known of all post-war manufacturer–consultant designer relationships. By
the 1950s, Eames had become a leading international figure. Like Robin
and Lucienne Day a little later in Britain, Charles and his wife Ray Eames
represented a modern couple who created for themselves a highly desirable
modern lifestyle. They even made a film about their house in Santa Monica,
which was filled with their own designs and objects they had collected on
their travels. The idea of the beautiful couple living in a modern idyll,
created by themselves for themselves, provided a role model for others. By
implication it was an idyll that was accessible to other people through the
purchase of an Eames-designed, Herman Miller chair.

Pat Kirkham described the way in which Eames was very aware of the
power that this reputation afforded him and suggested that he was reluctant
to share it with his wife.[6] Her biographical account of the couple set out to
redress that imbalance and to show that Ray Eames made a significant
contribution to the couple's achievements. She pointed out that the Eameses
were very conscious of their sociocultural role and the significance of the
way in which they lived their lives to the extent that they paid enormous
attention to their appearance, retaining a level of artistic bohemianism in
their dress, for instance, rather than wearing more conventional clothes.
'They bought or had specially made high-quality clothing', Kirkham
explained, 'chosen...for reasons of utility as well as beauty and never
ostentation. In clothes, as in other areas of design, the Eameses were stick-
lers for detail and quality'.[7] Like Le Corbusier – who was always
photographed wearing his signature circular glasses – before them, the
Eameses understood that the culture of design was greater than the creation
of a new chair. It was, rather, part of a much bigger sociocultural process of
adding value, both culturally and commercially, through an injection of

creative individualism that distinguished designer-goods from the world of ordinary mass-produced artefacts.

Eames first exhibited his chairs in New York's Museum of Modern Art (MoMA) in 1940 and again in 1946. In the post-war years, under the curatorship of Edgar Kaufmann Jr, the museum took on a role as an important arbiter of taste and its seal of approval became internationally recognized. The British Furniture company, Hille, first encountered the work of its long-term collaborator, Robin Day, at the prestigious New York museum and many other manufacturers looked to it for guidance. MoMA set out its stall as an authoritative arbiter on the subject of good design which it equated with the concept of modern design. Kaufmann's rhetorical description of the concept of good design stressed the qualities of 'integrity, clarity and harmony'.[8] Significantly, the examples he cited were all chairs, created by early modernists – Marcel Breuer and Le Corbusier among them – as well as by a number of later adherents of the same school of design, including the Scandinavian designers, Finn Juhl and Bruno Mathsson and the Americans, Charles Eames and George Nelson. Just as Pevsner had created a stable of pioneer modernists back in the mid 1930s, so Kaufmann's work at MoMA established an élite group of second-generation innovative designers who became known internationally. The agenda of MoMA was clear. Modernism was alive and well in post-war Scandinavia and the USA, epitomized by the work of a group of designers. Above all, in the resounding words of Kaufmann, 'Streamlining is not good design'.[9] The USA clearly sought to define its post-war design strategy by emulating Europe, rather than by acknowledging its indigenous, modern industrial design movement of the inter-war years, which it considered vulgar by comparison. The spectre of the superiority of European taste still lingered on.

As designer culture became increasingly reinforced in both Europe and the USA in the post-war years, so the professional framework for design practice and the educational system that supported it became strengthened. The professional status of different designers remained uneven, however, depending on their backgrounds, the disciplines within which they worked and the national design strategies that supported them. In Italy, for example, most designers working in the 1950s and 1960s had been trained as architects in the rationalist (modernist) tradition of the 1930s. As a result of the lack of architectural projects and the enthusiasm of the transformed furniture and product manufacturers to work with them in the post-war years, they redefined themselves as designers but, like the American consultants before them, they retained the ability to work across a wide range of goods, from chairs to vacuum cleaners to ashtrays. While the flexibility of the Americans was rooted in their broad backgrounds in commercial design, the breadth of the Italian designers derived from their training as modernist architects committed to the idea of the *Gesamtkunstwerk*.

Scandinavian designers had craft skills that were applied to an industrial context. As a consequence, many of them maintained a level of specialization, working with a limited number of materials: clay, glass or metal for the most part (Figure 8.3). The American model of consultant design also penetrated those countries, however. The Swede, Sixten Sason, had a background in graphic design and was responsible for, among other designs, a car for Saab, a vacuum cleaner for Electrolux and a camera for Hasselblad.[10] In Britain, a handful of American-style consultant designers also emerged in the post-war years. Douglas Scott worked in Raymond Loewy's London office in the 1930s before he was engaged by London Transport in the 1950s to work on its buses, while Kenneth Grange, trained in fine art in the early post-war years, was given his first commission by Kodak to work on a camera.[11] It was to be some time, however, before the work of either designer was to be openly acknowledged as the companies presented their anonymous products in the marketplace.

Figure 8.3 Tapio Wirkkala's 'Kantarelli' vase for Iittala, Finland, 1957
(courtesy of Iittala/Fiskars Home)

Interior design, graphic design, fashion design and automotive design all expanded as specialized areas of professional design practice in the post-war years. Rooted within the ideology of modernism, the newly defined interior-design profession broke away from the older, premodern discipline of interior decoration, which had become tainted by its links with amateurism, femininity and domesticity. An international community of interior designers, including figures such as Richard Neutra in the USA, Jean Royère in France, Edgar Horstmann in Hamburg, Alfred Altherr in Switzerland and Jaap Penraat in Holland, created a new language for the modern interior characterized by open bookcases, low buffets, suspended lamps, splayed-legged chairs, exposed staircases and textured walls. It appealed to taste-conscious clients who could afford their services.[12] By that period, most interior designers were trained as architects and, in the spirit of the modernist idea of the *Gesamtkunstwerk*, saw the interior as a natural extension of their work.

The idea of using a designer's name to sell a product had originated in the world of high fashion in the nineteenth century. In the early post-war years, the élite fashion-design profession, which had based its reputation upon the names of a handful of well-known individuals, was still centred in the couture houses of France and, increasingly, of Italy. Figures such as Christian Dior, Pierre Balmain, Jean Patou and Pierre Lanvin continued to dominate the picture. The inter-war years had also seen the formation of a designer-led sports clothes phenomenon in the USA and, by the late 1950s, the Italian fashion industry had begun to move into a similar arena, with companies such as MaxMara targeting a new level of the market. Middle and mass-market clothing resisted naming its designers, however, and was recognized, instead, by the name of its manufacturing company. The link between designer culture and luxury goods was thereby maintained.

The maturation of the graphic designer as a specialized professional also occurred in these years. Between the wars, the term 'commercial artist' had still been widely used to describe the mostly fine-art trained individuals who had applied their skills to commerce in a number of ways. After the Second World War, with the expansion of mass travel, new communication technologies, advances in paperback publishing and the growth of corporate identity programmes, the opportunities for work increased and the term 'graphic designer' came into being. In time, that gave way to yet another term, 'visual communicator'. As the new profession defined itself, it also adopted a more proactive role, attempting to push, rather than simply being pulled by, the industries it served and implementing the lessons learnt through its engagement with modernism.[13] That tactic was reinforced by the expansion of graphic-design education, especially in Germany.

One area of professional design practice concealed the name of its practitioners in favour of the brand names of manufacturing companies until very late in the twentieth century. It even avoided the word 'design'. Automotive 'styling' was so described to differentiate it from automotive engineering. As a result, the élite products of carriage-builders, which had been marketed through the names of their creators, were joined by cars that were only known by their branded identities – the combination, often, of evocative, invented names added to that the manufacturer which produced them – the Ford Thunderbird, for example. In that industry, designers continued to be highly specialized, in-house individuals who worked anonymously as part of a team (Figure 8.4).

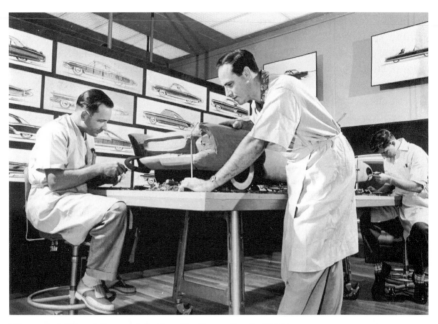

Figure 8.4 The Advanced Styling Studio at Ford, 1950s
(© Detroit Public Library, National Automotive History Collection)

Alongside the emergence of designer culture as a key international marketing strategy, designers were being redefined professionally and developing new identities for themselves. Education played an important role in helping designers to define themselves in preparation for their professional lives ahead. For the most part, post-war design education – whether at London's Royal College of Art, Germany's Hochschüle für Gestaltung in Ulm or the USA's Institute of Design in Chicago or the Cranbrook Academy of Art, all of which adopted different models of design pedagogy, rooted itself within the ideology of modernism and encouraged potential designers to see their role as cultural as well as economic. Through the 1950s and 1960s, designers increasingly positioned themselves as educated professionals through the organization of their own associations and events, among them the celebrated Aspen conferences in the USA which provided designers, across a range of specialisms, with a forum at which they could air their opinions and exchange ideas.[14]

The bubble of designer culture began to burst in the 1950s, however, when Vance Packard and others began to criticize American designers for their role in the process of product obsolescence.[15] It was not until the late 1960s, however, that, together with dominant political and economic systems, designers became the butt of criticism in Europe. Seen as the hand-maidens of capitalism and the creators of conspicuous consumption, some designers and architects, particularly in Italy, where design debates were at their hottest, were able to divert the attacks by becoming their own critics and, by seeking, sought a cultural role outside the commercial system. Teamed up in groups with anonymous names such as 'Gruppo Strum' and 'Gruppo NNNN', they attacked the superstar designers whose primary task had been to create high levels of consumer desire, to sell the products of industrial manufacture and thereby to perpetuate the capitalist system.[16] For a while, the designer faded into the wings, only to re-emerge, however, in the 1980s.

The new designers

> In our consumerist world the designer again rules. Yet this new designer is very different from the old.[17]

The early post-war years had witnessed the emergence of a second genera-tion of modernist designers whose names entered the public arena through the mass media. Thus, as we have seen, in the 1940s and 1950s, companies such as Herman Miller, Knoll Associates and IBM in the USA, Hille in Britain, Braun in Germany and Artemide, Kartell, Cassina and others in Italy, promoted many of their stylish products through the names of the designers who had created them. Design criticism and scholarship followed their lead in reinforcing the value of attributing names to designed goods. The result was an alignment of design with fine art. As a result, design jour-nals focused on the work of the relatively small community of designers whose work was recognized internationally thereby and a taste divide emerged between those goods that had a designer's name attached to them and those that did not.

From 1970 onwards, however, goods aligned to popular culture became as powerful in the marketplace as others linked to high-cultural modernism. Also, following the attacks of Vance Packard and others against the high level of waste incurred through conspicuous consumption, designer culture had to redefine itself, adjusting itself to the new context in which it found itself. A new generation of signature designers emerged who embraced post-modernism, championing it in the same way that an earlier generation had modernist design. The cult of personality remained firmly in place, becom-ing increasingly powerful as a form of identity formation and cultural communication. Now, however, it functioned within the mass market, designers taking a place beside film stars and football players. By the media-dominated final decades of the twentieth century, the idea of celebrity had become a powerful mass-cultural force, extending the potency of the Hollywood star system of the inter-war and immediate post-war years and the pop idol concept of the 1960s.[18]

As had been the case since the nineteenth century, fashion design led the way in transferring designer culture to a more popular context. From the 1960s onwards, the democratization of fashion, combined with the effects of the pop revolution that had disenfranchised the élite group of creators which had previously held sway in the fashion worlds of France and Italy, a growing number of young designers and retailers looked to the street for inspiration, appropriating the subversive styles and idioms that they found there. They rapidly transformed them into fashion garments and combined catwalk shows with forms of retailing and promotion aligned with youth culture. Catherine McDermott's 1987 study focused on a group of young British design professionals who worked within the transitional space that existed between youth culture and the established high-cultural world of the designer.[19] Within that new setting, the British fashion designers, Vivienne Westwood and Katherine Hamnett, and the graphic designers, Malcolm Garrett and Neville Brody, among others, created a new identity for the designer that was half pop-star, half style guru. Most significantly, they presented a new image of designers as media-conscious messengers whose role was to create cultural codes and, in the process, sell products and services.

In the 1980s, the idea of designers as named individuals visible in the media, conscious of their role within contemporary culture, underpinned the work of the group of designers who worked together under the umbrella of the Memphis experiment, which was led by Ettore Sottsass from his Milanese base. Perpetuating the tradition of the 1960s Italian radical groups, the Memphis designers harnessed the power of the media to communicate their message about the inadequacy of modernism to meet the cultural needs of contemporary society (Figure 8.5). A series of small exhibitions was held in Milan, in which the designers in question exhibited prototype furniture items that incorporated a range of visual shock tactics, attracting a significant amount of press attention. The strategy was likened to a fine-art performance, although Memphis' message spread through mass emulation as its bold surface patterns were reproduced on everyday graphic items, from carrier bags to magazines and advertising brochures. Within that process, the concept of the designer-star was heavily exploited and Sottsass became the subject of numerous articles and interviews within both the specialized and the international popular press.[20] With his long career as a radical designer behind him, Sottsass was skilled at using the media to his own ends, as a means, that is, of disseminating his radical ideas to the widest possible audience. The model he and the young designers around him developed involved acting, first and foremost, as agents of cultural change through their controlled presence in the mass media. The model used was borrowed from the early twentieth-century world of avant-garde

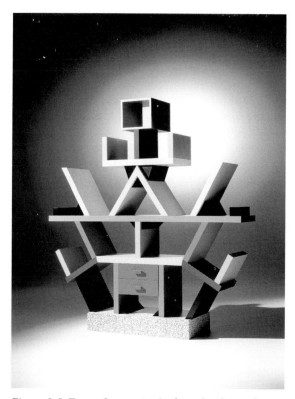

Figure 8.5 Ettore Sottsass's 'Carlton' bookcase for Memphis, Italy, 1981
(© Aldo Ballo; courtesy of Memphis)

fine art when figures such as Marcel Duchamp had acquired reputations for transgressing the norms of the cultural status quo. Within the context of postmodernism, however, that strategy ceased to be subversive but simply generated a new stylistic option in the marketplace.

A programme undertaken by the Italian company, Alessi, at that time, consciously aligned itself with the commercial face of designer culture. As part of its strategy to move its image forward and become linked in its customers' minds with a cultural programme, the company, which had been producing metal table and kitchenware since the early century, invited a number of well-known international postmodern architects and designers – including the Italian, Aldo Rossi, and Americans, Michael Graves, Robert Venturi and Charles Jencks – to create a series of 'tea and coffee-landscapes'. The resulting designs were intended for museum and exhibition purposes only.[21] The project was part of a more extensive Alessi campaign that lasted for many years, which involved producing books and catalogues to accompany its merchandise. The link with museums was a strategic means of blurring the boundaries between culture and commerce such that the goods which Alessi presented in specialist retail outlets resembled museum objects displayed for cultural purposes. Indeed, the shops in which Alessi chose to retail its goods looked more like art galleries than shops.

Alessi's decision by to engage with designer culture resulted in a number of designed artefacts, the iconic and cultural significance of which went way beyond their utilitarian functions and which came to represent the idea of the designer-object at its most extreme. Michael Graves' and Richard Sapper's kettles, for example, took the concept of design to a new level of meaning. They communicated a complex sociocultural message to a wide community of consumers without ever having to perform their primary util-itarian function, in their case to boil water. The kettles stood for design awareness and social aspiration as those participating in their consumption, whether as purchasers or as the recipients of the objects as gifts, were mark-ing their entrance into a middle-class, culturally aware social group. The knowledge that they had been created by well-known designers and manu-factured by a design-conscious company that only sold its goods through selected retail outlets was not apparent in the object itself but was known, nonetheless, by the participants in the process. Most importantly, it distin-guished those consumers who possessed that knowledge from those who did not. The fact that the designs themselves demonstrated the narrative and ironic qualities of what had become to be associated with Italian radi-cal design of that era undoubtedly added to their desirability.

The sociocultural potency of Alessi's products was also visible in the work of one of the most media-loved designers of the 1980s and 1990s, the Frenchman, Philippe Starck (Figure 8.6).[22] It was also extended to the work of a number of other designers who came to the fore in the 1990s whose personalities were almost as important as the forms they bestowed upon products. The London-based designers, Ron Arad and Nigel Coates, for example, created objects that performed a similar sociocultural role to that of Alessi's kettles. Several members of that generation of designers empha-sized reputations as *enfants terribles* through the way they dressed and lived their lives, a strategy that served to sustain the myth that they were linked to members of the early twentieth-century avant-garde. However, what had been originally conceived as radical gestures in a modernist, fine-art context was normalized within postmodernism.

The automobile was one of the last areas of modern, mass-produced material culture to embrace designer culture and to utilise what had, by the 1990s, become both familiar and effective strategies in a number of other design areas. Like fashion items, automobiles had long operated within a system of high stylistic turnover, the annual model change having been introduced in the 1930s. Unlike fashion design, however, with which car design shared many other features, the cult of the personality, epitomized by well-known couturiers, from Coco Chanel to Yves Saint Laurent, the names of automotive designers or stylists were not promoted in the popular arena.

Figure 8.6 Philippe Starck's 'M5107' television set for Saba, France, 1994
(© Thomson 2003)

Instead, as we have seen, brands, such as those of Ford, General Motors, Volkswagen, Fiat, Citroen, Rover, and so on, were heavily promoted. By as late as the 1980s, only a handful of Italian designers – Battista Pininfarina and Giorgetto Guigiaro among them – who worked in a tradition that was still linked to the individualistic, craft-based world of Italian coach-building, had achieved public notoriety. In the USA, Germany, Britain, Japan and elsewhere, however, the names of car designers were known only to a very small and select community.[23]

In the late 1990s, however, that situation changed dramatically and car designers began to become public property for the first time, appearing in both television and magazine commercials. Peter Schreyer of Audi was one of the first to show his face. That new marketing approach coincided with a new focus on the imagery of cars which, as their technology ceased to be their main attraction, and more women entered the marketplace, increasingly became their key selling point. Mass-produced cars became cultural commodities first and foremost as never before.[24] In that new context, the image of the car designer shifted significantly and values that had hitherto been restricted to Alessi kettles and Philippe Starck fruit-juicers were extended to the motor-car. As Ford's head of design, J. Mays (responsible for bringing back and updating the famous 'Thunderbird') explained, the task of the automobile designer in the year 2002 was to 'tell stories'. The concept of narrative had finally entered the world of automotive design.[25]

The identification of designers' names with goods gradually broadened across an increasingly wide spectrum, with traditional decorative objects at one end (Alessi kettles) and new, high technology goods at the other (Mays' 'Thunderbird'). Even computers and vacuum cleaners became designer-goods as the visibility of Jonathan Ive, in both the design and the popular press, and James Dyson's growing reputation as a designer of radically different vacuum cleaners – the word 'dyson' gradually replacing that of 'hoover' – increased. As cars and products embraced designer culture, however, fashion – the design area that had pioneered the concept of the signature-designer – began to move in a new direction. As mass producers became increasingly efficient at translating catwalk designs into items for the high street, often making them available before the fashion houses could do so themselves, designer-fashion became the preserve of a rarefied few (Figure 8.7).

Figure 8.7 John Galliano, dress design for Christian Dior, spring/summer 2002
(courtesy of AP Photo/Remy de la Mauviniere)

With this crisis came a new interest in what could be described as mass luxury fashion. Mass-produced branded designer-fashion became increasingly popular and labels, such as 'Calvin Klein', 'Gucci' and 'Versace', acquired new levels of desirability within youth markets. Mass-manufactured, brand name, designer culture was quick to invade the high street Moving rapidly beyond clothing, it embraced accessories and perfumes as well creating lifestyle scenarios that appealed to a market in search of new identities. Countries such as China produced vast numbers of copies of branded luxury goods. Within that context the word 'designer' took on a new significance. Based upon the fundamental contradiction that implied that people could both belong to a group and be individuals at the same time, the term came to denote a world of craftsmanship and luxury that was far removed from the reality of mechanized mass production and media-led mass consumption while simultaneously, ironically, being totally dependent on them.

Such was the new dynamic of designer culture that names once familiar only to a restricted group moved, within a short space of time, into the wider community of aspiring consumers according to the laws of the fashion system. The result was the creation of a constantly shifting picture that allowed new names to enter the frame on continual basis. The art schools provided a flow of new designers while cultural institutions and the media – including, in Britain, London's Design Museum, the specialist design press and Sunday newspaper supplements – helped to disseminate the work and reputations of a continual flow of new names. Designers' kept that socio-cultural system and the economy, in motion. By helping to create constantly new patterns of desire, it fuelled consumption.

By the early twenty-first century, the designer star system had become increasingly popularized through its visibility in the mass media. Even Philippe Starck, probably the best known and most highly revered designer-superstar of the late twentieth century, succumbed to the thrill of being broadcast to a mass television audience and entered the world of celebrity culture, alongside footballer David Beckham and his pop star wife, Victoria, among others. Starck's BBC2 2009 series, *Design for Life*, which encouraged a group of young people to engage in designing and inviting them to work in Paris alongside the French designer-hero took a hitherto élite phenomenon to a mass audience. Inevitably, some of the earlier mystique that Starck had developed around his personality was sacrificed in the process. Writing in *The Observer* newspaper, the British design writer, Stephen Bayley, vehemently attacked both the series and designer culture at the same time, 'He [Starck] tickles the ego of desire', he wrote, 'without gratifying the more profound demands of the id's lasting needs. Far from tidying up the world, he has contributed to excess. As Karl Kraus said of psychoanalysis, Starck's work is a symptom of what it purports to cure. Meretricious? Sure, so he is ideal for television, the most meretricious medium of them all... Starck's greatest achievement was to design his own celebrity. He is a god, but a false one'.[26] The 'both/and' culture of post-modernism advocated by Robert Venturi several decades earlier had become a reality for designer culture which, by the early twenty-first century, was linked, in true postmodern fashion, both to an unachievable ideal and to an everyday reality available to all, at the press of a button, on the television screen.

The designer-hero maintained a presence into the twenty-first century. Jonathan Ive maintained celebrity status as the designer responsible for Apple's key products, while James Dyson continued to represent the successful designer-entrepreneur, even opening his own design school. What was significant about these two individuals, however, was that Ive was on the board of Apple Inc. and reported directly to its CEO, Steve Jobs, while Dyson owned his own design-led company. Both men had the power and authority not just to create design icons but to be closely involved with key business decisions and therefore to integrate design into the hearts of their respective consumer product-based businesses.

Increasingly, designer culture entered the mass market as well. In Britain, for example, the furniture designer, Matthew Hilton, created a range of sofas and chairs for the low-priced mass retail chain, John Lewis. While his name was linked to the products in the brochure and online, it was not overplayed, however. The assumption was that the design literate would recognize his name while other potential purchasers would simply like the minimal lines of the furniture pieces themselves. This was soft designer culture, more fitting to the recession years of the early twenty-first century than the heavier branding that had accompanied the sales of designer-jeans and handbags a couple of decades earlier.

Of course, many other designers worked anonymously, outside the star system. Through the 1980s and 1990s, there was an increasing need for designers to work in a number of new commercial areas, including branding, corporate identity, software, computer games, multimedia, web pages, art direction, exhibitions and events and lifestyle marketing. In several of those contexts, the input of the individual was considered less important than team work and interdisciplinarity. A number of large, interdisciplinary design companies – from frogdesign in Germany to IDEO in the USA's Silicon Valley – encouraged designers to think flexibly as part of a team.

IDEO was formed in 1991 as a merger between David Kelley Design and ID2, which was run by British designer, Bill Moggridge. In the early years, it concentrated on designing user-friendly high technology goods, from computers to cameras, but quickly became one of the first teams to move from designing objects to designing experiences. In the process, the idea of the named designer was much less relevant than the interdisciplinary team that included, in addition to designers, social scientists, architects and engineers, among others. A 2003 project undertaken for the American health organization, Kaiser Permanente, for example, brought such a group together to work with the client's nurses, doctors and facility managers.[27]

The aim was to attract more patients and cut costs. The discoveries made by the team included the facts that checking in was a nightmare, waiting rooms were uncomfortable and the doctors and medical assistants sat too far away from patients. The cognitive psychologists brought in by IDEO found out that that patient's friends and families were not allowed to talk to the doctors with them and the sociologists discovered that patients did not like the examination rooms because they were frequently left in them half-naked for up to twenty minutes. The final conclusion was not that new buildings or products were needed but that the patient experience needed changing. As one journalist put it, 'Kaiser learnt from IDEO that that seeking medical care is much like shopping – it is a social experience shared with others'.[28]

The concept of 'design thinking' was much discussed in the early years of the twenty-first century. IDEO's British chief executive officer, Tim Brown, explained that it involved both working with consumer/user insights and employing rapid prototyping to get quick, innovative results that might or might not relate to product development. In his words the aim was, 'to get beyond the assumptions that block effective solutions'.[29] The emphasis on prototyping showed the way in which the design process, as it had been developed through its collaboration with manufacturing industry over two centuries, could be applied to a new context and provide a new way to reach innovative solutions to problems of all kinds. It offered a means of seeing quickly how problems could be solved visually and physically as well as conceptually. Going one step beyond the traditional business-related process of brainstorming it brought a new and imaginative method with which to deal with high-level problems and provide imaginative solutions.

The kind of designing that IDEO initiated in the early years of the twenty-first century, and which was rapidly emulated by consultancies worldwide, sat somewhere between the traditional practice of design and business consultancy. Although the American consultant designers of the inter-war years had been business advisors as well, the new design-rooted advice was less linked to industry and manufacturing and more to business practice. The idea of design work resulting in a design icon only existed at one end of what became an increasingly broad spectrum, therefore.[30] In that new context, the dominance of the architect/craftsman was displaced to a significant extent by a generation of young designers, from a wide range of backgrounds, who openly embraced the new opportunities on offer.

In Britain, as Guy Julier has explained, after the recession of the early 1990s, 'design consultants would offer an increasing range of services: this meant, for instance, that graphics specialists would offer more three-dimensional orientated facilities such as exhibition stand design, while product designers would diversify to graphic design. Furthermore, some consultancies began to offer other strategic services, carrying out, for instance, design audits of companies, assessing their product and market. Indeed, many of the more prominent design consultancies dropped the word "design" from their name altogether or added the word "strategy"'.[31] Thus, as the public became increasingly aware of a cultural concept called 'design', visible in the media and on their television screens, large numbers of professional designers began to transform their practices and move into new areas of work that were less visible to the general public. The added value they offered was directed less at the consumer in the first instance but and more at the business community to which it brought new levels of imagination, increased efficiency and enhanced profits.

The gap that began to appear between design as a form of added value in the marketplace, and as an expanding professional activity within the new communications and leisure-related industries and linked directly to business processes, was reflected in the direction in which design education moved in the last years of the twentieth and the first years of the twenty-first century. The Institute of Design at Umeå in Sweden, for example, among several other educational institutions located across the globe, pioneered a new approach that focused on erasing boundaries between traditional design specialisms. It had been founded in 1989 by Bengt Palmgren, a partner in the influential Swedish design firm Ergonomi Design Group that had focused on the idea of inclusive design by creating innovative objects and tools that served both the disabled community as well as the able-bodied simultaneously. The Institute of Design took Palmgren's farsighted approach forward for a new generation of designers. As a student on the interaction design course explained, 'Of course there are universal stars such as Philippe Starck and Jasper Morrison but the majority of industrial designers are rarely seen in the spotlight of fame. Nevertheless, they are well educated and creative and they have a broad knowledge of everything from human behaviour to material engineering and production methods. But they are not solo artists. They play their part as creative and driving forces in development processes which involve constructors, marketing managers, product planners, production engineers, and many other experts'.[32] The Institute put a strong emphasis upon working on current and urgent problems and its teachers' pedagogic methods involved concentrated on the problem-solving face of design. However, the most important question addressed by the students was not 'how can this problem be solved' but rather 'is it a problem worth solving?'.[33] The student body was and remains international and many projects focus on the health and transportation sectors and the communications industry. Interaction design plays a special role in the Institute's curriculum, based on the understanding that it is not the design of the physical object that is the issue but rather what the product can do. Importantly, the Institute sees the interaction design discipline as being rooted in industrial design, although it is conscious that practitioners need to work in teams that also include behavioural scientists.

By the end of the twentieth century, therefore, on a number of levels, designer culture – a legacy from the pioneer American consultant designers of the 1930s – was being replaced by experience-culture, within which designers played an even more important role. Although designer culture still filled the pages of mass circulation magazines and was represented in television adverts promoting a wide range of goods and services, by the early twenty-first century, the potency it had acquired by the 1980s was wearing thin. The language of modernity and the notion of creative individualism, which had been inherited from the era of early modernism and was still going strong eight decades later, remained a powerful way of selling goods but the culture it represented had a tired look to it. Partly as a result of its appropriation by global, mass-market retail organizations such as IKEA, the message of design had been diluted. Consumer desire needed to be reinvigorated in new ways.

One of the ways in which the notion of desire was readdressed was, in fact, to sidestep it and replace it by the concept of need. In that new context, the designer had to completely reinvent himself/herself and move away from the design legacy s/he had inherited. Inasmuch as it was predicated upon interdisciplinarity and cooperation the new need-focused approach built on the work of firms such as IDEO. 'Co-design', as it came to be called, was less business focused than the work of IDEO, although the two approaches necessarily overlapped to a considerable extent, united by the application of design thinking. Co-design combined the new team thinking with an enhanced sense of social commitment and engagement, however. IDEO also engaged in numerous socially focused projects across the globe. However, one example involved rethinking how a woman could get fresh water on a daily basis in Hyderabad in India. Another concerned itself with mosquito net distribution in Africa. The solutions to both involved the rethinking of systems rather than the redesigning of products.

On a more local level, many designers became increasingly involved with the issue of social sustainability and brought together social and environmental ideas. Theory lagged somewhat behind practice, however and several terms – from user-led design to transformation design to participatory design to action design to experience-based design – were used interchangeably to denote what was, in effect, a new approach towards designing. While there was a focus on a new set of skills – user research in particular – more traditional ones were still embraced as appropriate. In Britain, the designer Mary Cook, for example, a partner in the firm, Uscreates, which addresses social change through innovative design, and winner of the 2005 'Designer of the Year' competition, has described a number of co-design projects with which she was involved. They included one that took place in 2009 which aimed to increase smoking quit rates with female routine and manual workers over the age of forty, another that set out to reduce teenage pregnancy and yet another that related to the health and wellbeing of migrant worker communities in mid-Essex. All three projects involved extensive consumer research and sustained work with stakeholders. A method dubbed 'speed modelling' was used to generate multiple ideas as quickly as possible. Social marketing experts were involved and all decisions were made by teams that involved stakeholders. There was a growing sense through this kind of work that everybody could be a designer but, as Mary contended, that was not the case. She validated her view by citing the old adage that if Henry Ford had asked people what they wanted they would have said 'faster horses' rather than automobiles. It remained, she claimed, the designer's responsibility to provide expertise in the area of innovation.[34]

Just as the technological revolution of the late twentieth and early twenty-first centuries redefined the relationship between people and their machines and, as a consequence, redirected the efforts of designers from thinking less about what objects should look like to more about what they do, so the shift from thinking about consumer desire to addressing social needs demanded of designers a different skills set. Critical problem solving and innovation came to the fore, requiring designers to work in teams, to cross disciplines and, above all, to think creatively. The result was a diminution of the power of designer culture and the cult object and a growing realization that designers need to be integrated into many more activities, processes and areas of business and social life than they currently are and to be given a voice that extends beyond the studio and the factory floor.

9 Postmodernism and design

Modern design in crisis

> Pure function does not eliminate the need for stylistic choice...A neglect of the vital connection between form and expression is traditional.[1]

From the moment in the early twentieth century when the Viennese architect–designer, Adolf Loos, proclaimed that ornament should be equated with crime, an essentially rationalist approach to modern design began to dominate all other ways of thinking about the subject. Not only did that view give rise to a highly reductive philosophy of design, summed up by the oft-repeated maxim 'form follows function', it also generated a minimal aesthetic for designed artefacts, characterized by geometric forms, undecorated surfaces and a restricted use of colour (Figure 9.1). The underlying intention of the modernist architects and designers was both to reject the status-ridden definition of design that had dominated the world of Victorian material culture and to align it with the efficiency culture of mass-production industry, which aimed to continually maximize its output and increase profitability. In turn, the rationalism that underpinned modernism had its roots in eighteenth-century Enlightenment ideas that had been based on a belief in the power of reason to facilitate social progress.

By the interwar years, there were signs that another model of design was jostling for attention; one, that is, that looked to the irrational values of the marketplace and the emotion-laden world of consumption. It was partly the inevitable result of the impossibility of applying the rational, craft-based philosophy of 'form follows function', embraced by educators at the Bauhaus and elsewhere, to the complex consumer artefacts emerging from the new industries – vacuum cleaners, radios and automobiles among them. As we have seen, rather than revealing their inner structures, the seductively simple body casings of those consumer machines concealed their complex inner workings, thereby explicitly denying the rules of functionalism. With the arrival of the consultant industrial designer in the inter-war years, the orthodoxy that had been established by modernist architects was replaced

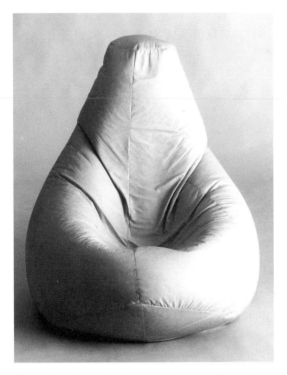

Figure 9.1 Gatti, Paolini and Teodoro's 'Sacco' seat for Zanotta, Italy, 1968
(courtesy of Zanotta Spa – Italy)

by a more pragmatic approach that supported the creation of simple body casings for complex products. In spite of their creators' claims to be following the high-minded principles of Le Corbusier and others, they disguised their functional components.[2] Ironically, the real machine aesthetic of those years contradicted the machine-inspired design principles of the early modernists.

In his 1955 essay, 'A Throw-away Aesthetic', the design critic, Reyner Banham, compared a Bugatti Royale Type 41 with a Buick, pointing out that such complex objects defied the simple formula of form follows function and demonstrated, instead, that there was no inherent link between geometric simplicity and function. 'We live' he explained, 'in a throw-away economy, a culture in which the most fundamental classification of our ideas and worldly possessions is in terms of their relative expendability'.[3] The illusion of objectivity residing in Platonic aesthetics, he went on to argue, had badly misled designers; the concept of objectivity underpinning laws of mechanical engineering did not translate directly into aesthetic laws and the concept of standardization had been misunderstood by being equated with an ideal rather than, as in engineering, with a momentary norm.

Banham's words were among the first to acknowledge the dramatic gap that existed between the ideals of the modernists and the realities of design as it operated in the commercial, post-war world. Back in the 1940s Edgar Kauffmann Jr, among others, had realized that, in the same way that jazz had replaced classical music in the popular imagination, popular design values had usurped the place of modernism in the marketplace.[4] Banham had opened the lid of a box that had been firmly sealed for several decades. His words were part of a bigger maelstrom, however, created by a number of individuals associated with the worlds of fine art, architecture and design, who came together in the early 1950s to articulate their shared belief that modernism need to be looked at again in the light of new and exciting ideas and values that had come to the fore through the joint influences of advanced technology and popular culture.

The Independent Group consisted of a number of people who were linked in various ways to the Institute of Contemporary Arts in London through the early 1950s. It included among its members the artists Richard Hamilton and Eduardo Paolozzi, the photographer Nigel Henderson, the art critic, Lawrence Alloway and the architectural and design critic Reyner Banham. They set out to debate and document the impact of new technologies and popular culture upon the arts in general. The historians, Nigel Whiteley and Anne Massey, have both acknowledged the Group's important role in recognizing the limitations of modernist thinking and its pioneering work in providing an intellectual basis for understanding design in the years following the Second World War.[5] In essence, the Independent Group set out to explore the ways in which ephemerality, popular appeal and desire had redefined the meanings of designed objects. It also developed new ways of evaluating the results of cultural practices that resisted modernist reductivism and the rules of good taste. Among the disciplines called upon to help in the task of developing that new evaluative methodology was anthropology, useful because it did not impose a hierarchy upon cultural practices but understood them, rather, in context. In his articles in *Architectural Review*, entitled 'The Expendable Icon' Independent Group member, John McCale, attempted a value-free analysis of contemporary popular culture along those lines.[6]

Attempts to define design in an early postmodern context were also emerging from other countries in the post-war years. In France, for example, the cultural critic, Roland Barthes, combined the anthropological ideas of Claude Levi-Strauss with the semiological work of Ferdinand de Saussure to develop an analytical model for a discussion of such popular cultural manifestations as 'Greta Garbo's face', 'Steak and Chips, and 'The Romans in Films'. The broad picture of contemporary popular culture that he both painted and analyzed also embraced material culture, in the form of the Citroën DS car and plastic products, both of which he maintained were potent messengers of contemporary life. For Barthes, the Citroën was 'the exact equivalent of the great Gothic cathedrals...the supreme creation of an era, conceived with passion by unknown artists, and consumed in image if not in usage by a whole population', while plastics represented the 'abolition of a hierarchy of substances'.[7] His emphasis upon the object in the context of consumption and his interest in the object's image, rather than its function, represented an important new direction for design studies at that time (Figure 9.2). Barthes' approach was formulated at a moment when the impact of the mass media, designed artefacts and images among them, was only just being fully understood. Although designers, it could be argued, had always tacitly understood the significance of the image, the critical rhetoric that had accompanied their work since the early years of the twentieth century had sought to equate their achievements with those of the architect and the engineer and had neither recognized nor acknowledged their skills as image creators.

Figure 9.2 Eduardo Paolozzi, 'Dr. Pepper', 1948
(© Eduardo Paolozzi, DACS; photograph © Tate)

The linguistic underpinning of Barthes' work rapidly became a feature of a more general approach to the analysis of designed artefacts. Through the 1950s, several other writers, such as Gillo Dorfles and Abraham Moles, also applied a semiotic approach to discussions about the meaning of objects, especially ones that did not conform to the conventional notion of good taste.[8] In Germany, teachers at the newly established Hochschüle für Gestaltung at Ulm, among them the Argentinian, Tomas Maldonado, also developed a linguistic approach to design analysis. The crisis of the theoretical underpinnings of modernism became increasingly apparent as the 1950s progressed and was expressed in a number of different quarters. In the USA, the home of so many of the popular cultural artefacts and images that had inspired the Independent Group, writers also focused upon the cultural shifts that were taking place. David Riesman, for example, noted the changing significance of the individual in the face of the masses, which had come to be defined as markets. Objects, he and others explained, were being redefined as images for a society that was increasingly defined by mass consumption. In *The Image*, written in 1961, Daniel J. Boorstin expressed his dismay at this overwhelming tendency, explaining that 'tempted, like no other generation before us, to believe that we can fabricate our experience – our news, our celebrities, our adventures and our art forms – we finally believe we can make the very yardstick by which all these are to be measured. That we can make our very ideals. This is the climax of our extravagant expectations. It is expressed in a universal shift in our American way of speaking; from talk about "ideals" to talk about "images"'.[9] His book pinpointed a significant moment in American mass culture in which, according to Boorstin, the American people had created an image of itself through its high, albeit unrealistic, expectations of, for example, 'compact cars which are spacious, luxurious cars which are economical'.[10] What Boorstin did not explain is that those expectations had been partly constructed by advertisers in collaboration with designers, encouraged in their efforts by consumers and their unquenchable desire for goods with which to express their new-found identities and aspirations.

Such was the power of the mass market in the 1950s that it could not be ignored by cultural theorists. The result was the death, or at the least the dramatic transformation, of modernism, and a reduction in the potency of its rhetoric. Stylistically, of course, modernist design remained one of the options available in the marketplace, but its ideological hegemony was destroyed. The idea that good design – the term that had come to denote the branch of design that was rooted within modernism – was in crisis dominated the work of many design critics and cultural theorists through the 1950s and 1960s. They located the cause of the crisis in the influence of American culture in Britain and in Western Europe. The spectre of Americanization, as one writer called it, was manifested in a variety of cultural forms – from food to music to literature to architecture to advertising to designed mass-produced consumer goods. As Peter Masson and

Andrew Thorburn have explained, 'the years following the Second World War saw an enormously expanded American influence in Europe, in terms of economic aid, business concessions, political influence and numbers of personnel'.[11] That new form of imperialism contained a strong cultural component and it quickly became apparent that the marketing-led approach to design, the consultant design profession and the stylistic idiom of streamlining had moved together across the Atlantic. Although inevitable modifications were made according to local tendencies – streamlining, as we have seen, took on a strongly sculptural quality in Italy for example – America's presence influenced the material culture of post-war Europe, especially on the popular level. Dick Hebdige also described the extent to which British writers and cultural critics – among them George Orwell, Richard Hoggart, and Raymond Williams – were suspicious of that influence, which they saw as a levelling down. As he explained, 'whenever anything remotely "American" was sighted, it tended to be read at least by those working in the context of education or professional cultural criticism as the beginning of the end'.[12]

Although the resistance to Americanization temporarily prolonged the belief in modernism and the concept of good design, in Britain, a new generation sought new values in their material goods. What came to be called the 'Pop' movement in design was a spontaneous outburst of expendable forms and materials, bright colours and provocative decoration (Figure 9.3). It represented a commitment to pleasure and instantaneity. As such, it resisted theorization and remained closely linked to the laws of the marketplace, determined, as it was, by consumer preference rather than by ideological beliefs. Focused specifically at and largely created by youth, it sought to represent the values of a generation that had not known wartime austerity and which had more expendable income than its parents to spend on clothes, music and other lifestyle accessories. Only a few people attempted to describe it, among them the journalist, Corin Hughes-Stanton, who wrote in the mouthpiece of the bewildered Design Council's *Design* magazine, that, 'it has cheerfully embraced Pop, Op and Surrealist Fine Art. Cottage pinewood furniture, Buckminster Fullerism, amusement arcades, hot dog stands and Archigram'.[13] Reluctantly, the chairman of the Design Council, Paul Reilly, also had to admit that Pop design had won the day and that the language traditionally used to describe design was going to have to be transformed.[14] Although, on one level, Pop design was a commercially oriented phenomenon that influenced transient lifestyle goods – fashion items, posters and other items of graphic ephemera and shop-fronts in particular – and which failed, with just a few notable exceptions, to penetrate the more durable worlds of product design and architecture, its long-term cultural impact was far from trivial. Pop served to break apart what had been seen, within modernism, as the inseparable concepts of form and function and to demonstrate the possibility that form, or rather image, and expression could, in the context of consumption, be closely linked

Figure 9.3 Paul Clark mug design, UK, mid 1960s
(courtesy of Paul Clark)

instead. This seemingly light-hearted design movement served, in fact, as a model for what later came to be known as postmodern design.

The aesthetic and cultural significance of Pop were strongly felt in Italy in the late 1960s and early 1970s, where groups of radical architects self-consciously adopted many of the spontaneous strategies of the British Pop designers. The Italian groups, Archizoom, Superstudio, Gruppo Strum and others, stepped sideways from the marketplace to demonstrate that design could become its own cultural critic. They believed that it could ally itself with the political context of the era by helping to break down the bourgeois consumerist ethic which, in turn, had been strongly allied with the Italian modernist design movement of the 1950s and early 1960s. The work that these groups showed in galleries and at events in the late 1960s acted as cultural irritants and, unlike their somewhat politically naïve British Pop design equivalents, sought to introduce a debate about design in Italy that had wide sociocultural and political ramifications. The work of the Italian designer, Ettore Sottsass, undertaken both for Olivetti and on a more individual basis, operated in a similar way, employing strategies borrowed from Pop designers – bright colours, strong imagery and transient forms – to achieve his radical ambitions.[15]

The most significant piece of theoretical work of the 1960s to articulate the crisis of modern design, *Complexity and Contradiction in Architecture*, was written by the American architect, Robert Venturi.[16] This book represented the first attempt at providing a theoretical framework for the shift in architectural and design values that had emanated from the impact of popular culture on them. Modernism had been culturally challenged, not by an articulated counter theory but by an erosion of its values by the reality of design as it functioned in the marketplace. Theory was, in effect, running to catch up with practice. Some brave attempts were made to renew the impetus of modernism in the post-war years. Germany's Hochschüle for Gestaltung at Ulm, as well as the German manufacturer of audio equipment, Braun, tried to revive pre-war rationalism, while the neo-modern design movement that emerged in Italy in the 1940s and 1950s had a strong element of idealism built into it.[17] By the 1960s, however, the power of the market and of the mass-cultural values embedded within it, ensured that those manifestations of pre-war thinking had lost their rhetorical potency, except as markers of national identity and modernization. They had become transformed, instead, into stylish statements, containing a high level of cultural capital, in a world in which consumer choice had become powerful than design idealism. In response to that market reality and the new energy that flowed from the material culture that emanated from it, critics and designers moved forward, in the 1970s and '80s, to embrace a range of new ideas that responded to the condition of postmodernity.

Postmodern design

> I have read that under the name of postmodernism, architects are getting rid of the Bauhaus project, throwing out the baby of experimentation with the bathwater of functionalism.[18]

The 1970s and '80s saw the emergence of a converging body of theoretical writings emanating from a number of different disciplines that focused on the concepts of postmodernity and postmodernism.[19] Their roots lay in the growing influence of mass culture on everyday life and the growing disillusionment with modernism.

What Jurgen Habermas called the 'project of modernity' was, claimed many of the theorists of postmodernism, initiated in the eighteenth century, the period of the Enlightenment, and lasted up until the late 1960s. For those theorists, the student uprisings in Paris and elsewhere of 1968 were a cultural watershed after which modernism was unable ever again to regain its position of authority.[20] Many of the writers regretted the end of the era of progress and experimentation and saw postmodernism as an abandonment of the grand ideals of the past. Positioning themselves within modernism, albeit at its end, they saw postmodernism as a movement in which consumption and the rules of the marketplace held sway and in which old ideas about value had become redundant. Certain writers, feminists among them, were more optimistic, however, seeing within postmodernism an opportunity for what had long been perceived as the 'other' to gain a level of credibility and authority. The sociologist, Janet Wolff, welcomed its 'destabilizing effects', explaining that, 'the radical task of postmodernism is to deconstruct apparent truths, to dismantle dominant ideas and cultural forms, and to engage in the guerrilla tactics of undermining closed and hegemonic systems of thought'.[21] Andreas Huyssen also saw it as an opportunity for a new space for the 'other', seen by him as wearing a feminine face.[22] By extension, postmodernism had the potential, many believed, to embrace cultural diversity and to make culture available to groups that had previously been excluded from it. The key debate centred on the issue of whether or not the culture (or cultures) in question was (or were) worth having. A market-based definition of design was, it could be argued, one of the many faces of the 'other' that was liberated by the crisis of values. It stood in opposition to the modernists' concept of good design which, in the face of social change, was being seriously challenged.

In spite of their anxieties about the new cultural movement, the less optimistic writers recognized the presence of what has been described as a new 'structure of feeling'.[23] At its most simple, that new structure related to the emergence of a pluralistic culture which no longer recognized absolute truths but which sought, instead, to embrace a set of truths. The question of value lay at the heart of the debates about postmodernism. While some welcomed the questioning about conventional values, which, they argued, had had an oppressive effect, others feared that relativism would rule the day and that value judgements would no longer be possible. The most optimistic of the supporters of postmodernism claimed that they did not want to stop making value judgments, however, but rather to open up the old rules that had suppressed the possibility of different kinds of cultural manifestations being valued equally. No longer, some suggested, should one speak about good design but rather about appropriate design.

Nowhere was the debate about postmodernism more relevant to design than in discussions relating to the sensitive issue of taste. A strict division between what was considered tasteful as opposed to tasteless (or kitsch) had long served to maintain class and gender differences within Western industrialized societies. The idea that all tastes could be considered equally valid had been anathema, for instance, to the theorists of the Frankfurt school – Theodor Adorno among them – who had repudiated the idea that mass culture brought new, equally valid, values to the fore. Their ideas underpinned those of many of the postmodern theorists, Frederic Jameson among them.[24] Work emerging in the social sciences, in anthropology in particular, began to consider the concept of taste from a new perspective, however, defining it socioculturally but stopping short of judging it. Pierre Bourdieu's 1979 publication, *Distinction: A Social Critique of the Judgment of Taste*, opened up a new discussion about taste. In his view, it was a relative concept, a product of education and a formative factor in class construction.

The postmodernists prioritized the consumption of goods, services, spaces and images over their production and reversed the modernists' distrust of consumption, considering it, rather, as the main arena in which meaning was formed. That view gave rise to an extensive body of theoretical work, emanating once again from a variety of academic disciplines, including anthropology, sociology, psychology, literary criticism, art and design history and cultural geography that built on the ideas of earlier theorists such as Thorstein Veblen and George Simmel. The aim was to find appropriate analytical tools with which to study consumption. Mary Douglas and Baron Isherwood led the way with *The World of Goods*, in which they set out to supplement the current ideas of economists in that arena and to explain that consumption was one of the most important ways in which social relations were formed.[25] Other studies, notable among them Daniel Miller's *Material Culture and Mass Consumption*, of 1987, which adopted a Hegelian perspective, and Grant McCracken's *Culture and Consumption* of 1988, which had the most to say about consumer goods and their meanings in the context of consumption, followed. By the end of the 1980s, a significant body of literature had emerged that took a value-free approach to the subject of consumption and, by implication, design.[26] The impact of that work for the designer and for the historian of design was significant. It helped to prioritize a new set of questions about design's relationship with culture, past and present, and to encourage a much wider discussion about its relationship with meaning, an area that had hitherto been restricted to the rather narrow field of product semantics. The new approach did not totally eradicate the need for judgments about design but it provided a set of new criteria according to which they could be formulated.

In her 2010 publication, *Design Anthropology: Object Culture in the 21st Century*, Alison J. Clarke, building on the 1980s work described above, stated that she thought that design history and theory had not focused enough on the people and the lives that give objects their meanings.[27] Her words demonstrated the continued existence of the debate about value and design in the early twenty-first century and what Clarke believed to be an ongoing over-concentration on objects in isolation. Within a capitalist economy, she claimed, they inevitably end up as commodities rather than recognizing the social relations that ultimately define them.

One body of theory that grew out of 1980s postmodernism and which had implications for the practice and understanding of design, focused on the idea of identity. That line of enquiry developed naturally out of studies of consumption which focused attention on the cultural relationships between designed goods, services, spaces, images and their consumers. In a media-dominated postmodern environment, characterized by the erosion of traditional social relations and their replacement by mediated, represented experiences, a search for identity, whether of the individual or of the group, was high on the agenda. In his seminal 1991 text, *Modernity and Self-Identity: Self and Society in the Late Modern Age*, the sociologist, Anthony Giddens, outlined the way in which he believed that the concept of the self had developed as modernity was itself transformed.[28] Other studies focused on the ways in which identifying cultural categories, such as gender, class, ethnicity and nationality, functioned within a world in which the mass media (including design) played an ever stronger role in helping to define them. The work of Edward Said, for example, explored the meaning of Arabic culture in the new, post-imperial environment in which the impact of colonialism and the culture it had brought with it was dying away.[29] As countries became independent, one of the ways in which they sought to create an identity for themselves was through an exploration of their indigenous craft traditions.

By the 1990s, the bodies of theory that had emerged under the umbrella concept of postmodernism were numerous, each one containing its own internal debates. Much of the work touched, to a lesser or greater extent, on the arenas of visual, material and spatial culture, although not always overtly. They were usually only referenced as cultural symptoms, rather than as active agents of cultural change. Unlike modernist architectural and design theory that had been largely developed by and for architects and designers, postmodern ideas were broader in nature, focusing on the general areas of knowledge, culture and politics and only touching on architecture and design when they helped to explain a broad cultural concept. Theory had become much less instrumental and its links with practice were indirect at best. Frederic Jameson was one of the few to acknowledge that a parallel activity was going on within cultural practice, noting, for example, the 'reaction against modern architecture and in particular the monumental buildings of the International Style'.[30] Grant McCracken pinpointed the importance of consumer goods in helping to bridge the gap between the 'ideal' and the 'real' in social life but was less interested in how that idea might feed back into practice.[31] For the most part, postmodern ideas were linked to design but they did not, as modernism had, provide practitioners with a new set of rules.

In the context of architecture and design, the new ideas provided, by implication, a new approach to practice but they were observational and analytical, rather than prescriptive in nature. In the final analysis, in contrast to their role within modernism – a social and cultural ideal to which architects and designers could sign up and make a difference – within postmodernism designers were, rather, part of the problem. Inasmuch as they had become an inherent part of the media industry and the process of late capitalism – the baselines of postmodernity – they were symptomatic of it rather than a response to it. As Jameson described it, postmodernism was not an ideal to be aspired towards but rather 'a periodizing concept whose function is to correlate new formal features in culture with the emergence of a new type of social life and a new economic order...the society of the media or the spectacle, or multinational capitalism'.[32] Design, therefore, was part of the message, impotent to stand outside the system of which it was an intrinsic part. Arguably, therefore, theoretically at least, there could be no postmodern critique, only compliance, the implication being that the critical design movements that emerged in the 1980s – Ettore Sottsass's Memphis among them – should be seen as markers of the end of modernism rather than of a stage beyond it.

Postmodernism did have an impact upon material culture, however, if only on the appearance of goods and images. As Jameson rightly observed, the rejection of high modernism opened the door to a new aesthetic paradigm that embraced decoration, irony, historicism, eclecticism and pluralism. It also served to help validate the 'other', which in the world of material culture was represented by all those areas of design that had been marginalized within modernism – luxury, feminine taste, the decorative arts and craft among them. To a significant extent, therefore, the postmodern 'structure of feeling' had a significant impact on visual, material and spatial culture.

Back in 1966, the architect Robert Venturi had developed ideas about 'both/and' rather than 'either/or' culture in his book, *Complexity and Contradiction in Architecture*.[33] He followed it in 1973 with *Learning from Las Vegas*, a text in which he set out to show how pop culture had developed its own valid aesthetic, one which, he claimed, could act as an inspiration for architects and designers seeking a way out of the modernist impasse. The pleasure to be gained from the experience of pop culture, explained Venturi, came from an appreciation of what it had to offer, namely expendability, decoration, fun, irony, historicism, eclecticism and pastiche – values that directly opposed those embraced by heroic modernism.[34] The appeal of Venturi's ideas to the architectural and design professions was one of a new-found freedom that enabled them to move beyond the rationalism and universalism to which all modernist practitioners had aspired. In a world in which popular values were increasingly a defining element of culture, the new level of pleasure to be found in embracing its forms was very appealing. Inevitably, the new zeitgeist was being criticized as an acceptance culture embracing relativism and rejecting so-called real values. However, on one level at least, architects' and designers' self-conscious responses to postmodernism did not result in a non-hierarchical culture but, in the final analysis, merely replaced the aesthetic content of goods with a high level of cultural capital. Where postmodern design was concerned, therefore, the shift could be seen as one fashionable style following another, a necessary strategy to keep the cogs of industry moving and capital flowing.

In 1977, the architect and theorist, Charles Jencks, published an influential text entitled *The Language of Post-Modern Architecture*. It was among the first uses of the term in the context of the built environment. Jencks used linguistic analysis in an attempt to unpack the rhetorical strategies of architects interested in what Jencks called 'multivalence', that is, the language of architectural eclecticism.[35] In fact, the book was written before the production of much of what was dubbed postmodern architecture – created by Michael Graves in the USA, Quinlan Terry in Britain and others – and Jencks had to use numerous historical examples elaborate his ideas. References were made to Jorn Utzon's Sydney Opera House and to Eero Saarinen's TWA terminal at John Kennedy Airport. The book was prophetic in certain ways, as the approach to architecture that Jencks documented was to be realized later in many designs of the 1980s and '90s, including Frank Gehry's design for the Guggenheim Museum in Bilbao. They embraced an expressive aesthetic language that distinguished it from the neo-modernist work that continued to be created alongside it in the same decades.

In spite of the enormous cultural shift that occurred from the late 1960s onwards, where design was concerned, the effects of postmodernism were primarily stylistic on one level. On another, the movement helped to open the definition of design up such it could respond to a wide range of socio-cultural stimuli. The term came to be identified with goods that had a self-consciously cultural self-definition and which, ironically, operated in the arena of high culture rather than in that of mass culture from whence postmodernism had emerged. Nowhere was that fact better exemplified than in the designs created for Alessi in the 1980s. Seen from one perspective, postmodern design, defined simply as an antidote to the high-cultural neo-modern furniture and product designs that had characterized Italian design in the late 1950s and early 1960s, had emerged in that country in the late 1960s manifested in the work of the radical design groups based in Florence and Milan. So potent had the cultural language of designed artefacts become in that country that design had acquired the capacity, in the manner of fine art, to act as its own critic. The result was the emergence of a radical design movement that operated outside the industrial system, finding its natural home in the art gallery.

The Memphis experiment of the early 1980s brought that trajectory to a head and, through the extensive media response to it, was quickly transformed from an avant-garde activity, in the early twentieth-century sense of the term, into a stylistic alternative to modernism in the marketplace. The power of the process of commodification and of the postmodern condition that prioritized the importance of material goods in the context of consumption, inevitably imbued Memphis products with a level of added value. While, at one level, it remained an élite, gallery-oriented phenomenon – the Memphis designers produced an annual show of handmade pieces through the 1980s – as its images were endlessly reproduced it also penetrated the mass market. The couture catwalk show, which served as an inspiration for mass-market fashion producers to copy what they saw there, provided the model.

The decision by Alessi in the 1980s to ask a group of well-known postmodern architects and designers to create objects for them was part of the same story. The same strategy was employed by a number of American companies which sought to imbue their products with added value in a similar way. Knoll International launched a set of furniture pieces created by Robert Venturi (Figure 9.4), while Swid Powell worked with a number of designers from the Memphis stable and Formica used similar names to work on its Colorcore series of objects.[36] By the end of the 1980s, the concept of postmodern design had, on one level, become synonymous with a highly self-conscious use of decoration, by an international group of architect–designers who sought to move beyond modernism.

Figure 9.4 Robert Venturi's 'Queen Anne' chairs and table for Knoll International, USA, 1984
(© Knoll International Ltd)

Japan was the only country to witness the emergence of a postmodern design movement that impacted on mass market goods. In the 1970s, that rapidly developing country had begun to reject its earlier marketing strategy of selling its products on the basis of technological virtuosity. Instead, it adopted a more culturally oriented view of its goods, as well as a more strategic use of design to capture its home market, especially its wealthy young consumers. That led, in the 1980s, to ranges of high technology goods, produced in a range of highly decorative colour schemes and clearly directed at female and youth markets. They were culturally sophisticated products that appealed on the level of their carefully selected aesthetic and lifestyle potential, rather than on their technological attributes. They were not expensive designer-goods, along the lines of the Alessi products, but were available, rather, in the general marketplace. It has been suggested that postmodernism was closely aligned to the Japanese love of contradiction and was therefore easily assimilated into Japanese culture.[37] Japan certainly led the way in injecting a consumption-led postmodern aesthetic into its mass-produced products.

By the 1990s, the term 'postmodernism' had faded from view. Its heritage lingered on, however, both on the level of theory and in the world of design practice. The theoretical studies relating to the themes of identity, post-imperialism and globalism that dominated that decade had their roots in the paradigm shift from modernism to postmodernism. In the world of design practice, the esoteric work of Alessi was reflected in a general reappraisal of the meaning of designed artefacts such that numerous modern objects, such as cars, refrigerators and vacuum cleaners, began to pull back from the need to express the future and linked themselves, instead, in a nostalgic manner, to their own modern traditions. Cars were among the objects to embrace that tendency. Volkswagen's new 'Beetle', designed by J. Mays and Freeman Thomas, for example, represented a new design hybrid of the present, future and past (Figure 9.5), as did Chrysler's 'PT Cruiser'

Figure 9.5 Volkswagen's new 'Beetle', Germany, 2006
(courtesy of Volkswagen AG)

and the BMW-produced new 'Mini'. Refrigerators created by Smeg also recalled that object's own streamlined past and Dyson's vacuum cleaners were as much fashion statements as household tools (Figure 9.6). A high level of decorative self-reflexivity entered the world of product design, a result of the enhanced emphasis upon consumption and the identity of the consumer. As the inspiration for a set of new, fashionable, styles, visible in the upmarket world of decorative arts, however, postmodernism had a limited life and, by the early 1990s, had vanished from sight. As a more profound cultural shift, it has had a longer life, however. Indeed, the new sensibility that it spawned can be seen to have generated much of the visual, material and spatial culture that dominates life in the early twenty-first century. Arguably, it still underpins the bewildering eclecticism of goods, images and spaces that surround us and was responsible for the expanding cultural importance of heritage within the post-industrial world, the consumer-led approach of designers, the close link between design and marketing, the dominance of the image over the object and that of the representation over reality, which characterize everyday life in the capitalist economy of the early twenty-first century.

Figure 9.6 James Dyson's 'Ball' vacuum cleaner, 2005

By the end of the twentieth century, the strongly aesthetic face of design beyond modernism was joined by a new awareness that was more process driven. It involved an analysis of the design process itself and an attempt to integrate it within a wider set of practices. Inasmuch as the new approach was rationally based, it arguably extended the principles underpinning modernism into the twenty-first century but, given that its very being was dependent upon a view of design that was immaterial and consumer/user-focused, it was closely aligned to the postmodern zeitgeist.

By the turn of the century, a growing disillusionment with design seen as the marriage of art and industry, as a form of added value – the icing on the cake – and as the key to consumer desire within the market economy, had led to a radical reassessment of its social, cultural and economic roles on the part of many theorists and practitioners. The electronics revolution had broken the bond that had linked design to the decorative arts for centuries and forced the former to redefine itself as a feature of the new post-industrial world. In that new context the question of style, now a synonym for lifestyle, remained an urgent one for many individual consumers in an increasingly globalized world and designers continued to respond that imperative. Simultaneously, however, designer culture increasingly lost its prominence and designers were replaced by new celebrities, young entre-preneurs, chefs and computer wizards among them, all of who were widely visible in the media. Arguably, the extension of design into areas such as food, gardening and website design – in which the amateur could become increasingly confident and active – made it ubiquitous and ironically, as a result, invisible.

Design theorists and practitioners pulled back from that inevitable dilu-tion of what design, in its heroic decades – the 1920s and '30s, the '60s and the '80s in particular – had been and looked elsewhere both to reform it and to revitalise its potential to bring about change. The phenomenon called 'design thinking' grew out of that moment of rebirth and developed a new role for design and designers.

Design thinking was embraced both by practising designers and design education. One of its earliest manifestations in an educational institution occurred at Stanford University's 'd-School' (Design School), also known as the Hasso Plattner Institute of Design. Established in the mid-1980s, by the first decade of the twenty-first century, the d-School aimed to use design thinking to inspire multidisciplinary teams to solve problems in ways that did not necessarily result in new products or services but which might produce new business implementation or strategic plans for companies or other stakeholders (Figure 9.7). While the majority of projects were busi-ness focused, some were more altruistic in nature, such as dealing with the aftermath of a disaster.

Pedagogically, the aim of the d-School was to produce innovators or, as its teachers called them, 'breakthrough thinkers and doers'.[38] They also referred to them as 'T-shaped people', meaning that they combined special-ist knowledge (vertical) with breadth/empathy with other disciplines (horizontal). Many of the live projects undertaken by the multidisciplinary teams – designers worked alongside business specialists and engineers, for the most part, but also with ethnographers, psychologists and artists, among others – were invented by members of the University's faculty. The

Figure 9.7 Stanford University's d-School

focus was on action rather than theorizing and on the combination of business issues (viability), technical issues (feasibility) and human issues/values (usability).

The problem-solving process used by the group was carefully prescribed. It began with quick initial research (including observation of users). Often, a video or spreadsheets were produced as a record. Prototyping was a key component, as it forced decision making without the need for references to quantitative data. Intuition was considered very important at all stages and all participants had to keep logs. Important also (and characteristic of the conventional design process) was the need to retain ambiguity and multiple options right up to the end of projects. There were no team leaders and it was left to the group to decide what was important at any one moment. The key question was to define the problem. The space in which the action took place was also crucial. It had to be flexible with lots of informal furniture and break out rooms.

Design thinking, as it was implemented at Stanford University, underpinned the ideas developed by IDEO at Palo Alto. By 2006, sixty per cent of IDEO's projects were strategic rather than design focused. They utilised the technique of storytelling and employed film makers and writers to help them in that area. They worked on the principle that designers have always had to understand a bit of everybody else's discipline and that they were natural 'T people'. Importantly, also, for IDEO, designers had to question briefs rather than merely fulfil them. Indeed, for Tim Brown, the company's CEO, 'figuring out the right problem' was the most important part of the process.[39] The work at both Stanford and at IDEO was premised on the idea that designers should be leaders. An example of significant innovation frequently referenced at that time, in addition to the achievements at Apple Computers, was the work of the American coffee retailer, Starbucks, cited because it had succeeded in providing a completely new space for teenagers that was not a bar, a school or a home. The company was also admired for the fact that it had redefined its customers rather than simply catering effectively for its existing clientèle.

Innovation was the core theme in design thinking and research in the early twenty-first century. It implied taking problem solving to a new level, such that the problem itself was redefined. In the process, the idea of dealing with material products was marginalized. This did not mean that products were no longer important. They were simply repositioned as a means to an end. In the case of an electric drill, for example, it was a hole that it created that was considered important, rather than the object itself. This dematerialized thinking aligned itself with the work being undertaken on interface design, where systems, rather than images or objects, became the focus.

In the first decade of the twenty-first century, a number of design consultancies followed the model of IDEO and engaged in multidisciplinary work. A smaller group based in San Mateo, California, for example, used the d-School model but added culture (what's desirable?) to the mix. The concept of innovation also underpinned all their activities. They defined it as 'invention with socio-economic impact'.[40]

The idea of design thinking quickly spread across the globe. It was embraced by design education, which was in search of a new pedagogy, by designers who wanted to redefine themselves and take on new kinds of work, by industry and business which looked to it to solve their large problems and by governments, which were looking for new ways to address the questions with which they were grappling. Design thinking represented a renaissance for design inasmuch as it gave it a higher profile than it had hitherto enjoyed within the marketplace and the context of consumption, and it gave the designer a new status alongside businessmen and engineers.

Through the new emphasis on problem solving, design thinking and its alliance with the wide agenda of innovation in the early twenty-first century, design was, on one level, realigned with its modernist roots, although it was the process rather than the outcome that had come to matter most. On another level, inasmuch as it depended completely on its relevance to a post-industrial world in which the design of services, business and the need to address a raft of social issues represented by the main challenges, design thinking can be seen as postmodern while capitalism dominated the economic systems of increasing numbers of countries (even China, which was still controlled by a Communist regime) and consumption still fulfilled the needs of individual and group identities, the future of the globalized world became increasingly challenged by the stability of its financial systems, the sustainability of its environment and its countless social and health problems. For the first time, design moved beyond the marketplace and rose to the level of those large-scale challenges and was accepted as a possible means of solving them. Importantly, designers, educators and researchers began to work together to redefine design and to make it more relevant, more useful and more effective in the context of the changing twenty-first century.

10 Redefining identities

Redefining the nation

As in the pre-war years, so after 1945 design continued to carry with it the potential to represent nations and their desire to project their identities on to the world at large. This was the case both for those countries that sought to cast off their links with pre-war fascism and those which had had democratic systems in place before the war. Thus, Germany, Italy and Japan all embraced modern design as a means of forging new, post-war modern identities for themselves, while Britain, the USA and Sweden, among other countries, also used it as a key strategic means of enabling them to enter new international marketplaces. In all cases, those countries used the sophisticated programmes that had been developed in the context of wartime propaganda in the context of peace. They all understood that the promise of a new lifestyle, provided by the consumption of new modern goods, was an important means of uniting their populations and of moving forward into a new era.

Several studies of design have focused on its national manifestations, seeking to identify key characteristics that distinguish them from each other. Frederique Huygen's book, *British Design: Image and Identity*, highlighted a number of themes understood by the author to be specifically 'British'. The first chapter, entitled, 'The Britishness of British Design', characterized its subject as being 'sane and forthright, ordinary, solid, not extreme, honest, modest, homely...' 'The postwar Design Council', maintained Huygen, 'considered good, solid and useable design to be of paramount importance.'[1] The present author's edited collection of essays, published in 1986, to mark the fortieth anniversary of the 'Britain Can Make It' exhibition held at the Victoria and Albert Museum, also set out to capture what was particular about British design in the early post-war years (Figure 10.1). The aim was less to arrive at a set of epithets that would link design to the British character, however, than to attempt to find out how design influenced everyday life and what role it played in influencing the way in which Britain had evolved economically, socially and culturally since the War.[2] In that context, the role of the Council of Industrial Design was

Figure 10.1 J. F. K. Henrion's aluminium sewing machine at the 'Britain Can
          Make It' exhibition, London, 1946
          (courtesy of the author)

paramount, especially in relation to its agency in the 1946 exhibition, its
links with industry and its campaign to raise the level of taste of the British
public. Indeed, the Council, it has been suggested, played a paternalistic role
up until the mid-1960s when the upsurge of popular taste of that decade
threw into question the modernist model of design that, under Gordon
Russell and Paul Reilly, it had been promoting for two decades. The model
of good design that they had backed had been linked to the familiar Arts
and Crafts-derived rhetoric of 'fitness to purpose', while the artefacts
approved by the Council had ranged from simple items of wooden and
metal furniture pieces to restrained products that avoided the excesses of
American streamlining. Both Huygen's and Sparke's accounts emphasized
the influence of Scandinavia on British good design; the important role
played by retailing within British material culture (epitomized by the opening of Terence Conran's Habitat store in 1964) and the strong tradition of
exhibition and graphic design in Britain that went back to the work of the
wartime Ministry of Information.

The same two accounts also highlighted the use of modern design to rein-force national identity for a country's home population, achieved through the creation of a sense of national cohesion and optimism such as that displayed at Britain's 1951 Festival of Britain (Figure 10.2). Conceived by a Labour government but realized by a Conservative one, the event sought to unite the nation in a shared experience of modern visual, material and spatial culture. A range of didactic displays providing accounts of Britain's past, present and future aimed to demonstrate that, while the new Contemporary style heralded a bright new future it also kept one foot in the past. The Festival successfully created a shared vision that worked for a number of years, manifested in projects such as the construction of New Towns around the country. Its message was ultimately diluted, however, by the emergence of the youth-oriented pop culture of the 1960s which was sceptical of centrally controlled modern visions, preferring to find its own voice in the chaos of the marketplace.[3]

Scandinavia's contribution to post-war design has been documented in a number of studies, including David McFadden's *Scandinavian Design, 1880–1980*.[4] The very concept of Scandinavian Design, an amalgamation of the modern design traditions of Sweden, Denmark, Finland, Norway and Iceland, was a strategic alliance formed for purposes of trade and public

Figure 10.2 The Festival of Britain, South Bank, London, 1951
(© Design Research Unit)

relations outside the countries concerned. It was less meaningful within them, however. The concept was initially formed for an exhibition that toured the USA and Canada from 1954 to 1957, the main purpose of which was to promote the craft-based modern designs from the Nordic countries in those buoyant economies. Organized by the heads of the crafts and design organizations in each participating country (Iceland was not represented), the exhibition's patrons included the presidents of the United States and Finland and the kings of Norway, Sweden and Denmark. It proved highly effective in bringing Scandinavian material culture to the notice of the American public, to unify a broad range of material objects and to create a new design brand that remained enormously influential internationally through the rest of the decade.[5] Through its chapter headings, which emphasized the craft areas – ceramics, glass, textiles, metal and furniture in particular – Ulf Hard af Segerstad's book, *Scandinavian Design*, published in 1961, made it very clear that the newly constructed design movement was craft-based and defined by its faith in the human hand to transform natural materials into objects of integrity and democracy.[6] It was a clear and attractive message to a world that had to come to terms with the impact of the mass media, of mass consumption and of advanced technologies. Through the 1950s, Scandinavian craftsmen and designers exhibited their work at important international venues, such as the Milan Triennales, impressing and delighting audiences wherever it was shown.

Among the numerous studies of national design movements in modern democracies Arthur Pulos's two-volume account of design in the USA has an important place. *The American Design Ethic*, covering the years up to 1940, was followed by *The American Design Adventure*, which documented American design in the period 1940–75. The second volume began with an account of the dream offered to the American public in 1939 in the form of the New York World's Fair. The American public continued to be invited to confront design through the medium of the exhibition in the 1940s and 1950s. None of the post-war events, held at New York's Museum of Modern Art, were conceived on the same scale or communicated the same level of popular excitement as the 1939 Fair, however. Nevertheless, the post-war years presented the American public with a concept of good modern design which, they were told, would improve their lives significantly. The good design campaign was not managed by federal government but was in the hands of the culture industry, which took on the task of helping manufacturers and retailers to persuade consumers to use discretion in their purchases. Culture and commerce worked closely in collaboration with each other, the Museum of the Modern Art with the Merchandise Mart in Chicago, for example. In 1950, the director of the Department of Industrial Design at the Museum, Edgar Kaufmann Jr., responded to a request from the Mart to help it publicize the notion of good, modern design to manufacturers and consumers. The result was the series of six annual Good Design shows. They proved very popular with the

American public and provided an opportunity for the concept to be debated in the press. Furniture and domestic items dominated the exhibition, a large percentage of which was either Scandinavian in origin or heavily influenced by the Scandinavian craft-based aesthetic. Two cultures of design were clearly emerging in post-war USA, one destined for the living room, which was strongly influenced by Europe with a clear social cachet attached to it, and the other, a more indigenous movement, with more popular origins and appeal, visible in the street and in the kitchen in the forms of automobiles and bulbous refrigerators. The Museum of Modern Art tried to bridge the cultural gap between these two schools of American design by holding two exhibitions, in 1951 and 1953, dedicated to the automobile. Its selection process, however, reflected its taste in furniture, as the cars selected for exhibition all had a strong European flavour.

The countries that sought to renew their national identities in the post war years and to throw off their links with earlier totalitarian regimes – Germany, Italy and Japan in particular – also utilised the concept of design as a means through which to create new identities, find new trading partners, and renew their populations' commitment to a democratic, modern future fuelled by the wide availability of attractive and accessible consumer goods. The 1980s saw the publication of a number of accounts of those nations' achievements, including the present author's accounts of Italian Design and Japanese Design.[8] Both these texts set out to chart the ways in which those two very different countries evolved post-war national identities that involved defining a particular approach to the concept of design. Neither country had a concerted plan of action, nor were their governments directly involved. Rather the efforts of manufacturers, practising designers and their professional organizations combined to develop commercial and creative cultures in each country that supported the rise of modern design movements. Much depended on what had gone on in the pre-war years – the influence of the Bauhaus was seminal in both countries, for example, as was European architectural modernism. Those forces had to be balanced with the influence of the American model of mass production, modern styling and private consumption, however, that was disseminated worldwide in the post 1945 years and which had a strong presence in both countries. Although Italy and Japan responded to the same stimuli and used similar strategies through which to develop modern design cultures and identities, they developed in quite distinctly different ways, dependent upon local conditions. While Italy emphasized its fine art orientation, Japan depended upon its advanced technology. The emergence of post-war design cultures in both countries represented attempts to develop nationally specific cultural and commercial identities. Both also successfully resisted the wholesale adoption of the American Fordist model; Italy through its craft traditions of small, family-based manufacturing (Figure 10.3) and Japan through its ability to combine small manufacturing concerns with very large ones using a system of sub-contraction.[9] In the decades following

Figure 10.3 Gio Ponti's 'Superleggera' chair for Cassina, Italy, 1957
(courtesy of Cassina)

the War, modern design proved itself to be a powerful tool for both countries as a means of developing new identities and in offering their populations opportunities to embrace modernity through consumption.[10]

Germany also used design as a means of creating a new post-war identity. Its innovative strategy was implemented at governmental level as well as by the private manufacturing sector. The *Rat für Formgebung* was established to mastermind a series of *Gute Form* (good form) exhibitions that built on the achievements of the pre-war Bauhaus. A number of manufacturers, including Braun AG and Bosch AG, also played key roles in defining the rational, technologically proficient character of modern Germany and its material culture, both at home and abroad. The collaboration of the Braun electrical company, for example, with the designer Dieter Rams, reinforced Germany's reputation as a producer of well-engineered, well-designed, neo-modern technological consumer goods (Figure 10.4). The continuing work of leading pre-war designers, Wilhelm Wagenfeld among them, served to bridge the gap between the pre-war and post-war years and to develop the modern aesthetic of the products of the German decorative arts industries, while electrical appliance companies, such as AEG, applied the same level of aesthetic rationalism to their high-tech products that they had in the early century, helping to earn Germany an international reputation for the creation of well-designed modern products. The image of German design at the Milan Triennale of 1954 suggested a highly efficient, hard-working country determined to provide all the members of its population with high-quality goods.

Figure 10.4 Dieter Ram's 'Studio 2' hi-fi system for Braun, Germany, 1959
(courtesy of Braun)

It was not only nations that were quick to utilise the visual and ideological rhetoric of design as a means of creating instant identities in the years
after 1945, however. Multinational companies also saw in design the potential to define global identities that would enable them to control markets on
a worldwide basis. Indeed, since the turn of the century, companies, such as
AEG, had understood that a harmonious, modern-looking identity that
extended beyond buildings and products into graphic design, was a huge
asset. While the post-war emphasis on nations as political, economic and
cultural units remained strong, a number of corporations began to define
themselves as transnational entities. This was especially the case in the USA,
as the economy became increasingly dependent upon global sales. Nowhere
was it more apparent than in the case of Coca-Cola, which, since its birth
in 1886, had continually expanded to embrace world markets. Indeed the
term 'coca-colonization' was frequently used to describe the impact of
American culture in general on the rest of the world after the Second World
War. Described as a megabrand the Coca-Cola product – a sweet liquid in
essence – was highly dependent upon design for its identity, both through
packaging but also, more subtly, through the company's corporate image.[11]
Much effort had gone into advertising and promoting the product and the
brand both before, and during, the war but the pace quickened after 1945
to concentrate on the product's position within a lifestyle. As an advertisement explained, 'Creative entertaining is part of today's good life...and
you can count on Coca-Cola to make its own contribution to the good taste
of your arrangements'.[12] Here was an example of design doing its work
without objects, an evocation of the concept of good taste in the abstract,
linked to a cold drink. As Stephen Bayley explained, 'By 1969 Coca-Cola

was very much more than a drink. It was a talisman'.[13] Although Coca-Cola was international, it was also, paradoxically, American. That national/international ambiguity characterized a number of corporate products and services in the post-war years establishing a model that remains in existence today in the form of a company such as IKEA which trades internationally on the basis of its inherent Swedishness.

In the 1950s, the American multinational company, IBM, also embraced the concept of good design employing Eliot Noyes, hitherto Head of the Design Department at New York's Museum of Modern Art, to design its typewriters and oversee it total corporate identity. In Italy, Olivetti, a patron of modern design since the inter-war years, employed the graphic designer, Marcello Nizzoli, to create its office machines, thereby buying into the internationally understood concept of good design, while retaining its Italian identity at the same time. The German company, Braun, worked with Dieter Rams in a similar way, although he was not directly employed by them. Unlike Coca-Cola, those engineering-based companies depended upon a production-oriented, modernist definition of design with which to sell their consumer machines. Arguably though, in the eyes of consumers, those engineered goods were essentially talismanic, suggestive of the same good life to which Coca-Cola drinkers also aspired.

One product that was sold on the basis of overtly national characteristics, if not stereotypes, and which had strongly national characteristics but was increasingly becoming part of a global industry, was the automobile. Swedish safety vied with German technical efficiency, French idiosyncrasy and Italian elegance in the international marketplace for cars. This was design semantics at its richest, the creation of a set of design languages that communicated to consumers and went beyond mere fitness for purpose in the products they accompanied.

The automobile industry also demonstrated the growing significance of national identity in the context of global trading. As the global context threatened their demise, the meanings of the local and national identities intensified. By 1970, the concept of national identity in design – which had had a high level of meaning in the immediate post-war years – had become little more than a set of linguistic devices that could be manipulated at will to influence the market. The real links, if they had ever existed, between material culture and a set of particular conditions and characteristics determining national identity, had been displaced by an ever expanding globalism. The former existed only as strategic marketing ploys, used to create an illusion of identity in a world in which, through the growing influence of the mass media, the process of identity formation was changing at a rapid pace.

After 1970, a number of newly formed countries joined in the activity of creating national identities for themselves through modern design – France, Spain (or rather Catalonia) and the former countries of the Eastern bloc among them – demonstrating that the acceptance of modernism, albeit with a local dialect, had become an intrinsic element of the process of national modernization. As more and more countries underwent the experience, real local and national characteristics and variations were lost and replaced by constructed ones. In their place, consumers were offered a variety of national versions of the modern dream that were, in the end, all part of the same dream – one, that is, of a modern lifestyle accessed through consumption.

Redefining design

From the mid-nineteenth century onwards, nations and corporations have used design as a tool with which to form and promote their identities. After 1970, as the mass media increasingly replaced the public exhibition as the primary mechanism through which identities were communicated, however, the context changed. While occasional World's Fairs and a few large-scale international events, such as the Olympic Games, continued to make an impact upon both national and international audiences, the power of the exhibition diminished significantly. However, design continued to facilitate the development of new kinds of identities, whether global, national or local or, in the case of individuals and groups, defined by gender, race, ethnicity, age, religious persuasion or, more recently, membership of a consumer group or a taste culture. It also strengthened its links with brands, whether those of nations, cities, commodities or celebrity designers. In turn, branding reinforced the importance of identities and facilitated their instant recognition (Figure 10.5).

Figure 10.5 Art Room mail-order catalogue, early 2005
(courtesy of Scotts of Stow) Art Room is a division of Scotts Ltd (© 2012)

Increasingly, as the twentieth century progressed, identities linked to place were determined less by inherited cultures and more by new patterns of consumption. Nations became linked, both within their boundaries but more frequently from outside them, with a range of cultural manifestations – designed products among them – that were frequently food, clothing, and lifestyle related. England, for instance, became identified in foreign eyes with an upper-class image evoked by Burberry mackintoshes, cashmere sweaters and Jaguar cars, while Italy became the home of the steel pasta maker and France that of the *cafetière*. Sometimes those identities were linked to longstanding practices with authentic origins but often they were invented traditions with shallower roots.[14] As more countries industrialized and sought modern identities, they increasingly depended upon design. Although, in the context of the rampant globalization that characterized the era, modern design shared broadly based characteristics across geographical boundaries it also, importantly, continued to build on local influences. In the 1950s, Scandinavia's adaptation of international design modernism, for example, had been linked with simple craft products made from indigenous natural materials, while several of Italy's striking neo-modernist designs of the following decade – Achille Castiglioni's famous Arco light, among them – had featured local marble, a material that had long distinguished Italy's decorative arts.

Several European countries felt the need to rebrand themselves. In the 1980s, France, for instance, under the presidency of Francois Mitterand and following the lead of his culture minister, Jack Lang, made huge efforts to promote its modern design achievements, conscious that it had fallen behind other countries, such as Italy. In addition to the numerous architectural works that were commissioned (referred to as the *Grands Projets*), French initiatives included the formation, in 1979, of *Valorisation de l'Innovation de l'Ameublement* (VIA), which financed individual furniture designers; in 1982, of the *Ecole Nationale Supérieure de Création Industrielle* (ENSI), a new school for design; and of the *Agence de Promotion de la Creation Industrielle* (APCI), a promotional agency for the creative industries. The collective efforts of those organizations generated a strong, internationally visible, modern French design movement through an association with which a number of designers, Philippe Starck among them, achieved near superstar status.[15] The country's new national design brand was widely promoted at exhibitions at home and abroad and in the media.

During the 1980s and '90s Barcelona – a capital city of a distinctive region rather than a nation – saw its local government and industry work together to renew its image. Following the collapse of Spain's Fascist regime, the city initiated a programme of modernization similar to that pursued by Italy nearly three decades earlier. While Italy had modernized its identity within the context of late modernism, however, Barcelona underwent a similar process in a global, post-industrial, postmodern context. In turn, Catalonia sought to differentiate itself from the rest of Spain by referencing its past reputation for progressive design, linked to the turn-of-the-century *Modernista* movement centred on Antoni Gaudí, and by exploiting Barcelona's position as a centre of production. In that city's transformation, the importance of consumption and of servicing a wealthy middle-class market that had been deprived of the experience of consuming modernity under the Fascist regime, were well understood. Barcelona's economic and cultural regeneration was a complex process involving private and public collaborations and design innovations in the areas of products, retail environments and public spaces. It also benefited significantly from the decision to hold the 1992 Olympic Games there which provided the leverage for a wholesale regeneration programme.[16] Most significantly, however, fundamental change was achieved through a thoroughgoing rebranding exercise and the encouragement of new patterns of consumption. The new brand combined technological competence and innovative design and it was couched in a global language that embraced local inflections. The designer, Oscar Tusquets, expressed that dualism, dubbing one of his chair designs 'Gaulino' thereby referencing both Gaudí and Carlo Mollino, an important designer within Italy's cultural reconstruction in the 1940s. His clever tactic reinforced the Catalonian city's use of design as an expression of economic and cultural rebirth.

Barcelona's rebranding was an expression of late modernism expressed in a postmodern context. Many of the changes made to England's national image in the 1980s were also symptomatic of the post-industrial, postmodern era, although its agenda was focused on the heritage industry rather than upon modernization. Returning to Britain in 1979 after spending time in Canada, Patrick Wright remarked, 'I had come back to a country which was full of precious and imperilled traces – a closely held iconography of what it is to be English – all of them appealing in one covertly projective way or another to the historical and sacrosanct identity of the nation.[17] From the 1980s onwards, the work of the National Trust, of English Heritage and of a number of other heritage agencies was intensified as they took on the task of conserving and renovating many of Britain's crumbling historical sites. In 1981, Robert Hewison explained that there were over forty-one Heritage Centres in Britain at that time.[18] They numbered among them the Wigan Pier and Heritage Centre, the Ironbridge Gorge Museum, the Beamish Museum and the renovated Albert Docks in Liverpool. From the 1980s onwards, the skills of many of Britain's designers were applied to the task of creating heritage experiences, whether within a museum setting or in a regenerated city centre. As England's manufacturing base continued to decline, many designers moved into a new interdisciplinary mode of working, crossing the traditional areas of interior design, exhibition design, furniture and product design and graphic design, to meet the needs of what came to be called 'experience design'. Film making and script writing were also embraced. The result was a new kind of designer, one who was more flexible and team-conscious than ever before and who moved away from a focus on objects towards one that emphasized experiences and immateriality.

Design played a role in the branding of many other nations in the years after 1980. The opening up of Eastern Europe provided an opportunity for Hungary, Poland, the re-united Germany, the Czech Republic and Slovakia, among others, to use design both to reinforce and communicate their craft traditions and to develop a modern face to show to the rest of the world.[19] Followed Japan's lead, several Far Eastern countries – Korea, Singapore, Taiwan and China, among others – began to inject modern design into their programmes of modernization.

By the first decade of the twenty-first century, it had become apparent that China had become an industrial power to reckon with on the global stage. Its rapid growth and competitive manufacturing costs meant that many European and American product-related companies, as well as others from the Far East, began to outsource their production to that country. Vast manufacturing plants appeared producing high-tech components and products for global firms. Foxconn in Shenzhen, for example, the largest of them, formed by the Hon Hai Precision Industry Co. Ltd in 1974, was soon producing electronic components for Apple's iPods and iPads, among numerous other products of that nature. 'Foxconn city', as it was called, embraced, '15 factories, workers' dormitories, a swimming pool, a fire brigade, and a city centre complete with a grocery store, bank, restaurants, bookstore, and hospital. While some workers live in surrounding towns and villages, others live and work inside the complex, which broadcasts its own television network, Foxconn TV'.[20]

As China developed as an industrial power, and as its urban population became increasingly wealthy, a new Chinese middle class emerged – mirroring the situation in nineteenth-century Britain – keen to demonstrate its new social status through the acquisition of goods. Given the enormous size of its population, the home market was a significant one for Chinese manufacturers. To be able to provide their customers with the added value that they were seeking, Chinese producers began to think not only about the quantity of their manufactured goods but also about their quality. As consumption expanded so consumer taste began to influence the appearance of Chinese products. Once again echoing developments in mid-nineteenth-century Britain and in the USA in the early twentieth century, in spite of the continuing control of the ruling Communist Party, China was transformed into a consumer society in which the taste of its middle-class consumers was reflected in the emergence of a highly conspicuous aesthetic. The concept of 'gold teeth design', as it has been called, emerged, confirming the fact that for new Chinese consumers it was even more important to look rich than to be rich. Urban middle-class consumers valued luxury brands very highly, quickly understanding that they acted as markers of instant social status that did not demand complex decoding. In turn, the Chinese packaging design profession expanded and many novel products – a perfumed cell phone among others – were developed that rein-forced the integration of branding and lifestyle with high-tech products.

The rapid shift in emphasis from production to consumption that occurred in China in the early twenty-first century closely mirrored the way in which Ford's principles of mass production had been replaced by those of the more market-oriented General Motors in 1920s USA. By the twenty-first century, however, that transformation had been made increasingly easily with the help of high-tech flexible manufacturing. Under the pressure of its home market and by the increasing need to compete with the quality, not simply the price, of goods produced elsewhere, China began to evolve its own model of modern design at that time. At first, it relied upon emulat-ing Western models. Sponsored by indigenous manufacturing companies, especially in the areas of *high-tech* products and automotives, Chinese design students were sent in significant numbers to study in European and American design schools. Most importantly, however, they were obliged to return to China to apply their new knowledge. The country's educational institutions also experienced a rapid expansion. By the end of the first decade of the twenty-first century, over two thousand art and design colleges were in existence although, in terms of an international reputation, a handful stood head and shoulders above the others. In 1998, the Chinese Ministry of Education declared that the term 'crafts' should be replaced by that of 'design' and teachers were obliged to retrain as a result.

Also, by the end of the first decade of the twenty-first century, the Chinese home market had become so important to international companies that they began not only to manufacture their products there but also to target Chinese consumers. The Finnish mobile phone manufacturer, Nokia, was among the first to transfer its design and research facility – led by a Chinese designer who had undertaken a PhD in Finland – to China as a means of acquiring a better understanding of the Chinese youth culture that represented its largest market.

As had been the case in the USA in the inter-war years, in the early twenty-first century Chinese companies increasingly understood that engag-ing with design was key to improving their competitiveness. The computer manufacturer, Lenovo, for example, founded in Beijing in 1984 and which produced the popular ThinkPad line of notebook PCs and ThinkCentre line of desktops, doubled the size of its design team, realizing that design aware-ness gave it an edge in the global marketplace.[21]

Once China realized that it had to embrace design, it moved fast to learn about it from models developed elsewhere. Importantly, however, it also sought to retain a sense of national identity in its development of a concept of Chinese modern design. Given the huge strengths of its traditional deco-rative arts, it made sense to ensure that its longstanding craft skills and ritualistic artefacts informed a Chinese modern design movement. While on one level that approach resulted in some interesting hybrids – examples included a General Motors-produced concept sedan that looked like a pagoda when viewed from the rear, a speaker phone based on traditional 'hot pot' and a corporate identity scheme for Pizza Hut China's website that made extensive use of China's traditional colours, red and yellow – on another it stimulated programmes of research that focused on revisiting and reviving the traditional Chinese applied arts – garden design, calligraphy and ceramics among them – as a means of offsetting the bland Westernized products that were increasingly filling the country's retail centres. The principles underpinning Daoism and Confucianism were also widely discussed in this context, alongside efforts to ensure that Chinese designers understood how to innovate.

China also understood the importance of ensuring that its key cities – Beijing and Shanghai – featured signature buildings that acted as icons of modernity and represented a level of internationalism. Following the model offered by Barcelona in 1992, Beijing used its 2008 Olympic Games as an opportunity to demonstrate and expand China's commitment to modern architecture and design. The Swiss architects, Herzog and de Meuron's highly original Olympic stadium – unanimously referred to as the 'Bird's Nest' – was probably the most striking and memorable of the buildings created especially for that event. Leading Chinese artist, Ai Weiwei, was the artistic consultant on the project.[22] At Shanghai's 'Expo', held two years later, the British architect, Thomas Heatherwick's impressive UK pavilion, known as the 'Seed Cathedral', which consisted of more than sixty thousand acrylic rods containing seeds from different plants, performed a similar function. While, on one level, China was cautious about importing too much from the West and some of the content of YouTube, Twitter, Google, Facebook and Flickr was thought by the Chinese authorities to be inappropriate, on another level, it worked hard to play catch up with the rest of the developed world.

Ex-British colonies, such as Canada, Australia and South Africa, also began to develop their own modern design movements as a way of moving beyond their imperial pasts. Canada, for example, made huge efforts to develop a modern design identity epitomized in such artefacts as the 'Skidoo'. By the early twenty-first century, the earlier domination of the field by the USA/Europe axis, through the first half of the twentieth century, had diminished as many other places – among them Latin America, India and parts of Africa – began to embrace modern design as a means of demonstrating their aspirations to become part of the developed world.

Design not only played a role in the creation of the identities of places, nations in particular, however, but also in the formation of people's identities across the globe. A number of definitions of globalization have been put forward, including one developed by the sociologist, Anthony Giddens, who has described it as 'an intensification of worldwide social relations which link distant localities in such a way that local happenings are shaped by events occurring many miles away and vice versa'.[23] Another way of thinking about globalization is as the result of the impact of new technologies and the enhanced mobility of people that either brought new experiences to people or took people to them. Globalization occurred through the homogenization of products, industries and technologies and, most significantly, through shared patterns of consumption. It also, paradoxically, facilitated diversity. That paradox is expressed in the process described as 'glocalization'.

Globalization developed gradually through the course of the twentieth and into the twenty-first century. It was the result of the expansion of commercial life, the opening up of international markets, the expansion of the media and transformations in the nature of consumption. The cultural changes that lay beneath the last – the shift, that is, from class-based, trickle-down consumption to the emergence of what Zygmunt Bauman has called 'neo-tribes' that cross the conventional cultural classifications of class, age, gender, ethnicity and nationality (among others) – were fundamental to the growth of globalization and expressed through design.[24]

One of the most visible ways in which design and globalization joined hands was in the concept of the corporate brand. Much work has been undertaken in analyzing the effects of multinational branding, such as that of Coca Cola which, as we have seen, brought American culture to the rest of the world in the twentieth century.[25] More recently studies have been made of the Italian fashion producer/retailer, Benetton, and of the Japanese producer of electronic goods, Sony, which have set out to unpack the complex working of the brand in the late twentieth century and early twenty-first centuries. Both Pasi Falk and Celia Lury have published work about Benetton which has attempted to get beneath the surface of that company's brand strategies.[26] Lury has explained that the brand functions through the way 'in which it can recoup the effects of the subject or consumer's action, constituting these effects as the outcome of the brand's own powers through the repetitive assertion of its ability to motivate the branded object's meaning and uses'.[27] She has suggested that, although the product is absent the brand anticipates it. It can work so well, she has argued, because we have seen 'an intensification of the imaging of the object' through the twentieth century such that we know it even if it is not there. When we see the Coca Cola logo, for example, we imagine the bottle and the drink without needing to see them. Benetton's brand was made visible in the last decade of the twentieth century through a programme of progressive global advertising that took globalization, rather than the company's products, as its main theme. A number of advertisements rejected representations of its products in favour of depictions of its worldwide consumers shown as young, happy people from a variety of ethnic origins. Lury was critical of the implications of those advertisements, claiming that they set out to naturalize racial difference, making it a matter of skin colour only.

In their study of the Sony Walkman, Paul du Gay, Stuart Hall, Linda Janes, Hugh Mackay and Keith Negus have looked at the globalization strategies of that Japanese company from technological and marketing perspectives.[28] Sony first launched its product in Japan, then introduced it into a range of countries using a different product name in each. In the early 1980s, it decided to standardize the name globally. To sell the Walkman internationally, however, Sony had to make it technologically consistent and guarantee its repair or replacement across the world. The company also decided to set up local manufacturing operations in a number of different countries, as a means of entering local marketplaces. Thus, the company's process of globalization worked on a number of fronts. From a design perspective, the product was standardized in the first instance but variants were quickly developed to ensure the Walkman a constant flow of customers. Those variants were directed at global niche-taste cultures, however, rather than at different local markets.

Many other companies developed along the lines that have been pioneered by Sony and others. Japanese companies were especially keen to establish local plants. That was especially evident in the car industry and from the 1970s onwards Japanese cars competed favourably with those of the USA and Europe in the international marketplace. Indeed cars had long operated on a global basis – Ford, General Motors and Chrysler had set up foreign manufacturing in the inter-war years in imitation of the earlier electrical industries, General Electric, Westinghouse and Siemens. Indeed, it was natural for the products of the new technology industries to pave the way for international trade as they had no cultural traditions behind them. With the gradual homogenization of the environment, however, came the taste for difference and a desire for the exotic on the part of consumers who had experienced foreign travel and wanted to bring that experience home. The success of retailers, such as Terence Conran with his Habitat store in the 1960s, was the recognition of the need for culturally diverse goods that, like all commodities, found their place within the fashion system such that, while their appeal was temporary, there was always another example of exotica to take their place.

The design profession was also globalized. By the mid-twentieth century, it had become commonplace for design consultancies to set up branches in countries where they had clients. Raymond Loewy's British and French firms had set a trend that was emulated by British consultancies around the globe in the 1980s. The 1990s saw the collapse of many of those firms, however. Britain continued to be a focus for international design, a fact that was confirmed in the early twenty-first century by the American Ford Motor Company's formation of a design centre in London. Named 'Ingeni', the group was located in a building designed by the architect, Richard Rogers, and described as 'a laboratory and a shop window all at the same time'.[29] The group's brief was to create products that would be marketed as part of the Ford brand. London was selected as it was seen to be the most internationally oriented of the world's major cities and the home of the globally oriented creative industries.

The creation of national identities for countries and of brand identities for global corporations, through the strategic use of design positioned closely alongside marketing, was a striking characteristic of the late twentieth century. Both depended strongly on the concept of branding and the role that design played within it. The cultural spin-off of both processes was the formation of identities for individual consumers, whether acquired through a sense of belonging, through an association with a particular place or through a link with a lifestyle promulgated by a commercial brand. A number of other cultural categories, among them gender and age, were also represented by designed artefacts in the marketplace, such that consumers could use them as a means of constructing individual and group identities for themselves. Just as national identities reasserted themselves when they were under threat from globalism, so overt representations of femininity and masculinity became more apparent in the marketplace as, in everyday life, those gendered identities became less distinctive. Publications such as Pat Kirkham's group of edited essays, *The Gendered Object*, and Katherine Martinez and Kenneth L. Ames' *The Material Culture of Gender: The Gender of Material Culture*, described that tendency.[30] The first covered a wide range of products, from guns to Barbie dolls to perfume, describing the subtle and not so subtle ways in which commodities play a role in gender identity formation. Pat Kirkham and Alex Weller's account of the male and female coding in the advertising of Clinique cosmetic products, for example, showed how the former communicated a rational and objective message that was less apparent in the female equivalent. 'By the time they are old enough to afford Clinique products', they explained, 'they [girls] do not need [like the men] to be 'educated' about them'.[31] In her essay on the subject of 'Perfume', Angela Partington explained that 'it [perfume] represents the contingencies of identity' and that 'the consumer produces something real – new ways of relating as gendered subjects – and design provides the raw material'.[32] Martinez and Ames' book adopted a more historically oriented approach.

In its capacity as a cultural force with the potential to fill the gap left by the increasing loss of traditional social relations, design has clearly come to play a fundamental role within everyday life in the early twenty-first century. As a tool to convey the power of nations, it has moved a long way from the nineteenth-century exhibitions filled with huge halls displaying early production machinery. National identity has come to be on display in the global marketplace. It is embedded in the mass media and experienced on a daily basis. As individuals, consumers have learnt to negotiate their identities and their sense of belonging, aware that it is made up of many elements including gender, age, ethnicity, lifestyle and locality. Aided by designed goods, services, spaces and images available at any one moment in the marketplace, individuals can negotiate their own identities and play an active part in the construction of life in the everyday world.

Glossary

Aalto, Alvar (1898–1976)   A Finnish architect–designer best known for his humanistic buildings executed in a modern, organic style (e.g., Viipuri Library, 1927–35 and Paimio Sanitorium, 1929–1933); his furniture, which was made from wood moulded into two-dimensional curves; his curvaceous glass vases; and his textiles.

Anti-Design   The name given to the Italian movement of the 1960s and its revival in the 1980s, which set out to disassociate design from commerce and position it within the cultural area. The term 'radical design' was used interchangeably. Ettore Sottsass played a key role in the movement from the 1960s onwards.

Arad, Ron (1951–)   An Israeli designer who made his impact in London, where he settled in 1974, selling his idiosyncratic designs through his shop in Covent Garden. He was associated with the High-Tech movement in the 1970s and he formed a company called One-Off. His best-known design is the Rover chair, made from a recycled car seat. He is Professor of Design at the Royal College of Art.

Archizoom   An Italian architectural group, formed in 1966 in Florence, which participated in the Anti-Design movement. Its early members included Andrea Branzi and Paolo Deganello. The group created a number of visionary environments and some fantasy furniture as part of its attempt to move Italian design away from its preoccupations with consumerism and high style.

Art Deco   The name of a design movement that emerged in France in the 1920s, taking its name from the 1925 *Exposition des Arts Décoratifs*, held in Paris. Although it was a term associated with exclusive objects in the first instance, it moved into the popular arena in the 1930s through its mass production and dissemination and its alliance with new materials, such as plastics.

Art Nouveau   The name of an international architectural and decorative arts movement which came into being in the 1890s but which had disappeared by 1914. It was characterized by its flowing, organic forms in France, Spain and elsewhere but it had more rectilinear manifestations in Scotland and Austria. It has been described as the first modern design style.

Arts and Crafts Movement A British architectural and design movement, based on the ideas of John Ruskin and William Morris in Britain, which sought to eliminate the bad effects of industrialization on material culture and revert to a pre-industrial model in which hand making played a part. The ideas and designs of the Arts and Crafts protagonists – C. F. A. Voysey and C. R. Ashbee among them – were enormously influential abroad and influenced the early development of modernism internationally.

Banham, Peter Reyner (1922–88) A British architectural and design historian, theorist and critic, who wrote prolifically in the 1950s and 60s about the Modern Movement and its demise. A member of the Independent Group in the 1950s, he introduced the topics of mass culture and design to its meetings. He taught at a number of institutions, including the University of Los Angeles at Santa Cruz where he was Professor of Art History.

Bauhaus The most influential design school of the twentieth century, the Bauhaus was formed in 1919 in Weimar by Walter Gropius and it subsequently moved to Dessau. It took a radical approach to design education, starting from scratch and developing forms in craft workshops in collaboration with fine artists. It was closed by the Nazis in 1933.

Behrens, Peter (1868–1940) Peter Behrens was an architect–designer who worked in the Art Nouveau idiom in Darmstadt before becoming a consultant to the AEG Company, for which he designed a complete corporate identity in 1907. Walter Gropius, Mies van der Rohe and Le Corbusier all spent time in his studio.

Bel Geddes, Norman (1893–1952) Norman Bel Geddes began his career as a portrait painter before moving into stage design, shop-window display and finally consultant industrial design. His 'streamlined' fantasies for transport designs were the most expressive of the 1930s, but his work for production was more mundane by comparison.

Bellini, Mario (1935–) The Milanese architect–designer Mario Bellini is best known for his elegant typewriters and office machines, which he created for Olivetti in the 1960s and 70s, as well as for his stylish furniture designed for Cassina. An innovative product designer, he also created a wedge-shaped tape deck for the Japanese firm Yamaha. He was much admired and widely emulated in the 1970s.

Boontje, Tord (1968–) A Dutch designer who first studied industrial design at the design academy of Eindhoven and subsequently at the Royal College of Art in London, where he now teaches. He founded Studio Tord Boontje in 1996 in London. He believes that design should evoke emotion and he has created ranges of glassware, lighting and furniture.

Brandt, Marianne (1893–1983) A German painter, designer and metalworker who established her reputation through her work at the

German Bauhaus, where she was a graduate. She went on to become the head of the metal workshop and she designed some highly geometric objects there, including a small teapot, which have become classic designs.

Branzi, Andrea (1938–)   A Florentine architect–designer who was a member of Archizoom in the 1960s and who moved later to Milan to play a central role in the second phase of Italian Radical design, which emerged at the end of the 1970s. He is also a teacher and writer.

Breuer, Marcel (1902–81)   The Hungarian architect–designer Marcel Breuer was trained at the German Bauhaus Weimar, where he designed his famous tubular-steel chairs. He went on to teach at that institution and, on its closure by the Nazis, came to England to work for Jack Pritchard's Isokon company, for which he developed chairs made from bent plywood. In 1937, he went to the USA to join Walter Gropius at Harvard.

Brody, Neville (1957–)   Born in London, the graphic designer Neville Brody worked on *The Face* magazine in the 1980s, developing radically new typefaces and layouts. He combined early modernist ideas with images emanating from contemporary subculture to create a new look that was highly influential. Brody moved on to work on record covers and a wide range of graphic design projects.

Castiglioni, Achille (1918–2002)   Of the three Castiglioni brothers, Pier Giacomo (1910–1968), Livio (1912–1952) and Achille, it was the last, a Milan-based designer, who had the greatest influence on twentieth-century design. His designs for furniture, lighting and appliances – among them the Tractor Seat (Mezzadro) for Zanotta and his Arco light for Floa – won him numerous prizes and made him an important force both in Italy and elsewhere.

Chanel, Coco (1883–1971)   The French fashion couturier Coco Chanel was a pioneer in the field, opening her first millinery shop in 1909 and moving on to create a highly influential fashion house in the inter-war years. She anticipated the idea of selling clothes as part of a lifestyle and launched her perfume, Chanel No. 5, to accompany her clothes, in 1923.

Cliff, Clarice (1899–1972)   A British ceramic designer who came out of the Stoke-on-Trent tradition but who went on to make a reputation for herself as a result of her brightly painted ceramics, which she sold through her own firm. Her pattern named 'Bizarre' was among her most successful designs. Her work is avidly collected.

Coates, Wells (1895–1958)   Born in Tokyo, Wells Coates came to Britain in 1929 and became a major figure in the British architectural and design modern movement. After working on shop interiors, he went on to design an apartment block for Jack Pritchard's Isokon firm and he pioneered modern industrial design through his work for the Ekco Radio Company.

Co-design   This approach to design works on the principle that all people have different ideals and perspectives and that any design process needs to deal with this. Co-designers set out to consider the interests of stakeholders in the design process and include interviews, focus groups and workshops within it to achieve that end.

Colombo, Joe (1930–71)   One of the most influential of the superstar Italian designers of the 1960s, Colombo is especially remembered for his brightly coloured plastic products designed for Kartell. He began life as a painter but went on to produce influential furniture and product designs for several Italian manufacturers, including Zanotta, Elco and Stilnovo.

Conran, Terence (1931–)   Trained as a furniture designer in London, Terence Conran's impact on post-war British and international design was through his role as a retailer of lifestyle products. He opened Habitat in London's Fulham Road in 1964 and went on from there to influence post-war taste and aspirations through his numerous retailing achievements. Latterly, he has moved into developing restaurants.

Constructivism   The name given to the modern movement in art, architecture and design which is linked to the abstract work that emanated from Russia in the years around the 1917 Revolution. It took its lead from engineering, seeking to move away from the decorative traditions of the applied arts.

Contemporary Style   A term used to describe the modern yet decorative domestic style of furniture and furnishings that emerged in the years after the Second World War in Britain. The work exhibited at the 1951 Festival of Britain was highly influential on this essentially popular style, which was characterized by its biomorphic forms and bright colours.

Cooper, Susie (1902–95)   A British ceramic artist and business woman who, like Clarice Cliff, grew out of the Stoke-on-Trent tradition but who moved on to sell her own highly abstract, modern work. Her 'Curlew' shape of 1933 was among her best known. In the 1960s, her company was absorbed by Wedgwood.

Coray, Hans (1906–91)   The Swiss designer Hans Coray is best known for his all-aluminium chair, which was shown at the Zurich exhibition of 1939 and is still in production today.

Day, Robin (1915–) and Lucienne (1917–)   Robin Day was one of Britain's leading furniture designers in the 1950s and 60s, working with the Hille Company, while his wife, Lucienne, was known for her textile designs, retailed through Heals. They collaborated on several interiors, notably at the Milan Triennale of 1954.

De Lucchi, Michele (1951–)   The Milan-based architect–designer, de Lucchi, played a leading role in the Memphis project of the early 1980s. He went on to combine his work for Olivetti and for other international product manufacturers with his own experimental work, in which he continued to push the cultural role of design into new areas.

De Stijl   The De Stijl Movement, which took its name from a Dutch magazine of the same name, was formed during the First World War in Holland. It combined the fine-art work of Piet Mondrian with the design, graphic and architectural work of several others, all of whom sought to find a new abstract, geometric aesthetic for their practices.

De Wolfe, Elsie (1865–1950)   A pioneer American interior decorator, who worked from both New York and Paris, who created a new consultant profession that entailed supplying interior furnishings to clients as a means of increasing the level of taste in their homes. She was one of the first to understand the close link, for consumers, between design, taste and lifestyle.

Design Thinking   Design thinking refers to a design-led method of defining problems and finding solutions in a variety of fields. It combines empathy for the context of a problem, creativity in the generation of insights and solutions and rationality to fit solutions to the context. The term is widely used in contemporary design and engineering practice, as well as in business and management. The aim is to use design-related ideation as a means of achieving innovation.

Deutscher Werkbund   One of the first European modern design reform bodies, created in Germany in 1907 as a state and industry partnership, which set out to promote modern design as a key component of trade and national identity. The Werkbund sponsored the Cologne Exhibition of 1914 and a number of others in later years. It provided a model that several other countries emulated.

Dior, Christian (1905–57)   The French fashion designer Dior launched his first collection with what he called the 'New Look' in 1947. It had an enormous impact and he helped establish Paris as the headquarters of post-war haute couture. Following his sudden death, Yves Saint Laurent took over the design direction of his fashion house. In 1996, the British designer John Galliano became the chief designer at Dior.

Dresser, Christopher (1834–1904)   Dresser was an English designer who began his career as a botanist but moved later into product design. His metalwork and textiles were greatly influenced by Japan (which he visited in 1877) and he became one of the first designers internationally to work with manufacturing industry on a freelance basis.

Dreyfuss, Henry (1902–72)   From his background in the theatre prop business, Dreyfuss, like Norman Bel Geddes, was a stage designer before he became a consultant industrial designer. His early clients included the Bell Telephone Company, the Hoover Company and the New York Central Railroad. He wrote about his anthropometric approach to design in his book *Designing for People*, published in 1955.

Dunne and Raby   A London-based design studio established in 1994 by Tony Dunne and Fiona Raby, who use design to stimulate discussion about the social, cultural and ethical implications of current and emerging technologies. Dunne heads the Design Interactions course at

London's Royal College of Art and Raby is Professor of Industrial Design at the University of Applied Arts in Vienna.

Dyson, James (1947–) A British industrial designer, and founder of the Dyson company, who is best known as the inventor of the bagless vacuum cleaner and the 'Ballbarrow', a wheelbarrow using a ball instead of a wheel. Dyson studied furniture and interior design at the Royal College of Art (1966–1970) before moving to engineering.

Eames, Charles (1907–78) and Ray (1912–88) The American architect–designer Charles Eames first came to public notice when his moulded plywood furniture, designed with Eero Saarinen, won a competition at the Museum of Modern Art in New York in 1944. He had a one-man show there two years later, at which he introduced furniture that combined moulded plywood with steel rod. He went on to design a number of even more innovative furniture items through the 1950s and 60s, as well as venturing, with his wife Ray, who worked collaboratively with him from the 1940s onwards, into experimental film making.

Earl, Harley (1893–1969) Earl began his career as a coachbuilder in Hollywood but was employed by Alfred. P. Sloan of General Motors (GM) in 1926 to make the company's mass-produced automobiles look more attractive. The 1927 Cadillac Lasalle made automotive history in this respect and Earl went on to head the Styling Section at GM until the 1950s.

El Lissitzky (1890–1940) A Russian graphic designer who worked for various architects up to 1917 and who subsequently became involved with the artistic propaganda of the Revolution. His work was executed in the Suprematist style, pioneered by the Russian artist Kasimir Malevich, and he is best known for his 'Proun' compositions of the early 1920s.

Esslinger, Hartmut (1945–) The founder of the German design consultancy frogdesign, which was based in his home town of Altensteig. In 1982, the consultancy opened a Californian office and Apple Computer became an important client, for whom frogdesign created the first all-white computer. Other clients have included Villeroy and Bosch and Sony.

Fowler, John (1906–77) A British interior decorator who adopted a historicist approach from the inter-war years onwards. He worked with the National Trust in the years following the Second World War, restoring dilapidated country houses with chintz fabrics. He was a partner, with Nancy Lancaster, in Colefax and Fowler.

Franck, Kay (1911–88) A Finnish ceramicist, textile and glassware designer who took a more subtle, everyday approach than that of his contemporary 'superstar' designers. He was a designer at the Arabia pottery for many years, responsible for numerous simple, practical wares, including his 1952 Kilta tableware.

Frank, Josef (1885–1947)   An Austrian modernist architect who settled in Sweden in 1934 and who became the chief designer for the Stockholm furnishings company, Svenskt Tenn. He modified his earlier purist aesthetic to include pattern and texture in his later furniture, lights and fabrics. An early exponent of the style known as 'Swedish Modern', he remained with Svenskt Tenn until his death.

Fuller, Richard Buckminster (1895–1983)   An American designer and visionary who embraced design and wrote and lectured extensively about it, as part of advanced technology in the service of mankind. He designed a Dymaxion house in 1927, a Dymaxion car in 1932 and, later, a series of geodesic domes.

Functionalism   A term used by design theorists to describe the ideas of the protagonists of the early twentieth-century Modern Movement in architecture, who sought to derive their forms through an abstract consideration of their object's function, a process akin to that of an engineer, rather than by adding decoration to its surface to make it desirable.

Gaudí, Antoni (1852–1926)   A Spanish architect and designer, based in Barcelona, who evolved his own idiosyncratic version of Art Nouveau. His buildings – including the Sagrada Familia of 1903–26, the Casa Vicens of 1878–80, and his Parque Guell, begun in 1900 – all displayed the same fantastic aesthetic as his furniture designs.

Giacosa, Dante (1905–96)   A designer–engineer who worked for the Italian automobile manufacturer Fiat from the late 1920s into the 1970s. His most influential designs included the Fiat 500 of 1936 and the little 600 of 1956. He approached the problem of style as an engineer and, as a result, worked very differently from his contemporary car stylists in the USA.

Giedion, Siegfried (1888–1968)   A Swiss art historian who, under the tutorship of Heinrich Wolfflin, developed an approach to 'anonymous' history, which he articulated in his major study *Mechanisation Takes Command*, published in 1948. The book became an important modernist design-historical text.

Giugiaro, Giorgio (1938–)   An Italian car designer who set up his own firm, Italdesign, in 1968. Since then Guigiaro has designed a number of very significant cars, including the Alfa Romeo Akfa Sud (1971), the Volkswagen Golf (1974) and the Fiat Panda (1980). He has also worked as a product designer creating, among other goods, a camera for Nikon.

Grange, Kenneth (1929–)   A British product designer who worked in the neofunctionalist style for, among others, the Kenwood company, from the late 1950s onwards. In 1972, he joined the Pentagram design consultancy in London, becoming its first product designer. He went on to work for many clients, including a number in Japan.

Gray, Eileen (1878–1976)   An Irish architect–designer who did most of her work while living in Paris, where she settled in 1907. From a background in luxurious, lacquered furniture she went on to participate in the Modern Movement, creating a number of seminal furniture designs including models in steel and leather in the 1920s. From the 1930s she dedicated her self to architecture.

Gropius, Walter (1883–1969) The German modernist architect Walter Gropius began his career in partnership with Adolf Meyer in 1910 – with whom he designed the Fagus Factory in the following year – and became the first director of the German Bauhaus in 1919. He went on to become Professor of Architecture at Harvard in the USA in 1937.

Gugelot, Hans (1920–65) The Dutch designer Hans Gugelot set up his own office in 1950 after having worked with Max Bill and collaborated with the Ulm design school, in his capacity as head of its development group, on designs for the Braun company in the mid-1950s. His work was neofunctionalist in style.

Heal, Ambrose (1872–1959) The British designer Ambrose Heal joined the family furniture business in 1893. He became linked to the Arts and Crafts Movement and began designing in 1896. The Heal's store was established in 1840 and Ambrose moved its emphasis from reproduction to simple, modern furniture. He became chairman of the business in 1913 and played a role in the formation of the Design and Industries Association in 1915.

Henrion, F. H. K. (1914–90) Graphic designer of French origin who came to Britain in the 1930s and worked there, throughout the Second World War and the post-war period, as one of the country's leading graphic designers.

High Tech An interior and furniture aesthetic popular among the young and stylish in the 1970s, which borrowed its look and its materials from the industrial sector and applied them to the domestic arena. Shelves made from scaffolding epitomized this brutal aesthetic.

Hille The British furniture manufacturing company Hille developed from a small business set up in the early part of the twentieth century to become a substantial firm after the Second World War, sponsoring modern furniture. Robin Day, Roger Dean and Fred Scott all worked for Hille, which was dissolved in 1983. Day's polypropylene chair of the early 1960s is the company's most influential product.

Hochschüle für Gestaltung, Ulm A German design school, founded in 1953, as a revival of the pre-war Bauhaus. The Swiss designer Max Bill was the first director of the school and he was replaced at the end of the decade by Tomas Maldonado. In the 1960s, the school was divided by strong internal ideological differences and it was forced to close in 1968.

Hoffmann, Josef (1870–1956) An Austrian architect and designer who worked in the studio of Otto Wagner but went on to become a founder member of the Viennese Secession and an influential designer of furniture and decorative objects executed in a strikingly modern, geometric style. He worked across of range of products destined for the domestic sphere.

Honda   The Japanese motor cycle company Honda was founded in 1948. Its first important product was the Super-Cub step-through motor cycle, which succeeded, through the aggressive marketing that accompanied it, in conquering the American market. Since then the company has diversified into power appliances and motor cars. The Civic, Prelude, Accord and, more recently, the Insight eco-car are all examples of successful Honda designs.

IDEO   An international design and innovation consultancy founded in Palo Alto, California, in 1991, from a merger of three existing design firms: David Kelley Design (founded by David Kelley), ID Two (founded by British designer, Bill Moggridge) and Matrix Product Design (founded by Mike Nuttall). The current CEO is Tim Brown. The company designs products, services, environments and digital experiences but it has become increasingly involved in management consulting and organizational design in recent years.

Inclusive Design   This approach means making the design of products and environments usable by all people without the need for adaptation or specialized design. By implication, a product designed for an elderly person with disabilities should, according to this approach, be usable by anyone regardless of age or ability. The terms 'design for all' and 'universal design' are also widely used.

Interaction Design   This approach to design is focused on satisfying the needs and desires of the people who will use the outcomes of the design process whether they are interactive digital products, environments, systems and services. The main focus is upon the anticipated behaviour of the user rather than the form of the product.

Issigonis, Sir Alec (1906–88)   A British car designer who is best known for his designs for the 1948 Morris Minor, the 1959 Austin Mini and the 1962 Morris 1100. Of these, the Mini made the greatest impact on world markets.

Itten, Johannes (1888–1967)   Itten was largely responsible for the preliminary course at the Bauhaus. His ideas were too mystical for Walter Gropius, who dismissed him in 1923. He went on to form his own school in Berlin and, later, to become the director of the art schools in Zurich and Krefeld.

Ive, Jonathan (1967–)   A British designer, who studied industrial design at Northumbria University. After university, Ive went on to become a cofounder of London design agency, Tangerine and, subsequently, the senior vice president of industrial design at Apple Inc., based in Palo Alto in the USA. He is best known for his designs for the iMac, the iPod, the iPhone and the iPad.

Jacobsen, Arne (1902–71)   The work of the Danish architect and designer Arne Jacobsen is synonymous with the concept of Danish modernism.

He was influenced by Le Corbusier and created highly influential bent-wood furniture items in the 1950s – 'Ant' and 'Swan' being the best known. His Cylinda Line stainless steel tableware for Stelton remains much admired internationally.

Jiricna, Eva (1938–) A Czech architect–designer who came to London in 1968 and became known through her retail interiors for the fashion-shop owner Joseph Ettedgui. Her simple modernist work became identified with the High-Tech style and was characterized by its use of glass and chrome. She went on to collaborate with several modernist architects on the interiors of their buildings.

Jongerius, Hella (1963–) A Dutch designer who studied design at the Industrial Design Academy in Eindhoven. She subsequently attracted international attention through her work for the Dutch design label, Droog Design. She established her design studio, JongeriusLab, in Rotterdam in 2000 and created a range of products, among them ceramic objects, textiles and furnishings.

Jugendstil The German name for the French term, Art Nouveau, *Judendstil* was used to describe the revolutionary, new, turn-of-the-century style that swept across Europe at that time. The term is used to describe its extensive manifestations in countries of the former Eastern Bloc.

Kåge, Wilhelm (1889–1960) Trained as a fine artist, Kåge began working for the Swedish ceramic company Gustavsberg in 1917 and was responsible for encouraging it to use modern, democratic designs. In the 1930s, he produced several ceramic ranges, including Praktika and Pyro, but in 1949 he returned to painting.

Kiesler, Frederick (1896–1965) Associated with the Viennese Secession group, the Dadaists and the De Stijl Group in Holland, Kiesler left Europe and went to the USA in the late 1920s, continuing to work as an artist/architect/designer in that country. His numerous designs included a range of aluminium furniture which he created in the 1930s.

Klint, Kaare (1888–1954) A Danish architect and furniture designer, working in the 1920s in Copenhagen, who developed an anthropometric approach to designing furniture. His 1933 deck chair is based on a vernacular model, as were several of his other designs. Rud Rasmussen produced many of his designs.

Knoll The Knoll furniture company was formed in the USA in the late 1940s by a German cabinet-maker, Hans Knoll, and his wife, Florence Schust, a graduate of the Cranbrook Academy. From the beginning they used modern designers, including Eero Saarinen and Harry Bertoia, and established a reputation as a manufacturer of progressive furniture designs.

Kuramata, Shiro (1934–91) A Japanese furniture and interior designer who opened his own office in Tokyo in 1965. Kuramata combined traditional Japanese minimalist ideas with contemporary influences to create his highly original furniture designs. He created interiors for a number of the shops of the Japanese fashion designer Issey Miyake.

Le Corbusier (1887–1968) Born Charles Edouard Jeanneret, this Swiss architect became one of the leading figures of the Modern Movement in architecture and design. His 1920s buildings were typically white and flat-roofed, in imitation of Mediterranean architecture, and he achieved a simplicity of form in all his work. Where his design is concerned, he is best known for his Grand Confort chair and his Chaise Longue which he worked on with his assistant, Charlotte Perriand.

Loewy, Raymond (1893–1986) Born in France, Loewy went to the USA in 1919 and became one of the city's first consultant industrial designers. His first client was Sigmund Gestetner, for whom he restyled a duplicator in 1929. Through the 1930s, 40s and 50s he went on to design many products for a number of clients including the Hupp Motor Company, Frigidaire, Lucky Strike and Studebaker.

Loos, Adolf (1870–1933) An Austrian architect who, in 1908, wrote a much-quoted article entitled 'Ornament and Crime' in which he outlined what he believed to be the decadence of architectural ornament. His own designs from the early century included the Steiner House and the Müller house.

Mackintosh, Charles Rennie (1868–1928) A Scottish architect who worked as part of a group known as the Glasgow Four. He created a number of buildings, interiors, furniture pieces and decorative items in what was seen at the time as a Scottish version of Art Nouveau. His designs were very influential in Vienna.

Magistretti, Vico (1920–) An Italian architect and furniture designer who was trained in Milan and worked there, after the Second World War, particularly for the Arflex and Cassina furniture companies. His brightly coloured, plastic moulded chairs of the early 1960s were among the first of their kind. He has continued to design influential furniture items, including his Sindbad chair of 1981.

Maldonado, Tomas (1922–) Born in Buenos Aires, the design theoretician Maldonado was invited by Max Bill to take over the directorship of the Hochschüle für Gestaltung at Ulm, where he remained until the mid-1960s. Maldonado favoured a systematic approach to the design process.

Marimekko A Finnish fabric company and shop established by Armi Ratia in Helsinki in 1951. Marimekko (which means Mary's frock) is best known for its bold printed fabrics which are made up into simple clothing.

Mathsson, Bruno (1907–88) A Swedish furniture designer who, with G. A. Berg and Josef Frank, was responsible for creating the Swedish Modern design movement. He used wood and hemp webbing rather than tubular steel and leather and his most famous chair, created in 1934, is still produced today by Dux Mobel.

Maugham, Syrie (1879–1955) An English interior decorator who took the ideas of Elsie de Wolfe forward in a British context. Maugham was known for her all-white rooms and for her use of modernist components, including rugs by Marion Dorn. She had a number of high-class clients, Wallis Simpson among them.

Mellor, David (1930–) A British designer, based in Sheffield, who established his own cutlery and product manufacturing company and kitchen-equipment retail outlets. Trained at the Royal College of Art in the 1950s, Mellor is best known for his designs for cutlery; 'Pride' won him a Design Council award in 1959.

Memphis Led in Milan by Ettore Sottsass and supported by a group of international colleagues and young associates, the Memphis project launched itself with a show of Pop-inspired furniture prototypes in Milan in 1981. Annual shows continued into the 1990s. The group's aim was to revitalise design as a cultural concept rather than one which was led by industry and commerce.

Mendini, Alessandro (1931–) A participant in the Italian Radical Design movement, Mendini began his professional career working for the architectural group, Nizzoli Associates. He went on to edit a number of design magazines, among them *Casabella*, *Modo* and *Domus*.

Mies van der Rohe, Ludwig (1886–1969) A German architect who, along with Walter Gropius and Le Corbusier, is one of the most renowned exponents of the Modern Movement in architecture and design. Mies was the last director of the Bauhaus. From there he went to the USA, where he worked in Chicago. In design terms, he is best known for his steel and leather furniture items, especially his Barcelona chair of 1929.

Miyake, Issey (1935–) Trained in Paris as a graphic designer, the Japanese fashion designer Miyake opened his own studio in Tokyo in 1970. He cleverly combined French couture (the influence of Vionnet was strong) with Japanese dress to create an internationally appealing new fashion idiom, as at home on the stage as the catwalk.

Modernism The general term used to describe the cultural phenomenon of the early years of the twentieth century that sought to ally cultural practice and the aesthetic it embraced with the flow of modern life and its influences. It was especially strong in the arena of architecture and design, which constituted the material stuff of modernity.

Modern Movement A term coined by Nikolaus Pevsner in 1936 to describe the collective efforts of architects and designers to develop a new philosophy and aesthetic that was in tune with the spirit of modernity, especially the realities of mass production and the dominance of the machine.

Moholy-Nagy, László (1895–1946) Born in Hungary, Moholy-Nagy moved to Berlin in 1920. In 1922, he became a staff member at the Bauhaus in Weimar. Influenced by Eastern European Constructivism be worked as a painter and photographer and went to Chicago in the

1930s to set up the New Bauhaus, later known as the Institute of Design.

Mollino, Carlo (1905–73)   An Italian furniture designer, based in Turin, who created furniture pieces in the 1940s and 50s, which he described as 'streamlined-surreal'. His baroque, wooden forms contrasted sharply with the more rational designs emerging from Milan in those years.

Morrison, Jasper (1959–)   A British furniture and product designer who introduced a new, slightly nostalgic but eminently modern aesthetic into design in the 1980s. Morrison has worked with many international clients including FSB in Germany and Cappellini in Italy.

Murray, Keith (1892–1981)   A New Zealander by origin, the architect-trained Keith Murray turned to designing ceramic and glass products in the 1930s, working with James Powell's Whitefriars Glassworks and Wedgwood, among others. His simple, geometric designs contrasted strongly with many others which emerged at that time.

Muthesius, Hermann (1861–1934)   A German diplomat who travelled to England at the end of the nineteenth century and wrote a book, *Das Englische Haus* (1905), about the architecture he discovered there. He was a major force behind the formation of the German Werkbund and did much to promote German design for industry in the early twentieth century.

Nelson, George (1907–86)   The American architect and designer George Nelson, who began his career as an architectural journalist, created numerous modern artefacts for progressive clients, including Herman Miller. He is best known for his Storagewall and his office designs from the years immediately following the Second World War.

Neo-Functionalism   A term used to describe the return to an austere, rational geometric aesthetic that occurred in Germany in the years after 1945. it was epitomized by the work of Dieter Rams for the Braun company and by many of the designs emerging from the design school at Ulm.

Newson, Marc (1963–)   Australian by birth the product designer finally settled in London and formed his own studio in the late 1990s. His characteristic organic form was injected into a wide range of products, from furniture to a car for Ford. He also created a number of interior spaces for shops and restaurants in a similar style.

Nike   The Nike training shoe manufacturer, based in the USA, was among the first to embrace the idea of developing many different stylistics in its products at any one time to make running shoes part of an ever-changing lifestyle choice on the part of the consumer. It was a marketing philosophy that depended upon rapid stylistic turnover and automated manufacturing.

Nizzoli, Marcello (1887–1969)   Trained as a graphic designer, Nizzoli was hired by Adriano Olivetti in 1938. He worked on the Italian company's electrical machines and produced some elegant typewriters in the 1940s and 50s – among them the Lexicon 80 and the Lettera 22. He also designed the Mirella sewing machine for Necchi in 1956.

Noyes, Eliot (1910–77) An American industrial designer who worked as a curator for the Museum of Modern Art in New York and was subsequently hired by Thomas Watson, the son of the founder of the IBM Company. From 1956, he worked with the graphic designer, Paul Rand, as the corporate design director creating a number of striking office machines.

Nurmesniemi, Antti (1927–2003) and Eskolin, Vuokko (1930–) Husband and wife designers. Nurmesniemi was a Finnish interior and industrial designer and his wife is a textile designer, who markets her fabrics under the name of Vuokko. Nurmesniemi set up his own design office in Finland in 1956 and worked on interiors for many clients, sometimes in collaboration with his wife and sometimes alone.

Olivetti, Camillo (1868–1943) and Adriano (1901–60) The former was the founder of the Olivetti Office Machinery Company in 1908. He designed the first typewriter himself. His son, Adriano, took over the reins of the company in the 1920s and was responsible for hiring some of the designers who worked with Olivetti, including Marcello Nizzoli and Ettore Sottsass.

Panton, Verner (1926–98) A Danish architect and designer, working in Switzerland, who is best known for his furniture designs from the 1960s. He created the first one-piece, cantilever plastic chair and his 1960 Stacking Chair was produced by Herman Miller.

Paulsson, Gregor (1889–1964) The Swedish architect Paulsson was the first Director of the Swedish design society – the Svenska Sjlšdfšreningen. In 1919, he wrote a book about design entitled *More Beautiful Everyday Things*, which was highly influential in Sweden. He made a significant contribution to the organization of the 1930 Stockholm Exhibition.

Pentagram A British design consultancy that was established in 1971 on the basis of a graphic design consultancy from the 1950s called Fletcher, Forbes and Gill. Among several the product designers, Kenneth Grange and Daniel Weil joined the group in the 1970s and 1990s, respectively.

Perriand, Charlotte (1903–99) Between 1927 and 1937, the French designer Charlotte Perriand worked with Le Corbusier on his furniture designs, making a significant input. Later she visited Japan and became an adviser on arts and crafts to that country. She continued to design after the Second World War, focusing on interiors.

Pesce, Gaetano (1939–) An Italian architect–designer who has worked in a highly individual way since the 1960s producing, among other designs, nihilistic, 'decaying' objects. He has worked with Cassina on several occasion and divides his time between Venice and New York, where he continues to practise and teach.

Pevsner, Nikolaus (1902–83)   A German-born art historian whose writings about modern architecture and design have been very influential. He helped to define and champion the idea of the Modern Movement in his book of 1936, *Pioneers of the Modern Movement* (later *Pioneers of Modern Design*).

Pininfarina, Battista (1893–1966)   With his roots in coachbuilding, the Italian car manufacturer and designer Pininfarina embraced a sculptural approach to his craft. His creations for Alfa Romeo and Lancia – including the Lancia Aprilia of 1937 – were ahead of their time stylistically and led into dramatic post-war designs such as the 1947 Cisitalia.

Ponti, Gio (1891–1979)   An Italian architect–designer and editor of *Domus* magazine, Ponti worked as a designer of architecture, furniture and decorative objects from the 1920s. He sustained his own, highly individualistic aesthetic through these years and his many clients include Fontana Arte, Arflex and Cassina.

Pop   The Pop design movement was a spontaneous British phenomenon of the mid-1960s. It focused on fashion and lifestyle accompaniments and stressed instant impact and ephemerality. It was a reaction, on one level, to the timeless forms of modernism.

Porsche   A Stuttgart-based car manufacturer, named after its founder, Ferdinand Porsche, the designer of the Volkswagen 'Beetle'. Known for its upmarket, stylish products the company created a number of what became classic cars from the 1960s onwards, including the models 911 (designed by 'Butzi' Porsche), the 928 and, most recently, the Boxster, designed by Harm Lagaay.

Postmodernism   The catch-all name given to all the architectural and design manifestations of the late 1980s onwards which deliberately sidestepped the strategies of high modernism and sought to relate to the sphere of consumption, rather than that of production. It was expressed in a number of different ways, from nostalgia to the use of strongly expressive forms of many kinds.

Race, Ernest (1913–64)   Trained initially as an architect, the British furniture designer Ernest Race established Race Furniture Ltd in 1946, the same year in which he designed an influential, aluminium-framed chair. He went to create a range of steel rod chairs for the 1951 Festival of Britain.

Rams, Dieter (1932–)   A German product designer who made a name for himself working with the Braun Company, from 1955. He created for them a number of domestic machines that came to typify the sparse, geometric style of much post-war German design.

Rationalism   The term used to describe Italy's contribution to inter-war architectural and design modernism, as expressed by Guiseppe Terragni and others. For a short period of time Mussolini flirted with Rationalism as his official style but he moved away from it towards a more classically inspired Italian modern style, known as Novecento.

Reich, Lilly (1885–1947)   A German interior and furniture designer, working in the modernist idiom, who collaborated with Mies van der Rohe from 1927. Their first project was for the Weissenhof exhibition of that year. She also worked with him two years later on the Barcelona exhibition and taught him at the Bauhaus from 1932.

Riemerschmid, Richard (1868–1957)   A German designer, based in Munich, who developed a range of standardized furniture for serial production in the first decade of the twentieth century. He was an early member, with Peter Behrens, of the Deutscher Werkbund.

Rietveld, Gerrit (1888–1964)   Born in Utrecht and trained as a cabinet-maker, the Dutch architect–designer became a member of the De Stijl group and created a number of highly influential chairs, among them the Red-Blue chair of 1917/18 and the Zig-Zag chair of 1934. Both have become classic designs.

Rodchenko, Alexander (1891–1956)   A Russian Constructivist sculptor–designer who – with his wife, the textile designer Stepanova, and others – worked on interiors and street constructions at the time of the 1917 Russian Revolution. In the 1920s he moved closer to Tatlin's idea of the 'artist-engineer' and began designing utility items, such as furnishings and clothing.

Rosenthal   A German ceramics manufacturing company, founded in Bavaria in 1897. Through the latter half of the twentieth century Rosenthal encouraged a number of international designers – Tapio Wirkkala, Raymond Loewy and Walter Gropius among them – to work with them on products presented as part of its Studio range.

Ruhlmann, Jacques-Emile (1879–1933)   An exponent of the exclusive, French decorative style of the 1920s Ruhlmann used exotic woods in his furniture and interiors. His Hôtel du Collectionneur pavilion at the 1925 Paris 'Exhibition of Decorative Arts' exposed his luxurious style to a large audience.

Saarinen, Eero (1910–61)   The son of Eliel Saarinen, the Finnish archi-tect–designer Eero Saarinen went to the USA with his father in 1923. He studied architecture at Yale and, in 1940, he worked with Charles Eames on a range of moulded plywood furniture pieces. In the 1950s, Knoll manufactured his furniture designs, among them the famous Tulip chair.

Sapper, Richard (1932–)   A German-born designer who gravitated towards Italy, worked in Milan in the office of Marco Zanuso, collab-orating with him on a number of projects for Brionvega, and set up his office there in the mid-1970s. His lighting designs have been especially influential and his Tizio desk-light is a design classic.

Sarpaneva, Timo (1926–)   A Finnish designer of glass, ceramics, textiles and metalwork who was employed by the Iittala Glassworks in 1950 and who showed his work at the Milan Triennale exhibitions of the 1950s, winning several prizes. He helped make the world aware of modern Finnish design.

Sason, Sixten (1912–69)   A Swedish consultant product designer who trained as a silversmith and who went on to work for Electrolux, Hasselblad and Saab Motors, for whom he designed the stylish Saab 92 automobile.

Sipek, Boris (1949–)   A Czech designer who settled in Holland, where he now works. Sipek is known for his designs for domestic objects, which combine modernism with luxurious decoration. His glass and ceramic designs, in particular, manifest a baroque quality.

Sony   The Japanese consumer electronics manufacturer that was the first to think about the aesthetic design of its products as well as their advanced technology. The Sony Walkman, launched in the early 1980s, combined innovative design and technology with an understanding about lifestyle.

Sottsass, Ettore (1917–)   An Italian architect–designer who set up a consultant practice in Milan in the years after the Second World War and who went on to become the leading figure in the world of Radical Design in Italy. He was a consultant for many years for Olivetti and masterminded the Memphis experiment of the 1980s.

Starck, Philippe (1949–)   A French product designer who is widely acknowledged as a 'designer-star'. His designs range from interior designs to mass produced consumer goods such as toothbrushes, chairs and even houses. Starck was educated in Paris at the École Camondo and, in 1968, founded his first design firm, which specialized in inflatable objects. He has worked independently as an interior designer and as a product designer since 1975 and in 1982 he designed the interior for the private apartments of the French President François Mitterrand.

Streamform   The name given to the organic style of American automobile and products of the inter-war years the forms of which had been determined by 'streamlining' – making them aerodynamic and fast-moving. In static objects, such as irons and fruit juicers, the style was transferred metaphorically to denote futurity.

Superstudio   Formed in Florence in 1966 Superstudio was one of the architectural and design groups that spearheaded the Radical Design movement in Italy in those years. The group worked on a number of experimental projects and designed a table that was manufactured by Zanotta.

Sustainable Design   Also referred to as environmental design, environmentally sustainable design and environmentally conscious design, this concept means designing physical objects, the built environment and services to support the principles of economic, social and ecological sustainability. Using recycled and ecologically sound materials is an important aspect of it as is the disassembly and reuse of products.

Swatch   A Swiss watch manufacturer, which rejected the idea of 'a watch for life' and introduced, in its place, the concept of the fashion watch that changed according to the clothes and tastes of its wearers.

Swedish Modern The term coined at the New York World's Fair of 1939 to describe the soft, humanistic version of modernism that was evolved by the Swedish designers such as Bruno Mathsson and Josef Frank. It became a very influential style in the post-war years.

Tatlin, Vladimir (1885–1953) A Russian Constructivist sculptor who turned, after the 1917 Revolution, to working on functional projects such as clothing. He is best known for his Monument to the Third International of 1919–20, in the creation of which he set out to work like an engineer in the service of the Revolution.

Teague, Walter Dorwon (1883–1960) A pioneer American consultant industrial designer of the 1930s, Teague is often called the 'dean of industrial design'. His office worked with Eastman Kodak for many years, among other clients, and he chaired the Board of Design for the New York World's Fair of 1939, as well as designing a number of its exhibits.

van de Velde, Henry (1863–1957) A Belgian Art Nouveau architect and designer who moved to Germany in 1900 to run the Weimar School of Applied Arts. He was influenced by William Morris, wrote extensively about design and was a founder member of the Deutscher Werkbund.

Van Doren, Harold (1895–1957) An American consultant industrial designer who, like his colleagues, worked with a number of companies throughout the 1930s, including Philco and Goodyear. He moved into this new profession from the museum world and in 1940 he published a book entitled *Industrial Design: A Practical Guide*.

Venturi, Robert (1925–) An American architect who, in 1966, wrote his influential book *Complexity and Contradiction in Architecture*, which heralded the advent of postmodernism in architecture and design. Through the 1960s and 70s, he worked on a number of Pop architectural projects and he designed a range of furniture pieces for Knoll in the early 1980s. More recently he designed an extension for London's National Gallery.

Wagenfeld, Wilhelm (1900–79) A German Bauhaus graduate who worked at the Lausitzer Glassworks from 1935 to 1947 and who went on to run his own design studio in Stuttgart. Considered one of Germany's leading designers, he worked on a wide range of products, from glass to ceramics to cutlery to lighting.

Wagner, Otto (1841–1918) An Austrian proto-modernist architect–designer who, in the 1890s, worked at the edge of Art Nouveau but who showed more classical tendencies by the end of the decade. He pioneered the use of aluminium in buildings – for example, in his design for the Post Office in Vienna and for the feet of some of his furniture designs from the turn of the century.

Westwood, Vivienne (1941–) A British fashion designer who emerged from the subculture of Punk in the 1970s and who has remained a subversive figure in spite of her commercial success. She is known for her nostalgic clothes and her unconventional approach towards fashion and the fashion industry.

Wirkkala, Tapio (1915–85) One of Finland's superstar designers of the post-war era, who was employed by the Iittala glass company in 1947 and who went on to create striking decorative art objects and designs through the next three decades. He came to international recognition through his work that was exhibited at the Milan Triennales in the 1950s. Outside Finland, he worked both for Venini and Rosenthal.

Wright, Russel (1904–76) An American product designer who made his name through his ceramic dinner services created in the 1930s, which were marketed under the name American Modern. He was one of the first to use aluminium in a progressive manner, again in hospitality objects. His furniture designs also reached a large audience.

Notes

Introduction

1 Foster, H. *Design and Crime*. London and New York: Verso; 2002. p. 22.
2 McCracken, G. *Culture and Consumption: New approaches to the symbolic character of consumer goods and activities*. Bloomington and Indianapolis: Indiana University Press; 1990. p. xi.
3 Huyssen, A. *After the Great Divide: Modernism, Mass Culture and Postmodernism*. (Bloomington and Indianapolis: Indiana University Press; 1986) and Bourdieu, P. *Distinction: A Social Critique of the Judgement of Taste* (London and New York: Routledge and Kegan Paul, 1986).

1 Consuming modernity

1 Saisselin, R. G. *Bricobracomania: The Bourgeois and the Bibelot* (London: Thames and Hudson, 1985), p. 64.
2 McKendrick, N., Brewer, J., Plumb, J. H. (eds) *The Birth of Consumer Society: The Commercialization of Eighteenth-Century England* (London: Hutchinson, 1982); Campbell, C. *The Romantic Ethic and the Spirit of Modern Consumerism* (Oxford, Basil Blackwell, 1987); Weatherill, L. *Consumer Behaviour and Material Culture in Britain 1660–1760* (London and New York: Routledge, 1988); and Vickery, A. *The Gentleman's Daughter: Women's Lives in Georgian England* (New Haven and London: Yale University Press, 1998).
3 Weatherill, 1988, p. 77.
4 See Logan, T. *The Victorian Parlour: A Cultural Study* (Cambridge: Cambridge University Press, 2001).
5 Girling Budd, A. 'Comfort and Gentility, Furnishings by Gillows, Lancaster 1840–1855' in McKellar, S. and Sparke, P. *Interior Design and Identity* (Manchester: Manchester University Press, 2004).
6 Fraser, W. H. *The Coming of the Mass Market, 1850–1914* (London and Basingstoke: Macmillan, 1981).
7 Bushman, R. L. The *Refinement of America: Persons, Houses, Cities* (New York: Vintage Books, 1993).
8 Bronner, S. J. *Consuming Visions: Accumulation and Display of Goods in America, 1880–1920* (Wintherthur, Delaware: The Henry Francis du Pont Wintherthur Museum, 1989).
9 Hultenen, K. 'From Parlor to Living Room: Domestic Space. Interior Decoration, and the Culture of Personality' in Bronner, 1989. pp. 157–189.
10 Walkowitz, J. *Prostitution and Victorian Society: Women, Class and the State* (Cambridge: Cambridge University Press, 1980) and Rappoport, E. D.

Shopping for Pleasure: Women in the Making of London's West End (Princeton, New Jersey: Princeton University Press, 2000).

11   Wolff, J. 'The Culture of Separate Spheres: The Role of Culture in 19th Century Public and Private Life' in *Feminine Sentences: Essays on Women and Culture* (Cambridge: Polity, 1990).

12   Wilson, E. *The Sphinx in the City* (London: Virago, 1991).

13   Leach, W. *Lands of Desire: Merchants, Power and the Rise of a New American Culture* (New York: Vintage Books, 1994).

14   These include Bowlby, R. *Just Looking: Consumer Culture in Dreiser, Gissing and Zola* (New York: Methuen, 1985) and Miller, M. B. *The Bon Marche: Bourgeois Culture and the Department Store 1869–1920* (New Jersey: Princeton University Press, 1981).

15   Bronner, 1989, p. 8.

16   Giedion, S. *Mechanisation Takes Command: A Contribution to Anonymous History* (New York: W. W. Norton and Co., 1948).

17   Giedion, 1948.

18   Sparke, P. *A Century of Car Design* (London: Mitchell Beazley, 2002), p. 10.

19   Wharton, E. and Codman Jr, O. *The Decoration of Houses* (London: Batsford, 1898).

20   Milan, S. 'Refracting the gaselier: understanding Victorian responses to domestic gas lighting' in Bryden, I. and Floyd, J. *Domestic Space: Reading the Nineteenth-Century Interior* (Manchester and New York: Manchester University Press, 1999).

21   Wilson, S. *Adorned in Dreams: Fashion and Modernity* (London: Virago, 1985) and Breward, C. *The Hidden Consumer, Masculinities, Fashion and City Life* (Manchester: Manchester University Press, 1999).

22   Barthes, R. *Mythologies* (London, Jonathon Cape, 1983).

23   Veblen, T. *The Theory of the Leisure Class* (London: Unwin, 1970 [originally 1899]).

24   Wulf, K. H. (ed.) *The Sociology of Georg Simmel* (Glencoe: The Free Press, 1950).

25   Beetham, M. *A Magazine of Her Own: Domesticity and Desire in the Woman's Magazine, 1800–1914* (New York and London: Routledge, 1996) and Scanlon, J. *Inarticulate Longings: The Ladies' Home Journal and the Promises of Consumer Culture* (New York and London: Routledge, 1995)

26   Hine, T. *The Total Package* (Boston: Little Brown, 1995).

27   Strasser, S. *Satisfaction Guaranteed: The Making of the American Mass Market* (New York: Pantheon Books, 1989).

28   Slater, D. *Consumer Culture and Modernity* (Cambridge: Polity Press, 1997).

29   Alexander, S. 'Becoming a Woman in London in the 1920s and 1930s' in Alexander, S, (ed.) *Becoming a Woman and Other Essays in Nineteenth- and Twentieth-Century Feminist History* (London: Virago, 1994), pp. 203–24.

30   Harrison, H. A. (ed.) *Dawn of a New Day: The New York World's Fair, 1939/40* (New York: New York University Press, 1980).

31   See Strasser, S. *Satisfaction Guaranteed: The Making of the American Mass Market* (New York: Pantheon, 1989) and Tedlow, R. S. *New and Improved: The Story of Mass Marketing in America* (New York: Basic Books, 1990).

32   Forde, K. 'Celluloid Dreams: The Marketing of Cutex in America, 1916–1935', *Journal of Design History* 2002; 15 (3): 175–90.

33   Scanlon, J. *Inarticulate Longings: The Ladies' Home Journal, Gender and the Promises of Consumer Culture* (New York and London: Routledge, 1995).

34   Forde, 2002, p. 178.

35   Peiss, K. *Hope in a Jar: The Making of America's Beauty Culture* (New York: Henry Holt & Co. Inc., 1998).

36 See Bayley, S. Harley Earl (London: Trefoil, 1990) and Clarke, S. 'Managing Design: the Art and Colour Section at General Motors, 1927–1941' *Journal of Design History* 1999; 12, (1): 65–79.

37 Clarke, 1999.

38 Frederick. C. *Selling Mrs. Consumer: Christine Frederick & The Rise of Household Efficiency* (New York: Business Bourse, 1929).

39 Frederick, 1929, p. 22.

40 Swiencicki, M. A. 'Consuming Brotherhood: Men's Culture, Style and Recreation as Consumer Culture, 1880–1930' in Glickman, L. B. *Consumer Society in American History: A Reader* (Ithaca and London: Cornell University Press), 1999, p. 207.

41 Swiencicki, 1999, p. 226.

42 Gartman, D. *Auto Opium: A Social History of American Automobile Design* (New York and London: Routledge, 1994).

43 Jeremiah, D. 'Filling Up: The British Experience, 1896–1940' *Journal of Design History* 1995; 8 (2): 97–116.

44 Lewis, D.L. and Goldstein, L. (eds) *The Automobile and American Culture* (Michigan: University of Michigan Press, 1980, 1983).

45 O'Connell, S. *The Car in British Society: Class, Gender and Motoring, 1896–1939* (Manchester: Manchester University Press, 1998), p. 43.

46 Gronberg. T. *Designing Modernity: Exhibiting the City in 1920s Paris* (Manchester: Manchester University Press, 1998), p. 62.

47 Gieben-Gamal, E. 'Feminine spaces, modern experiences: The design and display strategies of British hairdressing salons in the 19230s and 1930s' in McKellar, S. and Sparke, P. (eds) *Interior Design and Identity* Manchester: Manchester University Press, 2004).

48 Clarke, C. *Tupperware: The Promise of Plastic in 1950s America* (Washington and London: Smithsonian Institution Press, 1999).

49 Light, A. *Forever England: Femininity, Literature and Conservatism Between the Wars* (London and New York: Routledge, 1991.)

50 Ryan, F. S. *The Ideal Home Through the Twentieth Century* (London: Hazar Publishing, 1997)

51 Massey. A. *Hollywood Beyond the Screen* (Oxford: Berg, 2000).

52 Fine, B. and Leopold, E. *The World of Consumption* (London: Routledge, 1993).

2 The impact of technology

1 Ford, H. 'Mass Production' in *Encyclopaedia Britannica* (1926).

2 For a longer discussion see Fine, B. and Leopold, E. *The World of Consumption* (London: Routledge, 1993), in which the authors outline the concept of 'systems of provision', which cross the production/consumption divide.

3 Examples such as James Nasmyth's steam hammer of 1838 and James Wyatt's pumping engine of 1783 were among the many tools developed to exploit this new source of power.

4 Clark, H. *The Role of the Designer in the Early Mass Production Industry* (unpublished PhD thesis, University of Brighton, 1982).

5 Habakkuk, H. J. *American and British Technology in the Nineteenth Century: The Search for Labour-Saving Inventions* (Cambridge: Cambridge University Press,1962).

6 Giedion, S. *Mechanisation Takes Command: A Contribution to Anonymous History* (New York: W. W. Norton and Co., 1969 [1948]).

7 Hounshell, D. A. *From the American System to Mass Production, 1800–1932* (Baltimore and London: John Hopkins Press, 1984).

8   The Austrian Postal Savings Bank building of 1904–06 and the office building for the *Die Zeit* newspaper of the same years both used aluminium. For more examples of early work in aluminium see Nichols, S. *Aluminum by Design* (Pittsburgh: Carnegie Museum of Art, 2001).

9   Clifford, H. and Turner, E. 'Modern Metal' in Greenhalgh, P. (ed.) *Art Nouveau 1890–1914* (London: V & A Publications, 2000).

10 Friedel, R. *Pioneer Plastic: The Making and Selling of Celluloid* (Wisconsin: University of Wisconsin Press, 1983).

11 The interior decorator, Elsie de Wolfe, was responsible for this innovation.

12 Frederick W. Taylor developed a system of rationalization through the analysis of work which came to be known as 'time and motion studies'.

13 Beecher, C. and Stowe, H. B. *The American Woman's Home* (New York: J. B. Ford and Co., 1869).

14 Cowan, R. S. *More Work for Mother: The Ironies Household Technology from the Open Hearth to the Microwave* (New York: Basic Books, 1983) and Strasser, S. *Never Done: A History of American Housework* (New York: Pantheon Books, 1982.

15 Frederick, C. *The New Housekeeping: Efficiency Studies in Home Management* (New York: Garden City, Doubleday Page, 1913).

16 Sparke, P. 'Cookware to Cocktail Shakers' in Nichols, 2001.

17 Forty, A. *Objects of Desire* (London: Thames and Hudson, 1986).

18 Habakkuk, 1962.

19 Sparke, P. *Electrical Appliances* (London, Bell and Hyman, 1987).

20 P. Frankl, *New Dimensions* (New York: Payson & Clarke, 1928), p. 23.

21 Kwint, M., Breward, C., and Aynsley, J. *Material Memories: Design and Evocation* (Oxford: Berg, 1999).

22 Barthes, R. *Mythologies* (Paris: Editions du Seuil, 1957), p. 97.

23 Freidel. R. *Pioneer Plastic: The Making and Selling of Celluloid* (Wisconsin: University of Wisconsin Press, 1983).

24 Meikle, J. L. *American Plastic: A Cultural History* (New Brunswick, New Jersey: Rutgers University Press, 1995.), p. 6.

25 Meikle, 1995, p. 106.

26 Meikle, 1995, p. 118.

27 Bayley, S. *In Good Shape: Style in Industrial Products 1900–1960* (London: Design Council, 1979).

28 Nichols. S. (ed.) *Aluminum by Design* (New York: Harry N. Abrams, 2000).

29 See Sparke, P. 'Cookware to Cocktail Shakers: The Domestication of Aluminum in the United States, 1900–1939' in Nichols, 2000.

30 D. Dohner, 'Modern technique of designing' *Modern Plastics*, (14 March 1937), p. 71.

31 Grief. M. *Depression Modern: The Thirties Style in America* (New York: Universe Books, 1975).

32 Pulos, A. *American Design Ethic: A History of Industrial Design to 1940* (Cambridge, MA: The MIT Press, 1983), pp. 348–53.

33 Blaser, W. *Mies van der Rohe: Furniture and Interiors* (Hauppauge, NY: Barrons Educational Series, Inc., 1982), De Fusco, R. *Le Corbusier designer i mobile del 1929* Milan: Documenti di Casabella, Electa, 1976) and Wilk, C. *Marcel Breuer: Furniture and Interiors* (New York: Museum of Modern Art, 1981).

34 Davies, K. 'Finmar and the Furniture of the Future: the sale of Alvar Aalto's plywood furniture in the UK, 1934–1939' *Journal of Design History* 1998; 11 (2): 145–56.

35 Handley, S. *Nylon: The Manmade Fashion Revolution* (London: Bloomsbury, 1999).

3 The designer for industry

1   Clark. H. *The Role of the Designer in Early Mass Production Industry* (unpublished PhD thesis, University of Brighton, 1986).

2   Forty, A. *Objects of Desire* (London: Thames and Hudson, 1986).

3   Atterbury, P. and Irvine, L. *The Doulton Story* (London: Victoria and Albert Museum, 1979).

4   Sparke, P. *Electrical Appliances* (London: Bell and Hyman, 1987).

5   Quoted in Naylor, G. *The Arts and Crafts Movement: A Study of its Sources, Ideals and Influence on Design Theory* (London: Studio Vista, 1971).

6   Halen, S. *Christopher Dresser* (Oxford: Phaidon, 1990).

7   Schwartz, F. 'Commofirt Signs: Peter Behrens and the AEG, and the Trademark' *Journal of Design History* 1996; 9 (3): 153–84.

8   Aynsley, J. *A Century of Graphic Design* (London: Mitchell Beazley, 2001). p. 6.

9   Hine, T. *The Total Package* (Boston: Little, Brown and Company, 1995. p. 84.

10 Hine, 1995, p. 87.

11 Leach, W. *Lands of Desire: Merchants, Power and the Rise of a New American Culture* (New York: Vintage Books, 1994).

12 Walker, L. 'Women and Architecture' in Attfield, J. and Kirkham, P. (eds) *A Vire from the Interior: Feminism, Women and Design* (London: The Women's Press, 1989).

13 Howe, K. S., Frelinghuysen, A. C. and Voorsanger, C. H. (eds) *Herter Brothers: Furniture and Interiors for a Gilded Age* (New York: Harry N. Abrams, Inc., Publishers, in association with the Museum of Fine Atrs, Houston, 1994).

14 Peck, A. and Irish, C. *Candace Wheeler: The Art and Enterprise of American Design 1875–1900* (New Haven and London: Yale University Press, 2002).

15 Hampton. M. *Legendary Decorators of the Twentieth Century* (New York: Doubleday, 1992).

16 Kirkham, P. Sparke, P and Gura, J. B. ' "A Woman's Place…"'? Women Interior Designers' in Kirkham (ed.) *Women Designers in the USA 1900–2000: Diversity and Difference* (New Haven and London: Yale University Press, 2000).

17 Pevsner, N. *Pioneers of Modern Design* (Harmondsworth: Penguin, 1968), pp. 34–5.

18 P. McConnell, 'SID – American hallmark of design integrity' *Art and Industry* 1949; 47, p. 84.

19 Sloan, A. P. *My Years with General Motors* (New York: Mcfadden-Bartell, 1965).

20 Sloan, 1965, p. 269.

21 Meikle, J. L. *Twentieth Century Limited: Industrial Design in America, 1925–1939* (Philadelphia: Temple University Press, 1979).

22 Meikle, 1979, p. 8.

23 See Sparke, P. 'From a Lipstick to a Steamship: The Growth of the American Industrial Design Profession' in Bishop, T. (ed.) *Design History: Fad or Function?* (London: Design Council, 1978).

24 Ewen, S. *All Consuming Images: The Politics of Style in Contemporary Culture* (New York: Basic Books, 1988).

25 Ewen, 1988, p, 45.

26 Teague, W. D. *Design This Day: the Technique of Order in the Machine Age* (London: The Studio Publications, 1940).

27 Bel Geddes, N. *Horizons* (Boston: Little, Brown and Company, 1932).

28 Forty, A. *Objects of Desire: Design and Society, 1850–1980* (London: Thames and Hudson, 1986).

29   Bourdieu, P. *Distinction: A Social Critique of the Judgement of Taste* (London and New York: Routledge, 1986).
30   Bel Geddes Archive, Humanities Index, University of Texas, Austin, USA, File 199.
31   See Sparke, P. *Consultant Design: The History and Practice of the Designer in Industry* (London: Pembridge Press, 1983).
32   Wilk, C. *Marcel Breue: Furniture and Interiors* (New York: Museum of Modern Art, 1981).
33   Aynsley, J. *A Century of Graphic Design: Graphic design pioneers of the 20th century* (London: Mitchell Beazley, 2001), p. 15.
34   Rothschild, J. (ed.) *Design and Feminism: Revisioning Spaces, Places and Everyday Things* (New Brunswick, New Jersey and London: Rutgers University Press, 1999).
35   Seddon, J. and Worden, S. (eds) *Women Designing: Redefining Design in Britain between the Wars* (Brighton: University of Brighton, 1994).
36   Sparke, P. *As Long as It's Pink: The Sexual Politics of Taste* (London: Pandora, 1995).

4 Modernism and design

1   G. Dorfles, *Introduction à l'Industrial Design* (Paris: Casterman, 1974), p. 15.
2   Pevsner. N. *Pioneers of Modern Design* (Harmondsworth: Penguin 1960).
3   Banham, P. R. *Theory and Design in the First Machine Age* (London, Architectural Press, 1960).
4   Banham, p. 14.
5   Banham, p. 27.
6   Banham, p. 46.
7   Bourke, J. 'The Great Male Renunciation: Men's Dress Reform in inter-war Britain' *Journal of Design History* 1996; 9 (1): 23–33 and Burman, B. 'Better and Brighter Clothes: The Men's Dress Reform Party' *Journal of Design History* 1995; 8 (4): 275–90.
8   Naylor. G. *The Arts and Crafts Movement* (London: Studio Vista, 1971).
9   Steadman, P. *The Evolution of Designs* (Cambridge: Cambridge University Press, 1979), p. 33.
10   Durant, S. *Victorian Ornamental Design* (London: Academy Editions, 1972).
11   Schaefer. H. *Nineteenth-Century Modern: The Functional Tradition in Victorian Design* (London: Studio Vista. 1970).
12   Hounshell. S. *From the American System to Mass Production 1800–1932: The Development of Manufacturing Technology in the U.S.* (Baltimore and London: John Hopkins University Press, 1990).
13   Giedion, S. *Mechanisation Takes Command* (New York, Norton, 1948).
14   Greenough, H. *Form and Function: Remarks on Art, Design and Architecture* (Berkeley: University of California Press, 1947).
15   Greenough, 1947, p. 131.
16   Loos. A. 'Ornament and Crime' reprinted in Conrads, U. *Programmes and Manifestoes on Twentieth-Century Architecture* (London: Lund Humphries, 1970).
17   B. Colomina *Sexuality and Space* (Princeton, New Jersey: Princeton Architectural Press, 1992)
18   Greenhalgh, P. (ed.) *Art Nouveau 1890–1914* (London: V&A Publications, 2000).
19   Naylor, 1971, p. 184.
20   S. Tschudi-Madsen, *Art Nouveau* (London: Wiedenfeld and Nicholson, 1967), pp. 54–5.

21 Collins, P. *Changing Ideals in Modern Architecture* (London: Faber and Faber, 1965), pp. 267–8.
22 Greenhalgh, P. (ed.) *Modernism and Design* (London: Reaktion Books, 1990).
23 See Bojko, S. *New Graphic Design in Revolutionary Russia* (New York/Washington: Praeger Publishers, 1972).
24 Troy. N. *The De Stijl Environment* (Cambridge, MA: The MIT Press, 1983), p. 5.
25 Overy, P. *De Stijl* (London: Thames and Hudson, 1991).
26 Overy, 1991, p. 32.
27 Naylor, G. 'Swedish Grace... or the Acceptable Face of Modernism' in Greenhalgh, 1990, pp. 164–83 and Sparke, P. 'Swedish Modern: Myth or Reality' in *Svensk Form* (London: Design Council, 1981), pp. 15–20.
28 Sparke, 1980. p. 16.
29 Gropius, W. *The New Architecture and the Bauhaus* (London: Faber and Faber, 1935), p. 19.
30 Gropius, 1935, p. 51.
31 Klee, P. *Pedagogical Sketchbook* (London: Faber and Faber, 1953).
32 Gropius, 1935, p. 71.
33 De Zurko, E. R. *Origins of Functionalist Theory* (New York: Columbia University Press, 1957).
34 Collins, 1965.
35 Le Corbusier *Towards a New Architecture* (London: The Architectural Press, 1974 [1927]), p. 7.
36 Le Corbusier, 1974, p. 22.
37 Rietveld built the Schroder house in 1924/25 while Le Corbusier's Villa Savoie was created in 1927.
38 Bullock, N. 'First the Kitchen – Then the Façade' *Journal of Design History* 1988; 1 (3 & 4): 177–92.
39 Thomson, E. M. ' "The Science of Publicity": An American Advertising Theory, 1900–1920' *Journal of Design History* 1996; 9 (4): 253–69.
40 Bourke, J. 'The Great Male Renunciation: Men's Dress Reform in Inter-war Britain' *Journal of Design History* 1996; 9 (1): 23–33 and Burman, B. 'Better and Brighter Clothes: The Men's Dress Reform Party' *Journal of Design History* 1995; 8 (4): 275–90.
41 Greenhalgh, 1990, p. 9.
42 Gropius, 1935, p. 92.
43 Sparke, P. *As Long As It's Pink: The Sexual Politics of Taste* (London: Pandora, 1995).
44 Sparke, 1995, p. 118.

5 Designing identities

1 McCarthy, F. *A History of British Design 1830–1970* (London: George Allen And Unwin Ltd., 1979).
2 Heskett, J. *Design in Germany 1870–1918* (London: Trefoil), 1986.
3 Heskett, 1986. p. 58.
4 Greenhalgh, P. *Ephemeral Vistas: The Expositions Universelles, Great Exhibitions, and World's Fairs 1851–1939.* (Manchester: Manchester University Press, 1988).
5 See Naylor, G. *The Arts and Crafts Movement* (London: Studio Vista, 1971).
6 Ernyey, G. *Made in Hungary: The Best of 150 Years in Industrial Design* (Budapest: Rubik Innovation Foundation, 1993).
7 Exhibition catalogue, *Josef Hoffmann 1870–1956: Architect and Designer* (London: Fischer Fine Art Gallery, 1977), pp. 5–6.

8 See Crowley, D. 'Budapest: International Metropolis and National Capital' in Greenhalgh, P. (ed.) *Art Nouveau 1890–1914* (London: V&A Publications, 2000).

9 Ernyey, 1993.

10 Ernyey, 1993, p. 24.

11 Lamarova, M. 'The New Art in Prague' in Greenhalgh, P. (ed.) *Art Nouveau* (London: V&A Publications, 2000).

12 Campbell, J. *The German Werkbund: The Politics of Reform in the Applied Arts* (Princeton, NJ: Princeton University Press, 1978), Burckardt, L. *The Werkbund: Studies in the History and Ideology of the Deutscher Werkbund* (London: Design Council, 1980) and Schwartz, F. *The Werkbund: Design Theory and Mass Culture Before the First World War* (New Haven and London: Yale University Press, 1996).

13 Campbell, 1978, p. 10.

14 Schwartz, 1996.

15 McFadden, D. *Scandinavian Modern Design 1880–1980* (New York: Harry Abrams, Inc., 1982).

16 Opie, J. 'Helsinki: Saarinen and Finnish Jugend' in Greenhalgh. P., 2000, p. 375.

17 See Moller, S. E. (ed.) *Danish Design* (Copenhagen: Det danske Selskab, 1974).

18 Silverman, D. L. *Art Nouveau in Fin-de-Siècle France: Politics, Psychology and Style* (Berkeley: University of California Press, 1989).

19 Tiersten, L. *Marianne in the Marketplace: Envisioning Consumer Society in Fin-de-Siècle France* (Berkeley: University of California Press, 2001).

20 Hobsbawm, E. J. *Nations and Nationalism since 1780* (Cambridge: Cambridge University Press, 1990), p. 141.

21 Hobsbawm, 1990, p. 141.

22 See Hitchcock, H. R. and Johnson, P. *The International Style* (New York: W.W. Norton and Co. Inc., 1966).

23 Newman, G. 'A survey of design in Britain, 1915–1939' in *British Design* (Milton Keynes: The Open University, 1975).

24 Greenhalgh, P. (ed.) *Art Nouveau 1890–1914* (London: V&A Publications, 2000).

25 Gronberg, T. *Designs on Modernity: Exhibiting the City in 1920s Paris* (Manchester: Manchester University Press, 1998), p. 11.

26 Gronberg, 1998, p. 30.

27 Dell, S. 'The Consumer and the Making of the Exposition Internationale des Arts Decoratifs et Industriels Modernes, 1907–1925' *Journal of Design History* 1999; 12 (4): 311–25.

28 Doordan, D. *Twentieth-Century Architecture* (London: Lawrence King, 2001).

29 See Meikle, J. L. *Twentieth-Century Limited: Industrial Design in the USA, 1925–1939* (Philadelphia, USA: Temple University Press, 2001), p. 62.

30 Stuart Ewen *Captains of Consciousness: Advertising and the Social Roots of Consumer Culture* (New York: McGraw Hill, 1977).

31 Bowlby, R. *Shopping with Freud* (London: Routledge, 1993).

32 Frederick, C. *Selling Mrs. Consumer: Christine Frederick & The Rise of Household Efficiency* (New York: Business Bourse, 1929).

33 Sheldon, R. and Arens, E. *Consumer Engineering: A New Technique for Prosperity* (New York: Arno Press, 1932), p. 154.

34 'Building the World of Tomorrow' *Art and Industry* 1939; 26 (154) April: 126.

35 Susman, W. I. 'The People's Fair: Cultural Contradictions of a Consumer Society' in Harrison, H. A. and Cusker, J. P. *Dawn of a New Day: The New York World's Fair, 1939/40* (New York: Queens Museum of Art, 1980), p. 17.

36 Susman, 1980, p. 27.
37 See Woodham, J. 'Images of Africa and Design in British Empire Exhibitions between the Wars' *Journal of Design History* 1989; 2 (1): 15–33.
38 Woodham, 1989, p. 22.
39 Examples include the De La Warr Pavilion in Bexhill, London Zoo's penguin pool and the Highpoint, Quarry Hill and Lawn Road housing schemes.
40 Ryan, D. S. *The Ideal Home Through the 20th Century* (London: Hazar Publishing, 1997).
41 Elliott, D. 'Introduction' to *Devetsil: Czech Avant-garde Art, Architecture and Design of the 1920s and 1930s* (Oxford and London: Museum of Modern Art, 1990), p. 6.
42 Guidici, G. *Design Process: Olivetti, 1908–1983* (Torino, Italy: Edizioni di Comunità, 1983), p. 16.

6 Consuming postmodernity

1 Hopkins, H. *The New Look: A Social History of the Forties and Fifties* (London, Secker and Warburg, 1964), p. 231.
2 See Hebdige, D. 'Towards a Cartography of Taste 1935–1962' in Hebdige, D. *Hiding in the Light* (London and New York: Routledge, 1988), pp. 45–76.
3 De Grazia. V. 'Changing Consumption Regimes in Europe' in Strasser, S., McGovern, C. and Judt, M. *Getting and Spending: European and American Consumer Societies in the Twentieth Century* (Cambridge: Cambridge University Press, 1998), p. 61.
4 Merkel, I. 'Consumer Culture in the GDR' in Strasser, McGovern and Judt, *Getting and Spending: European and American Consumer Societies in the Twentieth Century* (Cambridge: Cambridge University Press, 1998), pp. 282–3.
5 Hopkins, 1964.
6 Galbraith, J. K. *The Affluent Society* (Harmondsworth: Penguin, 1958) and Carter. E. *How German is She? National Reconstruction and the Consuming Woman in the FRG and West Berlin 1945–1960* (Ann Arbor, MI: University of Michigan, 1996).
7 Williams, R. *Culture and Society 1780–1950* (London: Chatto and Windus, 1958).
8 See writings by Theodor W. Adorno and Max Horkeheimer on the subject, among them *Dialect of Enlightenment* (London: Verso, 1979 [1944]).
9 Williams, R. *Communications* (Harmondsworth: Penguin, 1968), p. 99.
10 Williams, 1968, p. 85
11 Marling, K. A. *As Seen on TV: The Visual Culture of Everyday Life in America in the 1950s* (Cambridge, MA: Harvard University Press, 1994).
12 See McDermott, C. 'Popular Taste and the Campaign for Contemporary Design in the 1950s' in Sparke, P. (ed.) *Did Britain Make It? British Design in Context, 1946–1986* (London: Design Council, 1986), pp. 156–64.
13 Wilson, R. *Only Halfway to Paradise, Women in Postwar Britain, 1945–1968* (London and New York: Tavistock Publications, 1980) p. 38.
14 Riesman, D. *The Lonely Crowd: A Study of the Changing American Character* (New Haven and New York: Yale University Press, rev. ed., 1970).
15 1948 Newson report, quoted in Wilson, E. *Only Halfway to Paradise: Women in Postwar Britain 1945–1968* (London and New York: Tavistock Publications, 1980).
16 Mort, F. 'Boy's own? Masculinity, style and popular culture in Chapman, R. and Rutherford, J. (eds) *Male Order* (London: Lawrence and Wishart, 1988).
17 Hine, T. *Populuxe: The Look and Life of America in the 1950s and 1960s,*

From Tailfins and TV Dinners to Barbie Dolls and Fallout Shelters (New York: Alfred A. Knopf, 1986).

18 During, S. (ed.) *Cultural Studies Reader* (London and New York: Routledge, 1993).

19 Massey, A. *The Independent Group: Modernism and Mass Culture in Britain, 1945–1959* (Manchester: Manchester University Press, 1995) and Whiteley, N. *Pop Design: Modernism to Mod* (London: Design Council, 1987).

20 Attfield, J. 'Inside Pram Town: A Case-Study of Harlow House Interiors, 1951–1961' in Attfield, J. and Kirkham, P. *A View From the Interior: Feminism, Women and Design* (London: The Women's Press, 1989), pp. 215–38.

21 Attfield and Kirkham, 1989, p. 17.

22 Friedan, B. *The Feminine Mystique* (Harmondsworth: Penguin, 1993 [1963]).

23 Hebdige, D. 'Object as Image': The Italian Scooter Cycle' in Hebdige, D. *Hiding in the Light* (London: Comedia, 1988), pp. 77–115.

24 See Clarke, A. *Tupperware: The Promise of Plastic in 1950s America* (Washington and London: Smithsonian Institution Press, 1999) and Peiss, K. *Hope in a Jar* (New York: Metropolitan Books, 1998).

25 See Moller, S. E. (ed.) *Danish Design* (Copenhagen: Der Danske Selskab, 1974).

26 See Venturi, R. *Complexity and Contradiction in Architecture* (New York: The Museum of Modern Art, 1966).

27 Venturi, 1966, p. 23.

28 Sparke, P. *Theory and Design in the Age of Pop* (unpublished PhD thesis, University of Brighton, 1975).

29 Lyotard, F. *The Postmodern Condition: A report on knowledge* (Manchester: Manchester University Press, 1984), p. 81.

30 Haug, W. H. *Critique of Commodity Aesthetics: Appearance, Sexuality and Advertising in Capitalist Society* (Oxford: Polity Press, 1986), p. 45.

31 Lehtonen, T. K. and Maenpaa, P. 'Shopping in the East Centre Mall' in Fall, P. and Campbell, C. (eds) *The Shopping Experience* (London: Sage, 1997).

32 Baudrillard, J. *Simulations* (New York: Semiotext(e), 1983).

33 Mort, F. *Cultures of Consumption: Masculinities and Social Space in Late Twentieth-Century Britain* (London and New York: Routledge, 1996).

34 Joanne Entwhistle '"Power dressing" and the Construction of the Career Woman' in Nava, M., Blake, A., MacRury, I. and Richards, B. *Buy This Book: Studies in Advertising and Consumption* (London and New York: Routledge, 1997).

35 Lunt, P. and Livingstone, S. M. *Mass Consumption and Personal Identity: Everyday Economic Experience* (Buckingham and Philadelphia: Open University Press, 1992).

36 Douglas, M. and Isherwood, B, *The World of Goods: Towards an Anthropology of Consumption* (Penguin, Harmondsworth, 1978), p. 59.

37 Du Gay, P., Hall, S., Mackay, H. and Negus, K. (eds) *Doing Cultural Studies: The Story of the Sony Walkman* (Milton Keynes: The Open University, 1997).

38 Bauman, Z. quoted in Warde, A. 'Consumers, Identity and Belonging: Reflections on Some Theses of Zygmunt Bauman' in Keat, R., Whiteley, N., and Abercrombie, N. *The Authority of the Consumer* (London and New York: Routledge, 1994).

39 Pavitt, J. (ed.) *Brand New* (London: V&A Publications, 2000).

40 Klein, N. *No Logo* (London: Flamingo, 2001), p. 4.

41 Dyson, J. *Against the Odds: An Autobiography* (London: Orion, 1997).

42 Hewison. R. *The Heritage Industry: Britain in a Climate of Decline* (London: Methuen, 1987), Samuel, R. *Theatres of Memory, Vol. I: Past and Present in Contemporary Culture* (London: Verso, 1995) and Wright, P. *On Living in an*

Old Country: The National Past in Contemporary Britain (London: Verso, 1985).

43 Urry, J. *Consuming Places* (London and New York: Routledge, 1995).

44 Wright. 1985, p. 5.

45 Urry, 1995, p. 177.

46 Eco, U. *Travels on Hyperreality* (New York: Harcourt Brace Jovanovich, 1986).

47 Zukin, S. *Landscapes of Power: from Detroit to Disneyland* (University of California Press, California, 1992).

48 Papanek, V. *Design for the Real World: Human Ecology and Social Change* (London: Thames and Hudson, 1972).

49 Jégou, F. 'Design and Social Innovation' *Azimuts* 2007; 29: 276.

50 Design Council. Case Studies: Design for Patient Dignity [http://www.design-council.org.uk/Case-studies/Design-for-Patient-Dignity/] (accessed 17.07.2012).

51 University of the Arts, London. Design Against Crime: A Practice-Led Design Initiative [http://www.designagainstcrime.com/about-us/background-history/] (accessed 17.07.2012).

52 Herman Miller, Inc. Environmental Advocacy [http://www.hermanmiller.com/About-Us/Environmental-Advocacy] (accessed 17.07.2012).

53 Nike, Inc. sustainable Business at Nike, Inc. [http://www.nikebiz.com/responsi-bility/] (accessed 17.07.2012).

7 Technology and design: a new alliance

1 *Dupont: The Autobiography of an American Enterprise* (Wilmington, Delaware: E. I. Du Pont de Nemours & Company, 1952), p. 119.

2 Hine, T. *Populuxe: The Look and Life of America in the '50s and '60s, From Tailfins and TV Dinners to Barbie Dolls and Fallout Shelters* (New York: Alfred A. Knopf, 1986), p. 70.

3 Hine, 1986, p. 128.

4 See Hogan, M. J. *The Marshall Plan: America, Britain and the Reconstruction of Western Europe, 1947–1952* (Cambridge: Cambridge University Press, 1987).

5 Sparke, P. *Italian Design: 1870 to the Present* (London: Thames and Hudson, 1988).

6 Sparke, 1988 and Sparke, P. *Japanese Design* (London: Michael Joseph, 1987).

7 White, N. *Reconstructing Italian Fashion: America and the Development of the Italian Fashion Industry* (London and New York: Berg, 2000), p. 21.

8 Sparke. P. 'The Straw Donkey: Tourist Kitsch or Proto-Design? Craft and Design in Italy, 1945–1960' *Journal of Design History* 1998; 11 (1): 59–69.

9 Palmer, A. *Couture and Commerce: The Transatlantic Fashion Trade in the 1950s* (Toronto: UBC Press, 2001).

10 Palmer, 2001, p. 20.

11 Pulos, A. J. *The American Design Adventure 1940–1975* (Cambridge, Mass: MIT Press, 1988).

12 Pulos, 1988, p. 79.

13 Jackson, L. *Robin and Lucienne Day: Pioneers of Contemporary Design* (London: Mitchell Beazley, 2001).

14 Catterall, C. 'Perceptions of Plastics: A Study of Plastics in Britain 1945–1956' in Sparke, P. (ed.) *The Plastics Age: From Modernity to Postmodernity* (London: V&A Publications, 1990), pp. 68–9.

15 Sparke, P. 'Plastics and Pop Culture' in Sparke, P. (ed.) *The Plastics Age: From Modernity to Post-Modernity* (London, Victoria and Albert Museum, 1990), pp. 92–104.

16   Attfield, J. 'The Tufted Carpet in Britain: Its Rise from the Bottom of the Pile, 1952–70' *Journal of Design History* 1994; 7 (3): 205–16.
17   Pile, S. 'The Foundation of Modern Comfort: Latex foam and the Industrial Impact of Design on the British Rubber Industry, 1948–1958' in *One-Off: A Collection of essays by Postgraduate Students on the V&A/RCA Course in the History of Design* (London: Victoria and Albert Museum, 1997).
18   Clarke, A. J. *Tupperware: The Promise of Plastic in 1950s America* (Washington and London: Smithsonian Institution Press, 1999).
19   Clarke, 1999, p. 10.
20   Handley, S. *Nylon: The Manmade Fashion Revolution* (London: Bloomsbury, 1999).
21   Sparke, P. *Italian Design: 1870 to the Present* (London: Thames and Hudson, 1988).
22   Blaszszyk, R. *Imagining Consumers: Design and Innovation from Wedgwood to Corning* (Baltimore and London: John Hopkins University Press, 2000).
23   Blaszszyk, 2000, p. 275.
24   Kron, J. and Slesin, S. *High Tech* (New York: Potter, 1978).
25   Du Gay, P., Hall, S., Janes, L., Mackay, H. and Negus, K (eds) *Doing Cultural Studies: The Story of the Sony Walkman* (Milrin Keynes: The Open University, 1997).
26   Riesman, D. *The Lonely Crowd: A Study of the Changing American Character* (New Haven: Yale University Press, 2nd rev. ed., 2001)
27   Postman, N. *Technolopoly: The Surrender of Culture to Technology* (New York: Vintage Books, 1993).
28   Postman, 1993, p. 7.
29   See *The Design Journal* 2011; 14 (2) June.
30   Ive, J. 'The Apple Bites Back' *Design* 1998; (1) Autumn: 36–41.
31   Hounshell, D. *From the American System to Mass Production 1800–1932: The Development of Manufacturing Technology in the US* (Baltimore and London: John Hopkins University Press, 1982).
32   Sparke, P. *Japanese Design* (London: Michael Joseph, 1987).
33   Sabel, C. F. *Work and Politics: The Division of Labor in Industry* (Cambridge: Cambridge University Press, 1982).
34   Wright, Paul K. *21st Century Manufacturing* (New Jersey: Prentice-Hall Inc., 2001).
35   *Brit Insurance Designs of the Year* (London: Design Museum, 2010), p. 56.
36   Design Museum. Droog Design Collective [http://designmuseum.org/design/droog] (accessed 17.07.12).
37   Wajcsman, J. *Feminism Confronts Technology* (Cambridge: Poloty, 1991), p. 137.
38   Scharff, V. 'Gender and Genius: The Auto Industry and Femininity' in Martinez, K. and Ames, K. L. *The Material Culture of Gender, the Gender of Material Culture* (Wintherthur, DE: Henry Francis du Pont Wintherthur Museum, 1997), p. 137.
39   Volvo Car Corporation. *YCC: Your Concept Car – by Women for Modern People.* Press Information [http://www.volvoclub.org.uk/press/pdf/presskits/YCCPressKit.pdf] (accessed 17.07.12) and Wikipedia. Volvo YCC [http://en.wikipedia.org/wiki/Volvo_YCC] (accessed 17.07.12).
40   Horowitz, R. *Boys and their Toys? Masculinity, Class and Technology in America* (New York and London: Routledge, 2001).
41   Manzini, E. *The Materials of Invention: Materials and Design* (Milan: Arcadia, 1986), p. 66.
42   Manzini, 1986, p. 68.
43   Antonelli. P. 'Aluminum and the New Materialism' in Nichols, S. *Aluminum by Design* (New York: Harry N. Abrams, 2000), p. 185.

8 Designer culture

1   See Jackson, L. *The New Look: Design in the Fifties* (London: Thames and Hudson, 1991, Jackson, L. *The Sixties: Decade of Design Revolution* (London: Phaidon, 2000) and Hines, T. *Populuxe: The Look and Life of America in the '50s and '60s, from Tailfins to TV Dinners to Barbie Dolls and Fallout Shelters* (New York: Alfred A. Knopf, 1986).

2   Day, R. 'At the Robin Days' in *Daily Mail Ideal Home Yearbook 1953–4* (London: Daily Mail Publication, 1954).

3   Race, E. 'Design in Modern Furniture' in *Daily Mail Ideal Home Book 1952–3* (London: Daily Mail Publication, 1953), p. 62.

4   Hard af Segerstad, U. *Scandinavian Design* (Stockholm: Nordisk Rotogtavyr, 1961), p. 16.

5   Sparke, P. *Italian Design: 1870 to the Present* (London: Thames and Hudson, 1988).

6   Kirkham, P. *Charles and Ray Eames: Designers of the Twentieth Century* (Cambridge, MA, and London: MIT Press, 1995).

7   Kirkham, 1995, p. 61.

8   Kaufmann Jr, E. *Introductions to Modern Design* (New York: The Museum of Modern Art, 1950), p 9.

9   Kaufmann, 1950, p. 8.

10 Bayley, S. *Art and Industry* (London: Boilerhouse Project, 1982).

11 *Kenneth Grange at the Boilerhouse: An Exhibition of British Product Design* (London: Boilerhouse Project, 1983).

12 See Aloi, R. *L'Arredamento Moderno* (Milan: Hoepli, 1955).

13 See Murgatroyd, K. *Modern Graphics* (London, Studio Vista, 1969) and Aynsley, J. *A Century of Graphic Design* (London, Mitchell Beazley, 2001).

14 Banham, R. (ed.) *The Aspen Papers: Twenty Years of Design Theory from the International Design Conference in Aspen* (London: Pall Mall Press, 1974).

15 Packard, V. *The Hidden Persuaders* (Harmondsworth: Penguin, 1957), Packard, V. *The Status Seekers* (Harmondsworth: Penguin, 1963) and Packard, V. *The Waste-Makers* (London: Longmans, 1961).

16 Ambasz, E. (ed.) *Italy: The New Domestic Landscape, Achievements and Problems of Italian Design* (New York: The Museum of Modern Art, 1972).

17 Foster, H. *Design and Crime* (London and New York: Verso, 2002).

18 Dyer, R. *Stars* (London: British Film Institute, 1992).

19 McDermott, C. *Street Style: British Design in the '80s* (London: Design Council, 1987).

20 Radice, B. and Sottsass, E. *Ettore Sottsass: A Critical Biography* (New York: Rizzoli, 1993).

21 Sweet, F. *Alessi: Art and Poetry* (London: Thames and Hudson, 1998) and *Alessi Design Factory* (London: Academy Editions, 1998).

22 Boissiere, O. *Philippe Starck* (Munich: Taschen, 1991) and Sweet, F. *Philippe Starck: Subverchic Design* (London: Watson-Guptil, 1999).

23 See Sparke, P. *A Century of Car Design* (London: Mitchell Beazley, 2002).

24 See Wollen, P. and Kerr, J. (eds) *Autopia: Cars and Culture* (London: Reaktion Books, 2002).

25 J. Mays, lecture given at the Design Museum, London, 15 August 2002.

26 Bayley, S. Philippe Starck's new reality TV show *The Observer* (6 September 2009) [http://www.guardian.co.uk/artanddesign/2009/sep/06/philippe-starck-reality-tv-show] (accessed 18.07.12).

27 Nussbaum, B. 'The Power of Design' *Bloomberg Businessweek* 2004; May 16: 6–7 [http://www.businessweek.com/stories/2004-05-16/the-power-of-design] (accessed 18.07.12).

28 Nussbaum, 2004.
29 Brown, T. and Wyatt, J. *Design Thinking for Social Innovation* (Palo Alto: Stanford Social Innovation Review, Winter 2012), p. 32.
30 Kelley, T., Littman, J. and Peters, T. *The Art of Innovation: Lessons in Creativity from IDEO, America's Leading Design Firm* (New York: Doubleday, 2001).
31 Julier, G. *The Culture of Design* (London: Sage, 2000), pp. 22–3.
32 Andersson, N. *Designed in Umeå* (Sweden: Infotain and Infobooks, 2009), p. 14.
33 Andersson, 2009, p. 116.
34 Rose, M. *The Emergence and Practice of Co-design as a Method for Social Sustainability under New Labour* (Draft PhD thesis, University of East London, Aug. 2011).

9 Postmodernism and design

1   Arnheim, R. 'From Function to Expression' *Journal of Aesthetics and Arty Criticism* 1964; Fall: 31.
2   Raymond Loewy, Norman Bel Geddes and others claimed to be following in the footsteps of the European modernists whom they admired.
3   Banham. R. 'A Throw-away Aesthetic' in Sparke, P. (ed.) *Reyner Banham: Design by Choice* (London: Academy Editions. 1980) pp. 90–3.
4   Kaufmann Jr, E. 'Borax or the Chromium-Plated Calf' *Architectural Review* 1948; August: 88–93.
5   Whiteley, N. *Pop Design: Modernism to Mod* (London: Design Council, 1987), Massey, A. *The Independent Group: Modernism and Mass Culture in Britain 1945–59* (Manchester: Manchester University Press, 1995), Massey, A. and Sparke, P. 'The Myth of the Independent Group' in *Block*, (Middlesex University, 10, 1985), pp. 48–56 and Hebdige, D. 'In Poor Taste: Notes on Pop' in *Hiding in the Light* (London and New York, Routledge, 1988), pp. 116–43.
6   McCale, J. 'The Expendable Icon' *Architectural Review* 1959; Feb/March.
7   Barthes, R. *Mythologies* (London, Jonathan Cape, 1972), pp. 88, 99.
8   Dorfles, G. *Kitsch* (London: Studio Vista, 1969) and Moles, A. *Le Kitsch* (Paris, Maison Mame, 1971).
9   Boorstin, D. J. *The Image* (London: Weidenfeld and Nicholson, 1962), p. 186.
10 Boorstin, 1962, p. 16.
11 Masson, P. and Thorburn, A. 'Advertising: the American influence on Europe' in Bigsby, C. W. E. (ed.) *Superculture: American Popular Culture and Europe* (London: Paul Elek, 1975), p. 98.
12 See Hoggart, R. *The Uses of Literacy* (New Brunswick and London: Transaction Publishers, 1998) and Williams, R. *Culture and Society 1780–1950* (London: Chatto and Windus, 1958).
13 Hughes-Stanton, C. 'What comes after Carnaby Street? *Design* 1968; 230 Feb: 42–3.
14 Sparke, P. *Theory and Design in the Age of Pop* (unpublished PhD thesis, Brighton University, 1975).
15 Sparke, P. *Ettore Sottsass* (London: Design Council, 1982).
16 Venturi, R. *Complexity and Contradiction in Architecture* (New York: Museum of Modern Art, 1966).
17 Lindinger, H. (intro.) *Hochschüle fur Gestaltung, Ulm: Die Moral der Gegenstande* (Berlin: Ernst & Sohn, 1987).
18 Lyotard, J. F. *The Post-modern Condition: A Report on Knowledge* (Manchester: Manchester University Press, 1984).

19 These included Jean-Francois Lyotard's *The Postmodern Condition: A Report on Knowledge*, originally published in 1979 by Editions de Minuit; Hal Foster (ed.) *The Anti-Aesthetic: Essays on postmodern culture* (Port Townsend: Bay Press, 1983); Frederic Jameson's essay 'Postmodernism, or the cultural logic of late capitalism' which appeared in *New Left Review* (1984; 146, July/Aug: 53–92); Andreas Huyssen's *After the Great Divide: Modernism, Mass Culture and Postmodernism* (London: MacMillan, 1986); David Harvey *The Condition of Postmodernity* (Oxford: Blackwell, 1989); and Linda Hutcheon *The Politics of Postmodernism* (London and New York: Routledge, 1989).

20 See Habermas, J. 'Modernity – An Incomplete Project' in Foster, H. (ed.) *The Anti-Aesthetic: Essays on postmodern culture* (Port Townsend: Bay Press, 1983).

21 Wolff, J. *Feminine Sentences: Essays in Women and Culture* (Cambridge, Polity Press, 1990), p. 87.

22 Huyssen, A. *After the Great Divide: Modernism, Mass Culture and Postmodernism* (London: Macmillan, 1986).

23 Harvey, 1989, p. 39.

24 Jamieson, 1984. See also Bourdieu, P. *Distinction: A Social Critique of the Judgement of Taste.* (London and New York: Routledge, 2010 [1979]).

25 Douglas, M. and Isherwood, B. *The World of Goods: Towards an Anthropoly of Consumption* (London and New York: Routledge, 1996 [1979]).

26 Featherstone, M. *Consumer Culture and Postmodernism* (London: Sage, 1983).

27 Clarke, A. J. *Design Anthropology: Object Culture in the 21st Century* (New York: Springer, 2010)

28 Giddens, A. *Modernity and Self-Identity: Self and Society in the Late Modern Age* (California: Stanford University Press, 1991).

29 Said, E. *Culture and Imperialism* (New York: Vintage Books, 1994).

30 Jameson, C. in Foster, H. (ed.) *The Anti-Aesthetic: Essays on postmodern culture* (Port Townsend: Bay Press, 1983), p. 111.

31 McCracken, G. *Culture and Consumption: New Approaches to the Symbolic Character of Consumer Goods and Activities* (London: John Wiley and Sons, 1990), p. 105.

32 Jameson, C. in Foster, H. (ed.) *The Anti-Aesthetic: Essays on postmodern culture* (Port Townsend: Bay Press, 1983), p.113.

33 Venturi, R. *Complexity and Contradiction in Architecture* (New York: Museum of Modern Art, 1966).

34 Venturi, R., Scott-Brown, D., and Izenour, S. *Learning from Las Vegas: The forgotten Symbolism of Architectural Form* Cambridge, Mass: MIT Press, 1972).

35 Jencks, C. *The Language of Post-Modern Architecture* (London: Academy Editions, 1977), p. 96.

36 See Collins, M. and Papadakis, A. *Post-Modern Design* (London: Academy Editions, 1989).

37 See Sparke, P. *Japanese Design* (London, Michael Joseph, 1987).

38 Multi-disciplinary Design Network. *Lessons from America: Report on the Multi-disciplinary Design Education Fact-Finding Visit to the United States* (London: Design Council, 2006).

39 Multi-disciplinary Design Network, 2006.

40 Multi-disciplinary Design Network, 2006.

10 Redefining identities

1 Huygen, F. *British Design: Image and Identity* (London: Thames and Hudson, 1989), pp. 19, 23.

2   Sparke, P. (ed.) *Did Britain Make It? British Design in Context, 1946–86* (London: The Design Council, 1986).

3   Oram, S. 'Constructing Contemporary': Common-sense Approaches to 'Going Modern' in the 1950s' in McKellar, S. and Sparke, P. (eds) *Interior Design and Identity* (Manchester: Manchester University Press, 2004).

4   McFadden, D. *Scandinavian Modern Design* (New York: Harry N. Abrams, 1982).

5   McFadden, 1982, p. 21.

6   Hard Af Segerstad, U. *Scandinavian Design* (London: Studio Books, 1961).

7   Pulos. A. *The American Design Ethic* and *The American Design Adventure* (Cambridge, MA: MIT Press, 1983 and 1988).

8   Sparke, P. *Italian Design, 1879 to the Present* (London: Thames and Hudson, 1988) and *Japanese Design* (London: Michael Joseph, 1987).

9   Sabel, C. F. *Work and Politics: The Division of Labour in Industry* (Cambridge: Cambridge University Press, 1982).

10   Sparke, P. 'Nature, Craft, Domesticity and the Culture of Consumption: The Feminine Face of Design in Italy 1945–60' *Modern Italy* 1999; 4 (1): 59–78.

11   See Bayley, S. *Coca-Cola 1886–1986: Designing a Megabrand* (London: The Boilerhouse, 1986).

12   Bayley, 1986, p. 63.

13   Bayley, 1986, p. 62.

14   Hobsbawm, E. *The Invention of Tradition* (Cambridge: Cambridge University Press, 1992).

15   *Design Francais 1960–1990: Trois Décennies* (Paris: Centre Georges Pompidou, 1990).

16   Narotzky, V. *An Acquired Taste: The Consumption of Design in Barcelona, 1975–1992* (unpublished PhD thesis, Royal College of Art, London, 2003).

17   Wright, P. *On Living in an Old Country: The National Past in Contemporary Britain* (London: Verso, 1985). p. 2.

18   Hewison, R. *The Heritage Industry: Britain in a Climate of Decline* (London: Methuen, 1987), p. 24.

19   Crowley, D. *National Style and National State: Design in Poland from the Vernacular Revival to the International Style* (Manchester: Manchester University Press, 1992).

20   Foxconn Electronics Co. About Foxconn [http://www.foxconn.com/CompanyIntro.html] (accessed 19.07.12) and [http://en.wikipedia.org/wiki/Foxconn] (accessed 19.07.12).

21   Lenovo Group Ltd [http://www.lenovo.com/uk/en/] (accessed 19.07.12) and [http://en.wikipedia.org/wiki/Lenovo] (accessed 19.07.12).

22   Beijing National Stadium [http://www.n-s.cn/en/] (accessed 19.07.12) and [http://en.wikipedia.org/wiki/Beijing_National_Stadium] (accessed 19.07.12).

23   Quoted in Franklyn, S., Lury, C., and Stacey, J. *Global Nature, Global Culture* (London: Sage, 2000), p. 2.

24   Zygmunt Bauman term 'neo-tribes' is referred to in Warde, A. 'Consumers, Identity and Belonging: Reflections on Some Theses of Zygmunt Bauman' in Keat, R., Whiteley, N. and Abercrombie, N. (eds) *The Authority of the Consumer* (London and New York: Routledge, 1994), p. 58.

25   Oliver, T. *The Real Coke: The Real Story* (London: Elm Tree, 1986), Pendergast, M. *For God, Country and Coca-Cola* (London: Weidenfeld and Nicholson, 1993) and Miller, D. 'Coca-Cola: a black sweet drink from Trinidad' in Miller, D. (ed). *Material Cultures: Why Some Things Matter* (London: UCl Press, 1998).

26   Falk, P. *The Consuming Body* (London: Sage, 1994), pp. 180–2 and 'The

Benetton-Toscani Effect: Testing the Limits of Conventional Advertising' in Nava, M., Blake, A., MacRury, I. and Richards. B. *Buy This Book: Studies in Advertising and Consumption* (London: and New York: Routledge, 1997) and Lury, C. 'The United Colors of Diversity' in Franklin, S., Lury, C. and Stacey, J. (eds) *Global Nature, Global Culture* (London: Sage, 2000), pp. 146–87.

27 Lury, 2000, p. 167.

28 Du Gay, P., Hall, S., Janes, L., Mackay, H. and Negus, K. (eds) *Doing Cultural Studies: The Story of the Sony Walkman* (Milton Keynes: The Open University Press, 1997).

29 *Newdesign Magazine* (London: Design Council, July/August, 2002), p. 22.

30 Kirkham, P. (ed.) *The Gendered Object* (Manchester and New York: Manchester University Press, 1996) and Martinez, K. and Ames, K. L. (eds) *The Material Culture of Gender: The Gender of Material Culture* (Winterthur, Delaware: Henry Francis de Pont Wintherthur Museum, 1997).

31 Kirkham, 1996, p. 199.

32 Kirkham, 1996, p. 205.

Bibliography

Introduction

Since the 1986 publication, the subjects of 'design' and 'material culture' have been discussed more widely in the English-speaking world than they had been before that date and a number of books have emerged which take a broad, analytical/critical approach to the subjects. These include:

Adamson, G. *The Craft Reader* (London: Berg, 2009).

Attfield, J. *Wild Things: The Material Culture of Everyday Life* (Oxford and New York: Berg, 2000).

Clark, H. and Brody, D. *Design Studies: A Reader* (London: Berg, 2009).

Dormer, P. *The Meanings of Modern Design: Towards the Twenty-First Century* (London: Thames and Hudson, 1990).

Fallan, K. *Design History* (London: Berg, 2010).

Foster, H. *Design and Crime (and other diatribes)* (London and New York: Verso, 2002).

Heskett, J. *Toothpicks and Logos: Design in Everyday Life* (Oxford: Oxford University press, 2002).

Highmore, B. *The Design Culture Reader* (London and New York: Routledge, 2008).

Inns, T. (ed.) *Designing for the 21st Century: Interdisciplinary Questions and Insights* (London: Gower, 2010).

Julier, G. *The Culture of Design* (London: Sage, 2000).

Kwint, M., Breward, C. and Aynsley, J. *Material Memories: Design and Evocation* (Oxford: Berg, 1999).

Lees-Maffei, G. and Houze, R. (eds) *The Design History Reader* (London: Berg, 2010).

Margolin, V. (ed.) *Design Discourse: History, Theory, Criticism* (Chicago: University of Chicago Press, 1989).

Margolin, V. *The Politics of the Artificial: Essays on Design and Design Studies* (Chicago and London: Chicago University Press, 2002).

Raizman, D. *History of Modern Design* (London: Laurence King, 2010).

Sparke, P. *The Genius of Design* (London: Quadrille Publishing), 2010.

Walker, J. *Design History and the History of Design* (London: Pluto Press, 1989).

Woodham, J. *Twentieth-Century Design* (Oxford: Oxford University Press, 1997.

A number of overviews of design in the twentieth century have also emerged, most of them focusing on a single design discipline. These include:

Aynsley, J. *A Century of Graphic Design* (London: Mitchell Beazley, 2001).
Breward, C. *Fashion* (Oxford: Oxford University Press, 2003).
Calloway, S. *Twentieth-Century Decoration: The Domestic Interior from 1900 to the Present Day* (London: Weidenfeld and Nicholson, 1988).
Crowley, D. and Jobling, P. *Graphic Design: Reproduction and Representation since 1800* (Manchester: Manchester University Press, 1996).
Doordan, D. P. *Twentieth-Century Architecture* (London: Lawrence King, 2001).
Edwards, C. *Twentieth-Century Furniture: Materials, Manufacture and Markets* (Manchester: Manchester University Press, 1994).
Forty, A. *Objects of Desire: Design and Society 1750–1980* (London: Thames and Hudson, 1986).
Massey, A. *Interior Design of the 20th Century* (London: Thames and Hudson, 1990).
Pile, J. *A History of Interior Design* (New York: John Wiley and Sons, 2000).
Sparke, P. *A Century of Car Design* (London: Mitchell Beazley, 2002).
Sparke, P. *The Modern Interior* (London: Reaktion Books, 2008).
Sparke, P., Keeble, T., Martin, B. and Massey, A. *Designing the Modern Interior: From the Victorians to the Present Day* (London, Berg, 2009).

Much of the work in the areas of design history and material culture undertaken over the last two decades has adopted a cultural slant. While a wide range of cultural issues have been focused upon, that of 'identity' has tended to dominate debates, especially in relation to gender but also, albeit to a lesser extent to date, in relation to race and ethnicity, especially in the context of post-imperialism and the unification of Europe. Class issues remain important to design historical work as well. Work on the relationship between women and design and material culture, influenced by concurrent work being undertaken within cultural studies, has been especially visible in the last two decades. Publications in this area include:

Attfield, J. 'Feminist Critiques of Design' in Walker, J. *Design History and the History of Design* (London: Pluto Press, 1989).
Attfield, J. and Kirkham, P. *A View from the Interior: Feminism, Women and Design* (London: The Woman's Press, 1989).
Buckley, C. 'Made in Patriarchy: Towards a Feminist Analysis of Women in Design' *Design Issues* 1986; 3 (2): 251–62.
Davis, F. *Fashion, Culture and Identity* (Chicago: Chicago University Press, 1992).
De Grazia, V. and Furlough, E. *The Sex of Things* (Berkeley: University of California Press, 1996).
Evans, C. and Thornton, M. *Women and Fashion: A New Look* (London: Quartet, 1989).
Ferguson. M. *Forever Feminine; Women's Magazines and the Cult of Femininity* (London: Heinemann, 1983).
Kirkham, P. (ed.) *The Gendered Object* (Manchester and New York: Manchester University Press, 1996).
Martinez, K. and Ames, K. L. *The Material Culture of Gender: The Gender of Material Culture* (Winthertur, Delaware: Henry Francis du Pont Wintherthur Museum, 1997).

McKellar, S. and Sparke, P. (eds) *Interior Design and Identity* (Manchester: Manchester University Press, 2004).

Sparke, P. *As Long as It's Pink: The Sexual Politics of Taste* (London: Pandora, 1995).

Most significantly, in relation to this publication, an enormous body of theoretical work emanating from tangential disciplines – including cultural studies, sociology, consumption theory, anthropology, social psychology, literary studies and cultural geography – has had a dramatic impact on the way in which work on the subjects of design and material culture has been undertaken. Among the many – too numerous to list here – important and useful studies are the following:

Apparudai, A. (ed.) *The Social Life of Things: Commodities in Cultural Perspective* (Cambridge: Cambridge University Press, 1986).

Baudrillard, J. *The System of Objects* (London: Verso, 1996).

Bourdieu, P. *Distinction: A Social Critique of the Judgement of Taste* (London and New York: Routledge, 1986).

Campbell, C. *The Romantic Ethic and the Spirit of Modern Consumerism* (London: Basil Blackwell, 1987).

Dittmar, H. 'Gender Identity: relation meanings of personal possessions' *British Journal of Social Psychology* 1989; 28: 159–71.

Douglas, M. and Isherwood, B. *The World of Goods: Towards an Anthropology of Consumption* (London and New York: Routledge, 1996).

Ewen, S. *All Consuming Images: The Politics of Style in Contemporary Culture* (New York: Basic Books, 1988).

Falk, P. *The Consuming Body* (London: Sage, 1994).

Fine, B. and Leopold, E. *The World of Consumption* (London and New York: Routledge, 1993).

Fiske *Understanding Popular Culture* (London: Routledge, 1989).

Haug, W. F. *Critique of Commodity Aesthetics* (Cambridge: Polity, 1986).

Hebdige, D. *Hiding in the Light: On Images and Things* (London and New York: Routledge, 1988).

Huyssen, A. *After the Great Divide: Modernism, Mass Culture and Postmodernism* (London: Macmillan, 1986).

Lund, P. and Livingstone, S. M. *Mass Consumption and Personal Identity: Everyday Economic Experience* (Buckingham and Philadelphia: Open University Press, 1992).

McCracken, G. *Culture and Consumption: New Approaches to the Symbolic Character of Consumer Goods* (Bloomington and Indianapolis: Indiana University Press, 1988).

McDowell, L. *Gender, Identity and Place: Understanding Feminist Geographies* (Cambridge: Polity, 1999).

Miller, D. *Material Culture and Mass Consumption* (Oxford: Basil Blackwell, 1987).

Mort, F. *Cultures of Consumption: Masculinities and Social Space in Late Twentieth-Century Britain* (London and New York: Routledge, 1996).

Stewart, S. *On Longing: Narratives of the Miniature, the Gigantic, the Souvenir, the Collection* (Durham and London: Duke University Press, 1993).

Sudjic, D. *The Language of Things: Design, Luxury, Fashion, Art: How We are Seduced by the Things Around Us* (London: Penguin, 2011).

The emergence of important journals – *Design History Journal* (Oxford University Press) and *Design Issues: History, Theory, Criticism* (MIT Press), *The Design Journal* (Berg), *Fashion Theory* (Berg), *Home Cultures* (Berg) and *Interiors* (Berg) – has helped to provide an outlet for work in this area.

1 Consuming modernity

Recommended reading

Many books deal with the relationship between consumer culture, material culture and modernity. While some focus on it through a single area of material culture, be it advertising, magazines, retailing or fashion, others, such as Don Slater's *Consumer Culture and Modernity* (Cambridge: Cambridge University Press, 1997) provide useful overviews; Simon J. Bronner's book of edited essays, *Accumulation and Display of Goods in America, 1880–1920* (New York and London: W. W. Norton and Company, 1989) shows how consumer culture and material culture worked together in the USA; Elizabeth Wilson's two books – *Adorned in Dreams: Fashion and Modernity* (London: Virago, 1985) and *The Sphinx in the City: Urban life, the Control of Disorder and Women* (London: Virago. 1991) – deal with issues relating to fashion, gender, the urban landscape and modernity; in *Lands of Desire: Merchants, Power and the Rise of a New American Culture* (New York: Vintage Books, 1994), William Leach focuses on the impact of the visual culture of the department store on the American urban landscape; while Thad Logan, in *The Victorian Parlour; A Cultural Study* (Cambridge: Cambridge University Press, 2001), provides a model for a cultural analysis of a room in the private sphere.

Further reading

Adburnham, E. S. *Shops and Shopping 1800–1914* (London: Allen and Unwin, 1981).

Beetham, M. *A Magazine of her Own: Domesticity and Desire in the Woman's Magazine, 1800–1914* (London and New York: Routledge, 1996).

Berman, M. *All That is Solid Melts into Air: The Experience of Modernity* (New (New York: Simon and Schuster, 1982).

Bowlby, R. *Carried Away: The Invention of Modern Shopping* (London: Haber and Faber, 2000).

Bowlby, R. *Shopping with Freud* (London: Routledge, 1993).

Bryden, I. and Floyd, J. (eds) *Domestic Space: Reading the Nineteenth-Century Interior* (Manchester and New York: Manchester University Press, 1999).

Bushman, R. *The Refinement of America: Persons, Houses, Cities* (New York: Vintage Books, 1993).

Chaney, D. 'The Department Store as a Cultural Form' *Theory, Culture and Society* 1983; 1 (3): 22–31.

Davidoff, L. and Hall, C. *Family Fortunes: Men and Women of the English Middle Class, 1780–1850* (London: Routledge, 1987).

Ewen, S. *Captains of Consciousness: Advertising and the Social Roots of Consumer Culture* (New York: McGraw Hill, 1977).

Forde. K. *Hope in a Jar: The Making of America's Beauty Culture* (New York: Henry Holt and Co. Inc., 1998).

Fraser. W. H. *The Coming of the Mass Market, 1850–1914* (London and Basingstoke: Macmillan, 1981).

Frederick, C. *Selling Mrs. Consumer: Christine Frederick and The Rise of Household Efficiency* (New York: Business Bourse, 1929).

Frisby, D. *Fragments of Modernity: Theories of Modernity in the Work of Simmel, Kracauer and Benjamin* (Cambridge: Polity, 1985).

Glickman, L. B. (ed.) *Consumer Society in American History: A Reader* (Ithaca and London: Cornell University Press, 1999).

Grier, K. C. *Culture and Comfort: People, Parlors and Upholstery 1850–1930* (New York: The Stron Museum, 1988).

Harris, N. 'The Drama of Consumer Desire' in *Cultural Excursions: Marketing Appetites and Cultural Tastes in Modern America* (Chicago: University of Chicago Press, 1990).

Hine, T. *The Total Package* (Boston: Little, Brown and Company, 1995).

Jeffreys, J. B. *Retail Trading in Britain 1850–1950* (Cambridge: Cambridge University Press, 1954).

Laermans, R. 'Learning to Consume: Early Department Stores and the Shaping of the Modern Consumer Culture (1860–1914)' *Theory, Culture and Society* 1993; 10 (4): 79–102.

Marchand, R. *Advertising the American Dream: Making Way for Modernity 1920–1940* (Berkeley: University of California Press, 1985).

Mason, R. *Conspicuous Consumption: A Study of Exceptional Consumer Behaviour* (Hampshire: Gower, 1981).

Miller, M. B. *The Bon Marche: Bourgeois Culture and the Department Store, 1869–1920* (Princeton, NJ: Princeton University Press, 1981).

Rappaport, E. D. *Shopping for Pleasure: Women in the Making of London's West End* (Princeton, New Jersey: Princeton University Press, 2000).

Richards, T. *The Commodity Culture of Victorian England: Advertising and Spectacle 1851–1914* (London and New York: Verso, 1990).

Saint, A. (introduction) *London Suburbs* (London: Merrill Holberton, 1999).

Scanlon, J. *Inarticulate Longings: The Ladies Home Journal, Gender and the Promise of Consumer Culture* (New York and London: Routledge, 1995).

Strasser, S. *Satisfaction Guaranteed: The Making of the American Mass Market* (New York: Pantheon Books, 1989).

Tester. K (ed.) *The Flaneur* (London and New York: Routledge, 1994).

Veblen, T. *The Theory of the Leisure Class* (London: Unwin, 1970).

2 The impact of technology

Recommended reading

The most important book to deal with the story of American industrialization and its effect upon material culture is, without doubt, David Hounshell's *From the American System to Mass Production 1800–1932: The Development of Manufacturing Technology in the US* (Baltimore and London: John Hopkins University Press, 1982), although he stops short of an analysis of 'design'. S. Giedion's *Mechanization Takes Command: A Contribution to Anonymous History* (New York: Norton, 1949) was an early attempt to look back at the effects of industrialization on the material culture of the USA. Ruth Schwartz Cowan's 'The

Industrial Revolution in the Home: Household Technology and Social Change in the 20th Century' in *Technology and Culture* (vol. 17, no. 1, Jan. 1976) provides a useful overview of the effects of technology in the domestic sphere. On the subjects of materials and modernity, the two most useful books are J. Meikle's *American Plastic: A Cultural History* (New Brunswick: Rutgers University Press, 1995) and Nichols, S. *Aluminum by Design* (New York: Harry N. Abrams, 2000), pp. 12–140. Robert Friedel's book, *Pioneer Plastic: The Making and Selling of Celluloid* (Wisconsin: University of Wisconsin Press, 1983), is also an important source.

Further reading

Arnold, E. and Burr, L. 'Housework and the Appliance of Science' in Failkner, W. and Arnold, E. (eds) *Smothered by Invention* (London: Pluto Press, 1985).

Bayley, S. *Harley Earl* (London: Trefoil, 1990).

Beecher, C. and Stowe, H. B. *The American Woman's Home* (New York: J. B. Ford and Co., 1870).

Bullock, N. 'First the Kitchen – Then the Façade' *Journal of Design History* 1988; 1 (3 and 4): 177–92.

Clifford, H. and Turner, R. 'Modern Metal' in Greenhalgh, P. (ed.) *Art Nouveau 1890–1914* (London: V&A Publications, 2000).

Cowan, R. S. *More Work for Mother: The Ironies of Household Technology from the Open Hearth to the Microwave* (New York: Basic Books, 1983).

De Wolfe, E. *The House in Good Taste* (New York: Century, 1913).

Dubois, J. H. *Plastics History USA* (Boston: Cahners, 1972).

Frederick, C. *Household Engineering and Scientific Management in the Home* (Chicago: American School of Home Economics, 1919).

Frederick, C. *The New Housekeeping: Efficiency Studies in Home Management* (New York: Garden City, Doubleday Page, 1913).

Horowitz, R. and Mohun, A. (eds) *His and Hers: Gender, Consumption and Technology* (Charlottesville and London: The University of Virginia Press, 1998).

Ierley, M. *The Comforts of Home: The American House and the Evolution of Modern Convenience* (New York: Three Rivers Press, 1999).

Katz, S. *Plastics: Design and Materials* (London: Studio Vista, 1978).

Kaufman, M. *The First Century of Plastics* (London: Plastics Institute, 1963).

Lupton, E. and Abbott Miller, J. *The Bathroom, the Kitchen and the Aesthetics of Waste: A Process of Elimination* (Cambridge, Mass: MIT Press, 1992).

MacKenzie, D. and Wajcman, J. *The Social Shaping of Technology* (Milton Keynes and Philadelphia: Open University Press, 1985).

Mayr, O. and Post, R.C. (eds) *Yankee Enterprise: The Rise of the American System of Manufactures* (Washington: Smithsonian Institution Press, 1981).

Meikle, J. 'New Materials and Technologies' in Benton, T., Benton, C. and Wood, G. *Art Deco 1910–1919* (London: V&A Publications, 2003).

Sparke, P. *Electrical Appliances* (London: Bell and Hyman, 1987).

Stage, S. and Vincenti, V. B. (eds) *Rethinking Home Economics: Women and the History of a Profession* (Ithaca and London: Cornell University Press, 1997).

Strasser, S. *Never Done: A History of American Housework* (New York: Henry Holt and Co., 1982).

3 The designer for industry

Recommended reading

There is a paucity of literature on the important subject of the emergence of the designer for industry and the cultural ramifications of that modern phenomenon. My book, *Consultant Design: The History and Practice of the Designer in Industry* (London: Pembridge Press, 1983), offers a brief, albeit dated, introduction to the subject, while my essay, 'From a Lipstick to a Steamship: The Growth of the American Industrial Design Profession' in Bishop, T. (ed.) *Design History: Fad or Function?* (London: Design Council, 1878), serves to open up the discussion about the origins about the modern industrial designer. Jeffrey Meikle's *Twentieth-Century Limited: Industrial Design in America 1925–1939* (Philadelphia: Temple University Press, 1979) is still the best subject on the inter-war American designer for industry seen from a cultural perspective, while Gregory Votolato's *American Design in the Twentieth Century* (Manchester: Manchester University Press, 1998) is a good complement to it. Isabelle Anscombe's *A Woman's Touch: Women in Design from 1860 to the Present Day* (London: Virago, 1984) is a useful introduction to all the female designers who have been left out of the picture.

Further reading

Atterbury, P. and Irvine, L. *The Doulton Story* (London: V&A Publications, 1979).

Bel Geddes, N. *Horizons* (New York: Dover Publications, 1977).

Buckley, C. 'Design, Femininity, and Modernism: Interpreting the work of Susie Cooper' *Journal of Design History* 1994; 7 (4): 277–93).

Callen, A. *Angel in the Studio: Women in the Arts and Crafts Movement* (London: Astragal Books, 1979).

Campbell, N. and Seebohm, C. *Elsie de Wolfe: A Decorative Life* (London: Aurum Press, 1992).

Cheney, S. and M. *Art and the Machine* (New York: McGraw Hill, 1936).

Clark, H. *The Role of the Designer in the Early Mass Production Industry* (unpublished PhD thesis: University of Brighton, 1982).

De la Haye, A. and Tobin, S. *Chanel: The Couturiere at Work* (London: Overlook Press, 1994).

De Marly, D. *Worth: Father of Haute Couture* (London: Elm Tree Books, 1980).

Dreyfuss, H. *Designing for People* (New York: Viking Press, 1955).

Flinchum, R. *Henry Dreyfuss, Industrial Designer: The Man in the Brown Suit* (New York: Cooper-Hewitt, National Design Museum and Rizzoli, 1997).

Halen, S. *Christopher Dresser* (London: Phaidon, 1990).

Hampton, M. *Legendary Decorators of the Twentieth Century* (New York: Doubleday, 1992).

Howe, K. S., Frelinghuysen, A. C. and Voorsanger, C. H. (eds) *Herter Brothers, Furniture and Interiors for a Gilded Age* (New York: Harry N. Abrams, Inc., Publishers, in association with the Museum of Fine Arts, Houston, 1995).

Loewy, P. *Never Leave Well Enough Alone* (New York: Simon and Schuster, 1951).

Naylor, G. *The Arts and Crafts Movement: A Study of its Sources, Ideals ands Influence on Design Theory* (London: Studio Vista, 1971).

Peck, A. and Irish, C. *Candace Wheeler: The Art and Enterprise of American Design 1875–1900* (New York: The Metropolitan Museum of Art, 2002).

Pulos, A. *The American Design Ethic* (Cambridge, Mass: The MIT Press, 1983).

Richards, C. *Art in Industry* (New York: Macmillan, 1922).

Schwartz, F. 'Commodity Signs: Peter Behrens, the AEG and the Trademark' *Journal of Design History* 1996; 9 (3): 153–84.

Seddon, J. and Worden, S. *Women Designing: Redefining Design in Britain Between the Wars* (Brighton: University of Brighton, 1991).

Sloan, A. J. *My Years at General Motors* (New York: Macfadden-Bartell, 1965).

Teague, W. D. *Design This Day: The Technique of Order in the Machine Age* (London: Studio Publications, 1946).

Thomson, E.M. '"The Science of Publicity": An American Advertising Theory' *Journal of Design History* 1996; 9 (4): 253–72.

Van Doren, H. *Industrial Design: A Practical Guide* (New York: McGraw Hill, 1940).

Weltge, S. W. *Bauhaus Textiles: Women Artists and the Weaving Workshop* (London: Thames and Hudson, 1998).

4 Modernism and design

Recommended reading

The literature relating to the subject of modern architecture and its theoretical underpinnings is extensive but that relating to modern design is less so. Because early twentieth-century design thinking took its lead from architecture a dependency on that literature exists to a significant extent. Thus Reyner Banham's *Theory and Design in the First Machine Age* (London: Architectural Press, 1960) is a seminal text on this context as is Benton, T. and C. and Sharp, D. (eds) *Form and Function: A Source Book for a History of Architecture and Design 1890–1939* (London: Crosby, Lockwood and Staples, 1975), which, although written some time ago, still provides a useful introduction to a study of modernist design. Paul Greenhalgh's book of edited essays, *Modernism and Design* (London: Reaktion Books, 1990), is the only one to focus directly on the relationship between this broad-based cultural movement and design, while Mark Wigley's *White Walls, Designer Dresses: The Fashioning of Modern Architecture* (Cambridge, Mass: MIT Press, 1995) is a more critical, retrospective analysis of architectural and design modernism.

Further reading

Bojko, S. *New Graphic Design in Revolutionary Russia* (New York and Washington: Praeger, 1972).

Bourke, J. 'The Great Male Renunciation: Men's Dress Reform in inter-war Britain' *Journal of Design History* 1996; 9 (1): 23–33.

Burnam, B. 'Better and Brighter Clothes: The Men's Dress Reform Party' *Journal of Design History* 1995; 8 (4): 275–90.

Collins, P. *Changing Ideals in Modern Architecture, 1750–1950* (London: Faber And Faber, 1965).

Colomina, B. *Privacy and Publicity: Modern Architecture as Mass Media* (Cambridge, Mass: MIT Press, 1994).

Colomina, B. *Sexuality and Space* (Princeton, New Jersey: Princeton Architectural Press, 1992).

Conrads, U. (ed.) *Programmes and Manifestoes on Twentieth-Century Architecture* (London: Lund Humphries, 1970).

De Zurko, E. R. *Origins of Functionalist Theory* (New York: Columbia University Press, 1957).

Frampton, K. *Modern Architecture: A Critical History* (London: Thames and Hudson, 1985).

Greenhalgh, P. (ed.) *Art Nouveau 1890–1914* (London: V&A Publications, 2000).

Greenough, H. *Form and Function: Remarks on Art, Design and Architecture* (Los Angeles: University of Californian Press, 1969).

Gropius, W. *The New Architecture and the Bauhaus* (London: Faber and Faber, 1968).

Jencks, C. *Modern Movements in Architecture* (Harmondsworth: Penguin, 1973).

Le Corbusier *The Decorative Art of Today* (Cambridge, Mass: MIT Press, 1987).

Le Corbusier *Towards a New Architecture* (London: The Architectural Press, 1974).

Loos, A. *Spoken into the Void: Collected Essays 1897–1900* (Cambridge, MA: MIT Press, 1982).

Naylor, G. 'Swedish Grace . . . or the Acceptable Face of Modernism' in Greenhalgh, P. *Modernism and Design* (London: Reaktion Books, 1990), pp. 15–20.

Naylor, G. *The Bauhaus Re-Assessed: Sources and Design Theory* (London; Herbert Press, 1985).

Overy, P. *Light, Air and Openness: Modern Architecture Between the Wars* (London: Thames and Hudson, 2008).

Pevsner, N. *Pioneers of Modern Design: From William Morris to Walter Gropius* (Harmondsworth: Penguin, 1960).

Schaefer, H. *Nineteenth-Century Modern: The Functional Tradition in Victorian Design* (London: Studio Vista, 1970).

Steadman, P. *The Evolution of Design* (Cambridge: Cambridge University Press, 1979).

Troy, N. *The De Stijl Environment* (Cambridge, Mass: The MIT Press, 1983).

5 Designing identities

Recommended reading

A number of studies have focused on design as an ideological tool in the hands of nations. Paul Greenhalgh's *Ephemeral Vistas: The Expositions Universelles, Great Exhibitions, and World's Fairs 1851–1939* (Manchester: Manchester University Press, 1988) provides an overview of all the important exhibitions in the first half of the twentieth century at which design made an appearance. Wendy Caplan's collection of essays, entitled *Designing Modernity: The Arts of Reform and Persuasion 1885–1945* (Miami and London: Wolfsonian/Thames and Hudson, 1995) is a useful account of the ways in which a number of nations sought to exploit the links between design and modernity. In his book, *Design in Germany 1870–1918* (London: Trefoil, 1986), John Heskett explores Germany's strategic relationship with modern design while, in *Designs on Modernity: Exhibiting the City in 1920s Paris* (Manchester: Manchester University Press, 1998), Tag Gronberg shows how France developed a quite different model of modernity through design.

Further reading

Aynsley, J. *Graphic Design in Germany 1890–1945* (London: Thames and Hudson, 2000).

Burckhardt, L. *The Werkbund: Studies in the History and Ideology of the Deutcher Werkbund* (London: Design Council, 1980).

Bush, D. *The Streamlined Decade* (New York: George Braziller, 1975).

Calkins, E. 'Beauty, the New Business Tool' *The Atlantic Monthly* 1927; 14 August: 145–6.

Campbell, J. *The German Werkbund: The Politics of Reform in the Applied Arts* (Princeton, New Jersey: Princeton University Press, 1978).

Commune di Milano *L'anni trenta, arte e cultura in Italia* (Milan: Mazotta, 1982).

Crowley, D. 'Budapest: International Metropolis and National Capital' in Greenhalgh, P. *Art Nouveau 1890–1914* (London: V&A Publications, 2000).

Crowley, D. 'Finding Poland in the Margins: The case of the Zakopane Style' *Journal of Design History* 2001; 14 (2): 105–16.

Crowley, D. *National Style and National State: Design in Poland from the Vernacular Revival to the International Style* (Manchester: Manchester University Press, 1992).

Fell, S. 'The Consumer and the Making of the *Exposition des Arts Decoratifs et Industriels Modernes, 1907–1925*' *Journal of Design History* 1999; 12, (4): 311–25.

Elliott, D. 'Introduction' to *Devetsil: Czech Avant-GardeArt, Architecture and Design of the1920s and 1930s* (Oxford and London: Museum of Modern Art, 1990).

Gebhard, D. 'The Moderne in the USA, 1920–41' *Architectural Association Quarterly* 1970; 2 July.

Gordon Bowe, H. (ed.) *Art and the National Dream: The Search for Turn of the Century Vernacular Design* (Dublin: Irish Academic Press, 1993).

Grief, M. *Depression Modern – the '30s Style in America* (New York: Universe Books, 1975).

Guidici, G. *Design Process: Olivetti, 1908–1983* (Torino, Italy: Edizioni di Comunità, 1983).

Harrison, H. A. (ed.) *Dawn of a New Fay: the New York World's Fair, 1939/40* (New York: New York University Press, 1980).

Hobsbawn, E. *Nations and Nationalisms since 1780* (Cambridge: Cambridge University Press, 1990).

Johnson, P. and Hitchcock, H. R. *The International Style* (New York: W. W. Norton & Co. Inc., 1966).

Lamarova, M. 'The New Art in Prague' on Greenhalgh, P. *Art Nouveau 1890–1914* (London: V&A Publications, 2000).

Light, A. *Forever England: Femininity, Literature and Conservatism Between the Wars* (London and New York: Routledge, 1991)

Opie, J. 'Helsinki: Saarinen and Finnish Jugend' in Greenhalgh, P. *Art Nouveau 1890–1914* (London: V&A Publications, 2000).

Schwartz, F. *The Werkbund: Design Theory and Mass Culture before the First World War* (New Haven and London: Yale University Press, 1996).

Sheldon, R. and Arens, E. *Consumer Engineering: A New Technique for Prosperity* (New York: Arno Press, 1976).

Silverman, D. L. *Art Nouveau in Fin-de-Siecle France: Politics, Psychology and Style* (Los Angeles: University of California Press, 1989).

Tiersten, L.*Marianne in the Market: Envisioning Consumer Society in Fin-de-Siècle France* (Berkeley: University of California Press, 2001).

Troy, N. *Modernism and the Decorative Arts in France: Art Nouveau to Le Corbusier* (New Haven: Yale University Press, 1991).

6 Consuming postmodernity

Recommended reading

A number of studies focus on the way in which the climate of mass consumption changed in the years after the Second World War. In *The Condition of Postmodernity: An Enquiry in the Origins of Cultural Change* (Oxford: Basil Blackwell, 1989), the geographer, David Harvey explores some of those changes. In his essay 'Towards a Cartography of Taste 1935–1962' in Hebdige, D. *Hiding in the Light* (London and New York: Routledge, 1988), pp. 45–76, the cultural critic, Dick Hebdige, looks at the influence of American culture on Britain in the early post-war years, while Frank Mort's essay, 'Mass Consumption in Britain and the USA since 1945' in Nava, M., Blake, A., MacRury, I. and Richards, B. (eds) *Buy This Book: Studies in Advertising and Consumption* (London and New York: Routledge, 1997), looks specifically at changing consumption patterns in those countries. Rob Shields' selection of essays in *Lifestyle Shopping: The Subject of Consumption* (London and New York: Routledge, 1992) show how the idea of lifestyle became linked to the acquisition of goods through the act of consumption in the years.

Further reading

Attfield, J. 'Inside Pram Town: A Case-Study of Harlow House Interiors' in Attfield, J. and Kirkham, P. (eds) *A View from the Interior: Feminism, Women and Design* (London: The Women's Press, 1989).

Baudrillard, J. *Simulations* (New York: Semiotext[e], 1983).

Bigsby, C.W. (ed.) *Superculture: American Popular Culture and Europe* (London: Paul Elek, 1975).

Boorstin, D. *The Americans: The Democratic Experience* (New York: Random House, 1973).

Breward, C. and Wood, G. *British Design From 1948: Innovation in the Modern Age* (London: V&A Publishing, 2012).

Carter, E. *How German is She? National Reconstruction and the Consuming Woman in the FRG and West Berlin 1945–1960* (Ann Arbor, MI: University of Michigan, 1996).

Cooper, R. *Constructing Futures* (London: Wiley-Blackwell, 2010).

De Grazia, V. 'Changing Consumption Regimes in Europe' in Strasser, S., McGovern, C. and Judt, M. *Getting and Spending: European and American Consumer Societies in the Twentieth Century* (Cambridge: Cambridge University Press, 1998).

Du Gay, P., Hall, S., Janes, L., Mackay, H. and Negus, K. (eds) *Doing Cultural Studies: The Story of the Sony Walkman* (Milton Keynes: The Open University, 1997).

Eco, U. *Travels in Hyperreality* (New York: Harcourt Brace Jovanovich, 1986).

Entwhistle, J. '"Power Dressing" and the Construction of the Career Woman' in Nava, M., Blake, A., MacRury, I. and Richards, B. *Buy This Book: Studies in Advertising and Consumption* (London and New York: Routledge, 1997).

Fuad-Luke, A. *The Eco-Design Handbook: A Complete Sourcebook for the Home and Office* (London: Thames and Hudson, 2009).

Galbraith, K. *The Affluent Society* (Harmondsworth: Penguin, 1958).

Gartman, D. *Auto Opium: A Social History of the American Automobile* (London and New York: Routledge, 1994).

Hebdige, D. 'Object as Image: The Italian Scooter Cycle' in Hebdige, D. *Hiding in the Light* (London and New York: Routledge, 1988), pp. 77–115.

Heller, S. *Citizen Designer* (New York: Allworth Press, 2003).

Hewison, R. *The Heritage Industry: Britain in a Climate of Decline* (London: Methuen, 1987).

Lewis, F. L. and Goldstein, L. (eds) *The Automobile and American Culture* (Michigan: University of Michigan Press, 1998).

Lowenthal, D. *The Past is a Foreign Country* (Cambridge: Cambridge University Press, 1985).

Lyotard, F. *The Postmodern Condition: A Report on Knowledge* (Manchester: Manchester University Press, 1984).

Marling, K. A. *As Seen on TV: The Visual Culture of Everyday Life in America in the 1950s* (Cambridge, Mass: Harvard University Press, 1994).

McDonagh, D. *Design and Emotion* (New York, CRC Press, 2003).

Merkel, I. 'Consumer Culture in the GDR' in Strasser, McGovern, C., Hudt, M. *Getting And Spending: European and American Consumer Societies in the Twentieth Century* (Cambridge: Cambridge University Press, 1998).

Mort, F. 'Boy's Own? Masculinity, style and popular culture' in Chapman, R. and Rutherford, J. (eds) *Male Order* (London: Lawrence and Wishart, 1995).

Norman, D. A. *Emotional Design: Why We Love (or Hate) Everyday Things* (London: Basic Books, 2005).

Proctor, R. *1000 New Eco Designs and Where to Find Them* (London: Laurence King, 2009).

Reisman, D. *The Lonely Crowd: A Study of the Changing American Character* (New Haven and London: Yale University Press, 1970).

Samuel. R. *Theatres of Memory, Vol. 1: Past and Present in Contemporary Culture* (London: Verso, 1995).

Schifferstein, H. N. J. and Hekkert, P. (eds) *Product Experience* (London: Elsevier Science, 2007).

Scranton, P. (ed.) *Beauty and Business: Commerce, Gender and Culture in Modern America* (New York and London: Routledge, 2001).

Urry, J. *Consuming Places* (London: Routledge, 1995).

Urry, J. *The Tourist Gaze: Leisure and Travel in Contemporary Societies* (London: Sage, 1990).

Warde, A. 'Consumers, Identity and Belonging: Reflections on some theses of Zygmuny Bauman' in Kear, R., Whiteley, N., and Abercrombie, N. *The Authority of the Consumer* (London and New York: Routledge, 1994).

Whiteley, N. *Design for Society* (London: Reaktion Books, 1994).

Williams, R. *Culture and Society 1780–1950* (London: Chatto and Windus, 1958).

Wilson, E. *Only Halfway to Paradise, Women in Postwar Britain 1945–1968* (London and New York: Tavistock Publications, 1980).

Wollen, P. and Kerr, J. (eds) *Autopia: Cars and Culture* (London: Reaktion Books, 2002).

Wright, P. *On Living in an Old Country: The National Past in Contemporary Britain* (London: Verso, 1985).

7 Technology and design: a new alliance

Recommended reading

One important aspect of the years following the Second World War was the shift to what has been called 'post-industrialism'. One face of this was linked to the move away from standardized mass production. This is the subject of Charles Sabel's and Jonathan Zeitlin's *World of Possibilities: Flexibility and Mass Production in Western Industrialisation* (Cambridge: Cambridge University Press, 1997). Two important books appeared in 1999 – Alison Clarke's *Tupperware: the Promise of Plastics in 1950s America* (Washington and London: Smithsonian Institution Press, 1999) and Susannah Handley's *Nylon: The Manmade Fashion Revolution* (London: Bloomsbury, 1999), both of which focus on the important links between materials, culture and design. Paola Antonelli's *Mutant Materials in Contemporary Design* (New York: Museum of Modern Art, 1995), shows how new materials and design worked together at the end of the twentieth century.

Further reading

Attfield, J. 'The Tufted Carpet in Britain: Its Rise from the Bottom of the Pile, 1952–70' *Journal of Design History* 1994; 7 (3): 205–16.

Berger, S. and Piore, M.J. *Dualism and Discontinuity in Industrial Society* (Cambridge: Cambridge University Press, 1980).

Blaszczyk, R. *Imagining Consumers: Design and Innovation from Wedgwood to Corning* (Baltimore and London: The John Hopkins Press, 2000).

Borries, F. Von *Apple Design: the History of Apple Design (AT)* (New York: Hatje Cantz, 2011).

Dupont: The Autobiography of an American Enterprise (Wilmington: DE: E. I. Dupont de Nemours and Company, 1952).

Hogan, M. J. *The Marshall Plan: America, Britain and the reconstruction of Western Europe 1947–1952* (Cambridge: Cambridge University Press, 1987).

Horowitz, R. *Boys and Their Toys? Masculinity, Class and Technology in America* (New York and London: Routledge, 2001).

Kron, J. and Slesin, S. *High Tech* (New York: Potter, 1978).

Lash, D. and Urry, J. *The End of Organised Capitalism* (London: Polity, 1987).

Lupton, E. *Mechanical Brides: Women and Machines from Home to Office* (New York: Cooper Hewitt National Museum of Design, 1993).

Manzini, E. *The Material of Invention* (Milan: Arcadia, 1986).

Nichols, S. *Aluminum by Design* (New York: Harry N. Abrams, 2000), pp. 140–89.

Norman, D. *The Design of Everyday Things* (London: Basic Books, 2002).

Palmer, A. *Couture and Commerce: The Transatlantic Fashion Trade in the 1950s* (Toronto: UBC Press, 2001).

Pile, S. 'The Foundation of Modern Comfort: Latex Foam and the Industrial Impact of Design on the British Rubber Industry, 1948–1958' in *One-Odd: A Collection of Essays by Postgraduate Students on the V&A/RCA Course in the History of Design* (London: Victoria and Albert Museum, 1997).

Postman, N. *Technopoly: The Surrender of Culture to Technology* (New York: Vintage Books, 1993).

Rogers, Y. *Interaction Design: Beyond Human–Computer Interaction* (London: John Wiley and Sons, 2011).

Sabel, C. F. *Work and Politics: The Division of Labour in Industry* (Cambridge: Cambridge University Press, 1982).

Sparke, P. *Italian Design* (London: Thames and Hudson, 1988).

Sparke, P. 'Plastics and Pop Culture' in Sparke, P. (ed.) *The Plastics Age: From Modernity to Postmodernity* (London: V&A Publications, 1990), pp. 92–104.

Sparke, P. 'The Straw Donkey: Tourist Kitsch or Proto-Design? Craft and Design in Italy, 1945–1960' *Journal of Design History* 1998; 11 (1): 59–69.

Tevfik, B. (ed.) *The Role of Product Design in Post-Industrial Society* (Ankara: Middle East Technical University, 1998).

White, N. *Reconstructing Italian Fashion: America and the Development of the Italian Fashion Industry* (Oxford: Berg, 2000).

8 Designer culture

Recommended reading

The maturation of designer culture which took place in the years after 1945 has still not been fully analyzed from a cultural perspective. However, a vast body of literature exists about the designers themselves, which offers many insights into the phenomenon. Hugh Aldersey-Williams is among the few to address the subject directly in his essay 'Starck and Stardom' published in *Industrial Design* (no. 34), pp. 46–51. Pat Kirkham's *Charles and Ray Eames; Designers of the Twentieth Century* (Cambridge, MA: MIT Press, 1995), is one of the best of its kind, while Andrea Brabzi's study of twentieth century design in Italy – *The Hot House: Italian New wave Design* (London: Thames and Hudson, 1984) shows the importance of designer culture to that country. P. Kunkel's *Digital Dreams: The work of the Sony Design Center* (New York: Universe Publishers, 1999) shows how, in contrast, Japanese industry sought to promote its products through the names of its corporations rather than of its designers.

Further reading

Alessi, A. *The Dream Factory: Alessi since 1921* (Milan: Electa/Alessi, 1999).

Ambasz, E. (ed.) *Italy: The New Domestic Landscape, Achievements and Problems of Italian Design* (New York: The Museum of Modern Art, 1972).

Brown, T. *Change by Design: How Design Thinking Creates New Alternatives for Business and Society: How Design Thinking Can Transform Organizations and Inspire Innovation* (London: Collins Business, 2009).

Caplan, R. *The Design of Herman Miller* (New York: Whitney Library of Design, 1976).

Cross, N. *Design Thinking: Understanding How Designers Think and Work* (London: Berg, 2011).

Drexler, A. *Charles Eames: Furniture from the Design Collection* (New York: Museum of Modern Art, 1973).

Dormer, P. (intro.) *Jasper Morrison: Designs, projects and drawings 1981–1989* (London: Architecture and Technology Press, 1990).

Ferrari, P. *Achille Castiglioni* (Milan: Electa, 1984).

Fossati, P. *Il Design in Italia* (Milan: Einaudi, 1972).

Gere, C. *Digital Culture* (London: Reaktion Books, 2002).

Ive, J. 'Apple Bites Back' *Design* 1998; (1) Autumn: 36–41.

Jackson, L. *The New Look: Design in the 1950s* (London: Thames and Hudson, 1991).

Jackson, L. *Robin and Lucienne Day: Pioneers of Contemporary Design* (London: Mitchell Beazley, 2001).

Jackson, L. *The Sixties: Decade of Design Revolution* (London: Phaidon, 2000).

Julius, G. *Design and Creativity: Policy, Management and Practice* (London: Berg, 2009).

Kelley, T. *The Art of Innovation: Lessons in Creativity from Ideo, America's Leading Design Firm* (New York: Doubleday, 2001).

Kenneth Grange at the Boilerhouse; An Exhibition of British Product Design (London: Boilerhouse Project, 1983).

Kirkham, P. (ed.) *Women Designers in the USA 1900–2000: Diversity and Difference* (New Haven and London: Yale University Press, 2000).

Larrabee, E. and Vignelli, M. *Knoll Design* (New York: Harry N. Abrams, 1989).

Martin, R. L. *Design of Business: Why Design Thinking is the Next Competitive Advantage* (Boston: Harvard Business School Press, 2009).

McCarty, C. *Marion Bellini, Designer* (New York: Museum of Modern Art, 1987).

Papanek, V. *The Green Imperative: Ecology and Ethics in Design and Architecture* (London: Thames and Hudson, 1995).

Pulos, A. *The American Design Adventure 1940–1975* (Cambridge, Mass: MIT Press, 1988).

Sudjic, D. *Ron Arad* (London: Lawrence King, 1999).

Sweet, F. *Philippe Starck: Subverchic Design* (London: Thames and Hudson, 1999).

9 Postmodernism and design

Recommended reading

Numerous writings exist which deal with the subject of 'postmodernism'. Not so many, however, relate that broad-based cultural phenomenon to the world of material culture and design. Anne Massey's *The Independent Group: Modernism and Mass Culture in Britain, 1945–1959* (Manchester: Manchester University Press, 1995) outlines ideas which showed that modernism was in crisis in the 1950s in Britain while Nigel Whiteley, *Pop Design: Modernism to Mod* (London: Design Council, 1987), showed where this crisis led in terms of material culture. In the USA Eobert Venturi diagnosed a similar crisis in American architecture in *Complexity and Contradiction in Architecture* (New York: Museum of Modern Art, 1966).

Michael Collins and Andreas Papadakis documented its effect on design production in the 1980s, in *Post-Modern Design* (New York: Rizzolu, 1989).

Further reading

Adamson, G. and Pavitt, J. (eds) *Postmodernism: Style and Subversion, 1970–90* (London: V&A Publishing, 2011).

Banham, R. 'A Throwaway Aesthetic' in Sparke, P. (ed.) *Reyner Banham: Design By Choice* (London: Academy Editions, 1981), pp. 90–3.

Boorstin, D. J. *The Image* (London: Wiedenfeld and Nicholson, 1962).

Featherstone, M. *Consumer Culture and Postmodernism* (London: Sage, 1983).

Dorfles, G. *Kitsch* (London: Studio Vista, 1969).

Foster, H. *Postmodern Culture* (London: Pluto Press, 1990).

Gablik, S. *Has Modernism Failed?* (London: Thames and Hudson, 1984).

Giddens, A. *Modernity and Self-Identity: Self and Society in the Late Modern Age* (California: Stanford University Press, 1991).

Hebdige, F. 'In Poor Taste: Notes on Pop' in *Hiding in the Light* (London and New York: Routledge, 1988), pp. 116–43.

Hochschüle fur Gestaltung, Ulm: Fie Moral der Gegenstande (Berlin: Ernst and Sohn, 1987)

Horn, R. *Memphis: Objects, Furniture and Patterns* (New York: Simon and Schuster, 1986).

Jamieson, F. 'Postmodernism, or the Logic of Late Capitalism' *New Left Review* 1984; 146: 53–92.

Jencks, C. *The Language of Post-Modern Architecture* (London: Academy, 1973).

Kauffmann Jr, E. *Introduction to Modern Design* (New York: Museum of Modern Art, 1969).

Massey, A. and Sparke, P. 'The Myth of the Independent Group' in *Block (Middlesex University)* 1985; 10: 48–56.

Moles, A. *Le Kitsch* (Paris: Maison Mame, 1971).

Packard, V. *The Hidden Persuaders* (Harmondsworth: Penguin, 1957).

Packard, V. *The Status Seekers* (Harmondsworth: Penguin, 1963).

Packard, V. *The Waste-Makers* (London: Longmans, 1961).

Sparke, P. *Ettore Sottsass Jr* (London: Design Council, 1982).

Sparke. P. *Reyner Banham: Design by Choice* (London: Academy Editions, 1981).

Sweet, F. *Alessi: Art and Poetry* (London: Thames and Hudson, 1998).

Thackera, J. (ed.) *Design after Modernism: Beyond the Object* (London: Thames and Hudson, 1988).

Venturi, R., Scott-Brown, D. and Izenour, S. *Learning from Las Vegas: The Forgotten Symbolism of Architectural Form* (Cambridge, Mass: MIT Press, 1972).

10 Redefining identities

Recommended reading

The globalism of the late twentieth century gave rise to a number of studies. These include Celia Lury's analysis of Benetton, 'The United Colours of Diversity:

Essential and Inessential Culture' in Franklyn, S., Lury, C. and Stacey, J. *Global Nature, Global Culture* (London: Sage, 2000). At the same time, with the destruction of the Berlin Wall, new nationalisms came into being and design was used to demarcate it. Studies of this new phenomenon include David Crowley's *Design and Culture in Poland and Hungary 1890–1990* (Brighton: Brighton University, 1992) and Gert Selle's 'The Lost Innocence of Poverty: On the Disappearance of Cultural Difference' in *Design Issues: History; Theory: Criticism* (Vol. 8, no. 2, Spring 1992), pp. 61–73.

Further reading

Aldersey-Williams, H. *Nationalism and Globalism in Design* (New York: Rizzoli, 1992).

Aynsley, J. *Nationalism and Internationalism in Design* (London: V&A Publications, 1993).

Banham, M. and Hillier, B. *A Tonic to the Nation: The Festival of Britain* (London: Thames and Hudson, 1976).

Breward, C., Conekin, B. and Cox, C. (eds) *The Englishness of English Dress* (Oxford and New York: Berg, 2002).

Bullig, M. *Banal Nationalism* (London: Sage, 1995).

Council of Industrial Design *Design in the Festival* (London: HMSO, 1951).

Erlhoff, M. (ed.) *Designed in Germany since 1949* (Munich: Prestel, 1990).

Ernyey, G. *Made in Hungary: The best of 150 Years in Industrial Design* (Budapest: Rubik Innovation Foundation, 1993).

Falk, P. 'The Benetton-Toscani Effect: Testing the Limits of Conventional Advertising' in Nava, M., Blake, A., MacRury, I. and Richards, B. *Buy This Book: Studies in Advertising and Consumption* (London and New York: Routledge, 1997).

Heskett, J. *Philips: A Study of the Corporate Management of Design* (London: Trefoil, 1989).

Julier, G. 'Barcelona Design, Catalonia's Political Economy and the New Spain' *Journal of Design History* 1996; 9 (2): 117–28.

Justice, L. And Xin Xinyang *China's Design Revolution (Design thinking, Design Theory)* (Cambridge, Mass: MIT Press, 2012).

Klein, N. *No Logo* (London: Flamingo, 2001).

Lury, C. *Consumer Culture* (Cambridge: Polity, 1996).

McDermott, C. *Made in Britain: Tradition and Style in Contemporary British Fashion* (London: Mitchell Beazley, 2002).

Marling, K. A. *Designing Disney's Theme Parks: The Architecture of Renaissance* (Paris: Flammarion, 1997).

Miller, D. 'Coca-Cola: a black sweet drink from Trinidad' in Miller, F. (ed.) *Material Cultures: Why Some Things Matter* (London: UCL Press, 1998).

Narotzky, V. *An Acquired Taste: The Consumption of Design in Barcelona, 1975–1992* (unpublished PhD thesis, Royal College of Art, London, 2003).

Oliver, T. *The Real Coke: The Real Story* (London: Elm Tree, 1986).

Pavitt, J. (ed.) *Brand New* (London: V&A Publications, 2000).

Sparke, P. '" A Home for Everybody?": Design, Ideology and the Culture of the Home in Italy, 1945–72' in Greenhalgh, P. (ed.) *Modernism in Design* (London: Reaktion Books, 1990), pp. 185–202.

Sparke, P. (ed.) *Did Britain Make It? British Design in Context 1946–1986* (London: Design Council, 1986).

Sparke, P. *Japanese Design* (London: Michael Joseph, 1987).

Vukic, F, *A Century of Croatian Design* (Zagreb: Meander, 1998).

Zukin, S. *Landscapes of Power: From Detroit to Disney World* (Berkeley: University of California Press, 1995.

Zukin, S. *The Cultures of Cities* (Cambridge, Mass: Blackwell, 1995).

Index